ALSO BY DAVID C. ANDERSON

Crimes of Justice
Children of Special Value

CRIME AND THE POLITICS OF HYSTERIA

CRIME AND THE POLITICS OF HYSTERIA

HOW THE WILLIE HORTON STORY CHANGED AMERICAN JUSTICE

David C. Anderson

RANDOM HOUSE

Library of Congress Cataloging-in-Publication Data

Anderson, David C.
Crime and the politics of hysteria : how the Willie Horton story
changed American justice / David C. Anderson. — 1st ed.
p.   cm.
Includes index.
ISBN 0-8129-2061-9
1. Crime—United States.   2. Criminal justice, Administration of—
United States.   3. Crime—Political aspects—United States.
4. Horton, William, 1952?–   .   I. Title.
HV6789.A65   1995
364.973—dc20   94-40619

9 8 7 6 5 4 3 2

First Edition

FOR BETSY

Acknowledgments

I am particularly indebted to Cliff and Angela Barnes for their willingness to discuss matters that still cause them much pain. I am also especially grateful for conversations with Joan Bamford, Charles Capace, Andrew Card, Dougie Cecil, Donna Cuomo, Anthony DiFruscia, Maureen Donovan, William Doucette, Michael Dukakis, Jeffrey Elliot, Michael Fair, Vincent J. Femia, Susan Forrest, Larry Giordano, Beth Henderson, Philip Johnston, Andrew Klein, Anthony McCarthy, Tom McManus, Jerome Miller, Bill Pedrick, Ed Rogers, Patrick Schiavone, Michael Stella, and Daniel Warner. (Former President George Bush declined to be interviewed.)

In addition, heartfelt thanks are owed:

To Jack Rosenthal of *The New York Times*, who understood my need to write this book and made generous allowances; to Sandra Ratkowsky, a fine secretary and loyal friend; to Peter Matson of Sterling Lord Literistic, a mainstay of my new life;

to Steve Wasserman of Times Books, who helped to shape the final product; to Mary, Michael, Sarah, Tom, Elspeth, and William, for their unselfish appreciation of my work; and finally to Kalil, source of constant inspiration as he embodies the hope of all the world.

Contents

CRIME AND THE POLITICS OF HYSTERIA

New York

1 9 9 5

I first heard of Willie Horton when most of America did, during the 1988 presidential campaign, and I had a chance then to participate, however marginally, in the national debate about him. In those days, I worked for the editorial board of *The New York Times*, and according to the board's informal allocation of subjects, I was responsible for criminal justice. So when Horton's name came up at one of our morning board meetings, the people responsible for politics turned to me.

What should we say, they wanted to know, about George Bush's use of the Horton case to embarrass his opponent, Michael Dukakis? The Massachusetts governor's administration had permitted a prison furlough program from which Horton, a murderer serving life without parole, had escaped. He went on to burglarize a house in Maryland, where he assaulted a man and raped the man's fiancée. Both were decent, middle-class people, randomly victimized. It all sounded out-

rageous. Was it therefore fair to suggest Dukakis was dangerously soft on crime?

Times editorial board meetings, conducted around a long
table with portraits of the publisher's family staring down
from the walls, were not a comfortable place at which to con-
fess either ignorance or the inability to form an opinion. So on
this day, as many of us did too often, I responded on the basis
of no more than what I had read in the paper, along with
whatever erudition might instantly have sprung to mind.

It didn't sound good, I said. Prison furloughs, as I understood them, were generally used as part of a pre-release program for inmates a few months from parole. Prisoners would
use the time on the outside to seek work and housing,
reestablish relationships with their families, generally get
ready for life back in the world. So why give a furlough to a
convict serving life without parole? It made no sense.

At the same time, I suggested, it didn't seem fair to hold
Dukakis responsible. Surely the operations of a prison furlough program were conducted at a level far below the level of
a governor's day-to-day scrutiny. Dukakis could not possibly
have given personal approval to the furloughing of a lifer like
Horton. In fact, he probably wasn't even aware of the policy.

Only much later would I think back to that day and realize
I had been wrong on both points: the furlough policy that led
to Horton's escape actually did make sense, and Governor
Dukakis not only had been aware of it; for a time in Massachusetts, he had spoken forcefully in defense of it.

But by then, my moment of glibness seemed a slight concern.
For the Horton story, I had learned, was about matters far
more important than the outcome of a presidential election.

• • •

The 1988 campaign came and went, and I found myself amazed that the Horton case wound up playing so big a role in it. Political commentators expressed dismay that voters might have made up their minds about a presidential candidate on the basis of a matter apparently so marginal as a foul-up in a prison furlough program. Others complained that supporters of George Bush had deliberately manipulated the issue of race—Horton is black; he had raped a white woman—as they exploited the case and broadcast a picture of Horton that made him look subhuman.

Phone calls to criminal justice people I knew in Massachusetts suggested that there was a lot to learn about Horton beyond what the Republicans had said about him in campaign ads and what the Democrats had said in their complaints about those ads. Up in the Merrimack Valley, north of Boston, Horton had been an obsession for most of the year before the presidential campaign began.

About that time, I also became aware of a recurring pattern in the news coverage of crime in New York. A particular kind of story appeared to dominate—one that always brought Willie Horton to mind. Five elements defined the pattern.

First, the crimes were luridly violent, involving homicide, rape, or aggravated assault that resulted in serious injury. Second, the victims were middle-class, usually white. Crimes committed by blacks against whites could add an ugly racial aspect to the story, though the race and social status of the criminal were not nearly so important as those of the victim.

Third, the victims were wholly innocent. They were not criminally involved, either in the incident that led to their victimization or in any other way—if they were, in fact, the news media and the politicians quickly lost interest. Nor had the victims put themselves in harm's way. Instead, they were typically attacked while going about a familiar daily routine, perhaps even while relaxing in their own homes.

Fourth, the criminals appeared to have chosen their victims entirely at random. Violence between neighbors or drinking buddies didn't count; neither did that arising from domestic conflict, sexual jealousy, or an unresolved previous relationship.

Finally, the criminals usually had some history of involvement with the criminal justice system, suggesting that if the system had only worked better, the terrible crime might have been avoided.

These elements—to qualify, a crime would have to include four of the five—signified an event that invariably stirred broad outrage and often provoked a political reaction. During the 1980s and '90s, the list was long.

There was, most famously, the case of the Central Park jogger, brutally gang-raped and left for dead by a group of teenage boys who ran in a pack through the park, assaulting any who crossed their path. There was the fatal stabbing of Alexis Ficks Welsh by Kevin McKiever, a total stranger with a long criminal record and a history of schizophrenia, who attacked her as she walked her dogs one peaceful morning in her Upper West Side neighborhood.

There was Juan Gonzalez, who visited a psychiatric emergency room and was held for forty-eight hours, only to be released on his promise to seek further treatment. The next day, he boarded a Staten Island ferry, carrying a Japanese ceremonial sword. He hacked two people to death and injured several others before he could be subdued. There was Larry Hogue, a brain-damaged man who turned violent and terrorized an Upper West Side neighborhood when he smoked crack. Though he was repeatedly arrested, the courts never seemed able to jail him for more than a short time or get him the psychiatric help he needed. And there was Colin Ferguson, who boarded a Long Island Rail Road train, pulled out a gun, and began shooting commuters at random.

There was the teenager from Utah, visiting the city with his family, who rushed to defend his mother from a group of young thugs trying to rob her on a subway platform; he died after one of them sank a knife into his chest. There was the Manhattan advertising executive murdered by a stranger who approached him as he made a call at a public telephone. And there was the drama teacher shot to death in Brooklyn by two young boys who were trying to steal the bicycle he was riding through Prospect Park.

Each case, its horrible details played over and over again for a period of days or weeks, affirmed a growing belief about the threat of random violence to decent people who do nothing wrong and about the incompetence of the authorities to deal with it.

Crimes that fit the Horton pattern carried such weight with the public that some criminals could turn it to their advantage. In October 1989, a Boston man named Charles Stuart called the police to report that a black mugger had stopped his car at gunpoint, murdered his wife, and shot him in the stomach. The Stuarts, a young suburban couple preparing for

7

the arrival of their first baby, had just come from a birthing class at a downtown hospital.

The crime inflamed the whole city. The news media erupted with outrage, and Mayor Ray Flynn demanded an aggressive search for the killer. After a manhunt that raised racial tension as blacks complained of heavy-handed police tactics, detectives arrested a black man, William Bennett. A few weeks later, however, Charles Stuart apparently committed suicide by leaping off the Tobin Bridge, and his brother pleaded guilty to charges related to the crime. He confirmed that Charles had actually murdered his wife, arranging for his own injury and concocting the story about the mugger to deflect suspicion.

A hauntingly similar case occurred in October 1994, smack in the middle of a mean-spirited off-year election in which crime headed the list of voter concerns. A young South Carolina mother named Susan Smith told police that a carjacker had forced his way into her car as she waited at a traffic light. She said that the man, whom she described as black and in his twenties or thirties, had driven her and her children away from town, then pushed her out of the car and sped away with the two young boys still buckled up in the back seat.

The crime quickly mobilized the news media. As the tearful mother and her estranged husband went on national television to plead for their sons' return, police distributed a sketch based on Smith's description. It depicted a black man in a plaid shirt and knitted watch cap. The publicity generated calls from coast to coast as concerned Americans said they had seen cars with South Carolina plates and boys who might have been the missing children.

But ten days after she first reported the crime, police arrested Smith herself, amid reports that she had confessed to drowning her sons by rolling the car down a boat ramp. They pulled the car from a nearby lake, the bodies of her sons still strapped inside.

As the Stuart and Smith cases underscored the power of random crime to inspire fear and outrage, they also reflected the discomfiting aspects of the Willie Horton story. I knew that random violence against the white middle class did not constitute the bulk of crimes, or even a very large minority of them. Why give them so much more than their share of attention? To do so seemed self-indulgent.

My friends in the criminal justice agencies remained preoccupied with other matters: ongoing daily violence in the city's ghettos, heavily armed teenage gangs, drug trafficking. To them, the cases of random violence against the white middle class were like lightning bolts that ignite publicity firestorms. They posed a danger, certainly, to any bureaucrat, and they could not be ignored. But they were no reason to alter one's basic approach to the job.

And I could find no reason to fault that attitude, even though I was hardly immune to outrage of my own. In the 1980s, fear had become an unavoidable, palpable part of everyday life for me along with everyone else. Shootings and stabbings occurred with disturbing frequency on West Forty-third Street across from *The New York Times* building, where I went to work each day. After a certain hour, my subway train might empty out, leaving me in the car with just one or two other people. Should they have decided to make me a victim, no one would even have known, much less have been in a position to offer help.

And though I lived on one of the more peaceable blocks of Greenwich Village, I, too, had seen drawn guns as plainclothes officers chased a suspect down the street one evening. In the early hours of another morning, I was even startled awake by gunfire—a semiautomatic handgun's unmistakable loud pops in quick succession—echoing off the townhouse façades. By the time I could stumble to a window, the shooter had disappeared, but the anxiety remained. That time, I even wrote a little editorial about what happened and how it made me feel.

But by now, I also knew something of criminal justice. As Americans had done more or less for two centuries, I continued to believe in a utilitarian approach based on crime control, which meant crime control for everyone. I wasn't aware of any foolproof strategy for giving potential middle-class victims special protection from random crime, even if one could get around the ethical problems of doing such a thing.

Furthermore, while I knew that in recent years crime control had become a lot more complicated than people liked to think, I also believed strongly that there were some effective ways to achieve it. During the 1980s, cops all over the United States had begun to experiment with community policing. Courts and probation departments in a number of places were developing effective new sanctions for huge numbers of young criminals that did not require sending them to the prisons that the taxpayers couldn't afford. Elsewhere states and cities were setting up special courts to push large numbers of drug-involved criminals into treatment programs rather than prison.

If the United States could not manage its crime problem, I felt, it was not for lack of sound policies so much as of focused commitment to a practical agenda and sufficient resources to back it up. But as time went on, I sensed the profound depth of public resistance to that idea. My editorials about criminal justice often drew letters—some were plaintive, describing at length a crime victim's suffering. Others were belligerent—demanding more use of the death penalty or mandatory incarceration of all serious criminals, including juvenile delinquents, for life. If there isn't enough prison space, some correspondents suggested, the government should build huge concentration camps in the deserts of the Southwest, on offshore islands, or in the wilds of Alaska.

Some letters accused me of ivory-tower arrogance. What did I know about crime in the city, since I surely lived in the suburbs and rode a limousine to work? Pondering such letters on my subway ride home to Greenwich Village, I eventually recognized that the charge of arrogance had to do with something more than *The Times*'s liberal elitist reputation.

For one thing, I saw that to dismiss the excessive focus on middle-class victims as self-indulgent missed a powerful point: the extent to which crime in general had eroded the social contract. Democracy depends on the willingness of citizens to give up certain freedoms, obey the laws, and pay taxes, in exchange for which the government provides certain benefits and protections. One of the most basic of these is a guarantee of physical security. And the Willie Horton stories suggested that the government could no longer provide that guarantee; in fact, the government's incompetence or negligence seemed to have increased the level of risk to public safety. The issue obviously had become more pronounced as the law-abiding, hard-working, taxpaying citizens who supported the society's basic values—in other words, the middle class—began to feel endangered.

Mike Reynolds, who campaigned for a tough sentencing law in California after the murder of his daughter, told *The New York Times:* "What these crimes have done is show people that you can do all the right things and it doesn't matter. You can lock your door, stay in the right neighborhoods. . . . When bad guys are killing bad guys, that's one thing. But when they start killing regular people, that's where you draw the line in the sand. That's what's driving people crazy."

His frankness was, on reflection, startling. It reinforced the view of cynics who lament the racism of a society in which crime becomes a powerful issue only when it spreads from minority ghettos (bad guys killing bad guys) to the white middle class (bad guys killing regular people). But the fact that the social contract had previously broken down—if it ever existed at all—for minorities and the poor was no argument for continuing to ignore it as the breakdown got worse. Self-indulgent it might be, but the special outrage of the middle class was sounding a loud alarm that many of the criminal justice bureaucrats I knew preferred not to hear. And it was not enough to answer it with statistics on improving crime trends and speculations about the promise of new law-enforcement strategies. There had to be a more fundamental response. Without one, volatile emotions set off by the Willie Horton stories ran wild.

Innocent victims, random choice: Those elements in particular piled an unbearable dose of mystery on top of pain and loss. Consider two fathers grieving for their sons. The first's son went to a bar known to be a hangout for members of a motorcycle club and made the mistake of propositioning a biker's girlfriend. The biker and his buddies beat the son to death in the alley outside. The second's son was pre-med at Columbia University. One fine spring afternoon, he took his books to Riverside Park instead of to the library. While he studied on a bench overlooking the river, a couple of young toughs approached him and demanded the gold chain he wore around his neck. When he refused to give it up, one took out a gun and shot him dead.

Both fathers suffer similar feelings of grief, but the first at least has a way to make moral sense of what happened. Had his son been more circumspect about approaching the woman, or about going into such a bar in the first place, the crime might have been avoided. It all could be explained as a tragedy of youthful poor judgment.

The second father isn't granted the comfort of an explanation. His son did nothing wrong. All he wanted to do was take advantage of a beautiful day. Why should he be put at risk for that? And why did his assailants happen to choose him? Surely there were other people in the park who might have been victimized instead. Why did sudden, inexplicable tragedy strike his son? Why is he left to deal with the pain of it for the rest of his life? The anguished questions, ancient as Job, engage elemental issues of human existence.

Even without direct experience of that kind of tragedy, the fear and vulnerability that I and millions of others felt from time to time as residents of the city touched on the same profound questions. The anxiety stirred by the thought of random crime against the innocent renewed itself with each new replay of the Willie Horton scenario.

Why should the fear have to be an issue when I went to work, did my errands, went out at night, lived my life? How was I supposed to handle it? More and more people I knew were taking matters into their own hands, carrying little canisters of Mace or pepper spray, installing elaborate alarm systems in their homes, even getting guns. On the subway late at night or turning down an empty street, I would sometimes clench my fist around my keys so that the tips stuck out between my fingers—brass knuckles!—or discreetly thumb open the blade of the Swiss Army knife I carried in my pocket.

But then I was luckier than most, for I had access to a therapy of sorts: I could go to work each day and write about crime. I could talk with experts and practitioners about what might work to reduce it, think hard about what I had learned, and try to make sense of it in print. As I did my job, I also managed my fear.

Millions of others weren't so fortunate. They felt the same anxiety, the same need to make sense of it, to manage the tension it produced. But they didn't have the same outlet I did. Instead, they had begun to handle it in another way, without realizing, perhaps, that they were turning back the clock.

The term "expressive justice" refers to laws, policies, and practices that are designed more to vent communal outrage than to reduce crime. Ancient as humanity, expressive justice has a rich history. It is the response to crime that prevailed in Western societies before eighteenth-century reformers and theorists like John Howard, Jeremy Bentham, and Cesare Beccaria proposed a more utilitarian penology based on crime control and rehabilitation.

In earlier times, communities accepted that there would always be evil people; the point was not to stop evil so much as to visit revenge on the perpetrators of it. As a result, criminals were humiliated, tortured, and executed by the thousands. They might be mutilated, stoned, branded, scalded, whipped, stretched on racks. They might be hung, burned at the stake, hacked to death with swords, slowly crushed with boulders, torn apart by horses driven in opposite directions. These punishments were carried out in public; that was the point: to give the community, as a community, its chance to exact satisfaction.

Expressive justice crossed the Atlantic with colonial settlers in America, who accepted the Calvinist idea of evil as a basic part of human nature. "They would combat the evil, warn, chastise, correct, banish, flog or execute the offender," the historian David Rothman writes. "But they saw no prospect of eliminating deviancy from their midst. Crime, like poverty, was endemic to society." They were satisfied with punishment that reinforced values of community, church, and family.

The Founding Fathers, however, thought more positively. The Constitution's Eighth Amendment, which bans "cruel and unusual punishments" reflects the influence of Beccaria, an Italian criminologist and economist, who argued that clarity of the law and certainty of punishment are more important than the severity of punishment. He proposed an end to torture and execution in favor of a rational, systematic approach to criminal sentencing.

Americans like Benjamin Franklin and Thomas Jefferson believed not only in Beccaria but also in the malleability of man. Beyond merely punishing crimes, the new country's justice system would attempt to reclaim lost souls. This led, in the late 1780s, to a new American invention, the penitentiary. Instead of being flogged or hanged, criminals would be required to follow regimens of work, Bible study, and solitary reflection.

The penitentiary would have a decidedly checkered career, but the guiding belief in the utilitarian goals of crime control and rehabilitation remained in place through much of the twentieth century. Now, however, in the 1980s and '90s, Americans gripped by fear appeared to be turning away from those original principles in a big way. Nobody was about to repeal the Eighth Amendment, certainly; so there could be no return to "cruel and unusual" torture and mutilation. But there could be a new form of expressiveness, one that had little to do with reducing crime or reclaiming deviant souls and everything to do with helping an anxious, angry public manage its feelings.

The biggest reflection of it was the death penalty, returning in the 1980s as a regular feature of American life after a hiatus that had lasted since the 1960s. By 1995, executions were occurring regularly at a rate of two or three per month, and only twelve states had resisted the political pressure to pass laws reinstating capital punishment according to new requirements set by the Supreme Court. The big crime bill passed in the summer of 1994 authorized execution as a punishment for about sixty federal crimes that result in death. They included car jackings, drive-by shootings, and rapes.

As always with the death penalty, there was absolutely no evidence that its return had had any effect on crime. No one could demonstrate that the execution of thirty or so murderers annually had made any difference at all to the twenty thousand murders occurring each year. But that wasn't the point. The point was the idea and the image: the once arrogant killer is led to the execution chamber, offers final words of remorse, defiance, or newfound religion, then writhes in the electric chair, gulps final breaths in the gas chamber, or succumbs quietly to the needle of death. Even if nowhere near frequent enough to make a practical difference, the event satisfied a craving for the symbolic reassertion of authority, the collective exacting of revenge. Once upon a time, executions in the United States were attended by solemn candlelight vigils of protest. Now they were also likely to draw raucous celebrations of support.

Legislatures have also responded to demands for expressive punishments with mandatory-sentencing laws. Typically, these laws established firm floors under prison terms for certain crimes: a mandatory minimum of five years, say, for the sale of a given quantity of drugs or the use of a gun in the commission of a crime. They might also require mandatory time in prison for a person convicted of a second felony or, more dramatically, a life sentence for someone convicted of a third—"three strikes and you're out." A few states and the federal government went so far as to jettison the whole process that gave a parole board discretion over when a convict could be released, substituting sentencing by formula: once a criminal was convicted, the judge would consult a chart that weighed the seriousness of the crime and the criminal's record and dictated the proper number of months or years behind bars.

There was an illusory aspect to all this. The vast majority of criminal cases in the United States aren't settled by trials but by plea bargains. Subject to a judge's approval, prosecution and defense agree on the charges to which the defendant will plead guilty, charges based more on the strength of the prosecution's case than the apparent seriousness of the crime. If the evidence isn't strong, the charges agreed to may bear little resemblance to what actually happened—a terrifying armed robbery, for example, gets settled with a plea to careless use of firearms.

So much for the legislature's well-publicized determination to punish armed robbery with a stern mandatory sentence. The main effect of the mandatory sentence is to strengthen the hand of the prosecutor a bit in the negotiations over pleas. Some laws stipulating mandatory sentences may also work against the cause of effective crime control, by, for example, filling state penitentiaries so full of nonviolent drug dealers that it becomes hard to find places for the rapists and armed robbers.

But as with the death penalty, effectiveness in controlling crime does not appear to be the point. Fearful people take comfort in the *idea* of a mandatory sentence. On paper, at least, it reinforces values: A second felony equals time in prison, period, with no need for more discussion. Mandatory sentences seem to put everyone on notice, criminal justice officials as well as criminals.

As important, demanding tough sentences and voting for them give people a way to feel as if they are doing something, a way to handle fear. It is no accident that voters often take advantage of ballot propositions and other such mechanisms to bypass legislatures and enact mandatory sentences themselves. Petition drives and other grassroots campaigning give large numbers of people the chance for direct participation; the political work becomes a massive exercise in group therapy.

By the 1990s, the expressive mood had reached down to lower levels of discipline, flirting with humiliation and corporal punishment. When a New Jersey sex offender, released from prison after serving his time, abused and murdered a young girl, pressure grew for more laws requiring that such offenders be forced to register with local authorities after they are released from prison so that their names could be made public. While supporters of the idea justify it in that it allows parents to protect their children from sex offenders in the neighborhood, it also recalls the era of the scarlet letter.

When Singaporean officials convicted Michael Fay, an American teenager, of vandalism and sentenced him to caning, the State Department and the president protested the Asian government's inflicting its outmoded, barbaric punishment on a U.S. citizen. But their voices were soon drowned out by those of Americans who heartily approved the idea of flogging some sense into a juvenile delinquent and who apparently consider Singapore's justice a praiseworthy model. As a result, legislators in some states introduced bills that would make whipping a sentencing option.

Here again, crime control had become secondary. It was far from clear how public notification of a released sex offender's presence in a community might play out in practical terms—

or even whether it could withstand constitutional challenge. As for the caning in Singapore, middle-class kids like Michael Fay might be genuinely terrified by the prospect of flogging. But in truth, America did not really have that much to fear from middle-class kids like Michael Fay. The bulk of the crimes that spread anxiety far and wide was committed by juvenile offenders from poorer neighborhoods, youngsters more familiar with physical violence on the street.

Whether these teenagers might feel the same terror of corporal punishment wasn't so clear. Many might well prefer the prospect of a whipping, over in a matter of minutes, to months of separation from friends, drugs, and the street. Much as time in adult prison had, scars from the whip might easily become marks of manhood, a way to gain respect.

But again, deterrence of crime didn't seem to be the point. News coverage of the Fay case reported Michael's terror at the prospect of being caned and described the humiliating, gruesome details: The offender is stripped naked and bound to a trestle; strokes of the cane to his bare buttocks draw blood, send chunks of flesh flying, and inflict excruciating pain. That is what millions of Americans found so fascinating, and satisfying, to read: For once, it was a young criminal who was being made to feel some fear and pain.

The Willie Horton stories, intensifying public anxiety, greatly accelerated the expansion of the new expressiveness and helped give it shape. Two features distinguish it from that of earlier eras. The first is that it makes special room for crime victims, allowing them to use politics as personal therapy, a device for managing their particular anger and grief. The second is that it makes a target of the criminal justice system, if not government in general—the authorities cannot expect to renege on the social contract and get away with it.

Think again about those two fathers whose sons were murdered. Suppose the police arrest the killers in both cases, and it turns out both had recently been released from prison and were on parole at the time of their crimes. In the first case, the issue seems marginal. Of course the bikers are bad guys with criminal backgrounds. The son should have known that. And if the one on parole hadn't been there to do the killing, another probably would have taken his place.

But in the second, more random case against a wholly innocent victim, the issue of parole becomes crucial. If the parole board hadn't released that kid, the anguished father might say, my son would be alive today. Suddenly there is an explanation for the unbearable mystery, a way, finally, to make sense of devastating confusion.

Two California cases, the murders of Kimber Reynolds and Polly Klaas, starkly illustrate the process. Eighteen-year-old Kimber died in 1992 when two young men on motorcycles tried to snatch her purse as she left a restaurant. When she struggled with one of them, he shot her in the head. Twelve-year-old Polly died at the end of 1993 after a man stole into her house during a slumber party. As her mother slept nearby, he abducted Polly, then murdered her, and dumped her body near an abandoned sawmill.

When Kimber's father, Mike Reynolds, learned that the man who shot Kimber had a long criminal record, he began gathering signatures to put a three-strikes-and-you're-out law before California voters in a general election.

Polly's murder, the following year, generated widespread publicity. The news media broadcast the wholly innocent circumstances of the girl's victimization nationwide, along with pictures of her. When it turned out that the man arrested for abducting and killing her also had a long criminal record, Reynolds's personal cause quickly escalated to a statewide landslide for the three-strikes law. California's media and politicians looked at Reynolds with new respect, comparing him with Howard Jarvis and Paul Gann, whose campaign for a ballot proposition on property taxes set off a national tax revolt, or Candy Lightner, who started Mothers Against Drunk Driving after her daughter's death.

Reynolds, a wedding photographer, had no previous experience in criminal justice. He freely acknowledged that he had undertaken the campaign mainly as a way to handle his personal grief, to make sense of his daughter's death. "You never stop reliving the last moments of your child's life and wondering what you could have done to prevent it," he told a reporter. Polly Klaas's father, Marc, speaking at a news conference after the girl's body was discovered, suggested that the widespread public outrage over his daughter's murder be focused on a campaign for stricter laws. "The bottom line is we cannot afford to ignore the right of our children to a safe world," he said. A general overhaul of criminal justice "would be the greatest memorial for Polly." The sympathy Reynolds and Klaas generated overwhelmed any reasoned discussion of the law they proposed.

Yet the law deserved to be discussed. The case for three strikes appears obvious: If it had been in effect when the murderers of Polly and Kimber had committed their third

crimes, wouldn't the girls be alive today? Yet there were reasons to question this assertion. With a three-strikes law in
effect, the killers might have plea-bargained earlier felony
charges down to misdemeanors or gone to trial and been
acquitted. Even if the law would prevent some crimes by
putting genuinely dangerous criminals away, it would also
needlessly impose life terms on others who weren't so dangerous, at enormous cost. Was that really the best use of tax-
payer dollars to control crime?

With the victims' families speaking out regularly, however,
California legislators weren't allowed to give these pragmatic
arguments any real consideration. Mike Reynolds and Marc
Klaas gained virtually invincible credibility. How could any
decent person deny them the satisfaction they sought? How
could anyone dare to shrug off their pain? Lawmakers began
with the assumption that to question the idea of three strikes,
not to mention vote against it, was to show callousness toward
two fathers who had lost their daughters under the worst circumstances a parent can imagine.

The legislators got the message: If law-enforcement officials
could not guarantee punishment and the removal from society
of the criminals who make such bad things happen, then the
people and their lawmakers would insist on making the guarantees ever more explicit in the law. The results might not
impress the experts, but at least they would teach the unfeeling, incompetent, or negligent public officials a lesson.

Some felt the sting of backlash. By 1994, California judges
were in revolt against the three-strikes law, refusing to give
life sentences for third crimes that seemed not to warrant the
drastic punishment. Beyond claiming to act in the name of

justice, however, the judges also clearly resented the law's slap at their competence. "Why are we having the judge go through the sham of sentencing if he has no discretion whatsoever?" one judge complained to a newspaper reporter. "We're going to have robots."

But for millions of Californians who had supported the law, inflicting such an insult was exactly the point.

The more I thought about Willie Horton, the more all of this came into focus. Not only had Horton committed serious crimes in Maryland against two innocent middle-class victims chosen at random. One of his victims, Cliff Barnes, made a point of using politics as personal therapy and was proud to say he did. The public joined in, expanding therapeutic use of the case nationwide, with consequences far more expressive than practical. Thus had the Horton case become the locus classicus for a new American folktale of crime and justice; it both arose from and encouraged a politics of fear that was now turning Americans away from principles that had governed their approach to law enforcement and penology for two centuries.

And from what I knew, this was a cause for real concern. For it seemed obvious to me, and to most of the experts I knew and trusted, that the more the expressive approach dominated debate, policy, and law, the longer it would take for the United States to gain control of its crime problem. The syndrome could easily perpetuate itself: continued crimes against random middle-class victims, continued ritual retellings of the Willie Horton story in all its permutations, continued expressive reactions absorbing attention, energy, and funds that might have been turned to serious methods of crime control. At the very least, I felt, the shift to expressive justice was not something that should happen by default, without a public airing that could clarify the issues and let people understand the real choice they were making.

Horton's files in Massachusetts and Maryland included voluminous court and prison records, plus a thick stack of newspaper clippings and boxes full of legislative hearing transcripts. There were plenty of people to talk to about his case, and they would have plenty to say. What I would find, after months of research and interviews, only deepened my concern.

Baltimore

1 9 9 2

The jumbled cluster of brick and stone structures covering several desolate blocks of downtown Baltimore houses well over five thousand souls in various stages of state custody. The spectrum extends from the Maryland Correctional Adjustment Center, a "supermax" for the most violent and disruptive felons, to the Baltimore Pre-Release Unit, for trustworthy inmates going out to work in the community each day.

By far the oldest of the structures, the 180-year-old Maryland Penitentiary, at the center of the complex, is a forbidding square castle of dark stone blocks with a domed cupola at the apex of its pyramidal roof and small steeples on each of four corner towers. Rooms in the towers have tall, narrow barred windows, like those from which Rapunzel might have let down her hair. A massive cellblock extends from one side, its façade dominated by intimidating arches over more barred windows. The building powerfully embodies the stern authoritarian statements nineteenth-century architects made with prisons. The buildings survive today because the stones and iron are heavy, firmly set and still apparently useful to society. The same might be said of the public sentiment behind them.

Finding the castle's entrance has entailed a number of false approaches and encounters with wary guards. Now I am sitting in the visitor's entrance, space that resembles the waiting room of an old railroad station, with four long wooden benches set up in a row before a uniformed figure at a desk behind a windowed cage. Near me sit a woman and two small children, one an infant in her arms, the other a restless toddler. She is accompanied by a second woman, her sister perhaps, along to help with the kids while she meets with their father inside. The mother of the children appears to be in her late twenties and is verging on the obese; her straight brown hair surrounds a pretty young face aging fast with worry. I feel guilty when my name is called before hers.

I submit to a search, surrender my wallet, change, and keys to a guard, pass through a metal detector, present my hand for stamping with invisible ink, and get fitted with a little plastic wristband bearing my name, much like those issued to hospital patients. Perhaps because I arranged the meeting through the correction department's public information office, or perhaps because I am to meet with one of the prison's stars, I am spared the main visitors' hall, where three long tables are arranged to form a large U. As guards keep watch here, anxious-looking women and a few men sit around the outside of the U, speaking in low voices across the tables to their convicted relatives on the inside.

Instead, I am escorted through the hall, down a flight of stairs, through rolling grates, and into a sizable, windowless room furnished with a long table and chairs.

He is waiting for me there, a black man of forty-one with a long, oval face, his dark hair and beard beginning to show flecks of white. I am immediately impressed with his height. One of his friends had described him as "a big country boy," and that he is, well over six feet and quite thin. He bears only a distant resemblance to the disheveled, barely human image that for a time became a kind of national icon and so took up permanent residence in the minds of millions. The straggly hair and beard are now carefully trimmed, and he is well turned out, in a beige suede jacket with knitted sleeves over a burgundy nylon T-shirt and cream-colored slacks. He rises nervously from a chair as I enter; as we shake hands, he avoids any eye contact, as he will throughout our meeting.

We begin to talk, and I find myself struggling to understand him against the dull prison roar—guards shouting, gates clanging—filtering into the room from outside. His sentences frequently end in unintelligible mumbles as he swallows his words, perhaps because he is missing a couple of teeth on the left side of his lower jaw.

I learn, nonetheless, that he has settled into the routine of doing his time and is working as a cook in the prison kitchen. He believes he may be better off here, all things considered; he fears that there are people who would like to kill him because of who he is. Assassination may be less likely in prison than on the street.

Because he continues to fear untimely death, he tells me, he has written down his story and signed it in hopes that it might survive him. I try not to betray too much interest, but it soon becomes clear that he is not about to let me see this document, if in fact it exists, or to grant my request for an extended interview about his background and his criminal activities.

In truth, I had not expected that he would—but neither had I anticipated the reason he gives. He is not concerned about more negative publicity; instead, he believes his story has some monetary value, and he doesn't think he should give it away for nothing.

I am not all that disappointed by his refusal. It would be impossible to take anything he might say at face value. And by now, the files his behavior has generated are voluminous enough to document a substantial biography. In any event, I have got much of what I came for: a sense of the man himself in three dimensions. He is a bit of a charmer, capable of an engaging smile when he relaxes, not smart so much as possessed of an instinctive gift for manipulating people and the truth.

Months later, I visit again in the company of a political science professor named Jeffrey Elliot, one of his friends and advisers. This time, apparently at Elliot's suggestion, my visitee has thought up some questions to ask me. As we get down to business, he opens a plastic portfolio and begins to read his questions from a notepad. How will my book be promoted? What overall impression of him will it give the reader? In what way would it be in his interest to help me out?

These are fair questions that deserve fair answers: At this point, I have no way of knowing how the book will be promoted; I hope to provide a balanced journalistic account that will benefit him to the extent it gives him a chance to tell his side of the story and correct some of the more lurid false-hoods still accepted as fact.

We go over all this for a bit, until he gathers himself for his big question, the one that has been on his mind from the beginning: What about money? He has a big need for cash, he explains, because he still hopes to hire lawyers to review his case and file more appeals. Should he give me his story, he goes on, he might forgo any returns he could realize from subsequently trying to publish it himself. Therefore . . .

The whole idea is ridiculous, given what I know about him by now. No way could I do anything that might help him get out or, more likely, help him finance dealings in contraband within the prison. So as not to seem too abrupt, I leave him with a promise to run the idea past my agent, though I know already what the response will be. As I leave, I adjust again to the idea of continuing without his help—and realize suddenly that he has greatly enjoyed our meeting, even without any lucrative result. I have, after all, granted him two hours away from his cell, away from the kitchen's grease and sweat, away from general boredom. On my account, there can be many more hours in which he can think it all over, review his options, scheme with Elliot over prospects that still seem deli-ciously plausible. For in spite of all that has happened, he has yet to lose his grip on the future or his sense of himself.

"Willie!" he had exclaimed disgustedly. "Willie! That's not my name. The press gave me that name. My name is William!"

Oxon Hill

1 9 8 7

The Tantallon South subdivision of Oxon Hill, Maryland, sits
on a square chunk of land along the east bank of the Potomac
River below Washington, D.C. It is bounded on the east by
Route 210, an arrow-straight commuter artery known as
Indian Head Highway, and on the north and south by two
Potomac tributaries, Broad Creek and Piscataway Creek,
which flow into the big river just before it first turns west on
its meander toward Chesapeake Bay and the open sea.

Though it feels relatively bucolic, the area remains convenient
to the capital and to Andrews Air Force Base, several miles to
the east. In the sixties and seventies, it made a logical choice for
developers who would build tidy neighborhoods for civil ser-
vants and mid-level professionals. Enough woodlots survived
around the shopping malls and residential tracts so that much of
the suburbanization remains out of sight on the ride out of the
District down 210, and a sense of rural serenity prevails.

Serenity and security: The homes on Proxmire Drive, running through the center of Tantallon South just west of the highway, preserve the cozy vision of suburban life that has symbolized middle-class America since the 1950s. Only a sizable number of black families, reflecting Washington's thriving African American middle class, distinguish the community from similar ones in thousands of suburbs across the United States.

The homeowners of Proxmire Drive, white and black, work hard and take pride in themselves and their lives, with no need for apology or excuse. They sought out such a place to live because it appeared to offer a low-key, comforting refuge from the city's stress and danger. Bad things are not supposed to happen here, and compared with much of metropolitan America, they rarely do. Through the late 1980s and early 1990s, the ten thousand residents of Tantallon South suffered only fifty to sixty violent crimes per year, a rate well below those for the rest of Prince George's County and the Washington, D.C., metropolitan area as a whole. The picture of Proxmire Drive on a warm autumn evening is one of tranquillity: Dads mow lawns before dinner while little kids ride bikes and teenagers tinker under the hoods of cars.

In February of 1987, Tantallon South welcomed two new neighbors, Angela Miller and Clifford Barnes, a young couple who moved into the rambling light-blue ranch house at the corner of Proxmire and Elkhurst Place along with their two poodles, Bandit and B. J. Cliff and Angie were an attractive, amiable pair. He was the natural extrovert, a man who said whatever was on his mind. That quality made it hard not to like and trust him and helped ensure his success as a service manager for an auto dealership in the District. She was a tall woman with long blond curls surrounding a wholesome Geena Davis face; she possessed a deep self-confidence that Cliff admired. In those days, he would say, she knew what she wanted and knew how to get it, whether at her job as a project analyst for a real estate development company or at home at night with him.

They were deeply committed to each other and planned to marry later that year. In the meantime, with two incomes and no real worries, they were already having a great time. They loved the new house with its yard, the cathedral-ceilinged family room, the little deck out back. Evenings they indulged the passion they shared for old movies, watching videos on one of their two VCRs, a VHS in the bedroom and a Betamax in the guest room down the hall. Weekends they partied with friends or tooled around the wide end of the Potomac in the big powerboat Cliff kept down at Port Tobacco, twelve miles to the south. Though still in their twenties, they had somehow achieved an enviable balance, giving as much to life as they got from it. It was all very good—and there was nothing to suggest it might wind up too good to be true.

Cliff and Angie went off to work as usual on the morning of April 3, a Friday, knowing they wouldn't see much of each other that evening. She had been invited to toast the birthday of a woman from work at a place called Randy's in the Best Western motel in Tyson's Corner, Virginia. He planned dinner with some friends at the Oxon Hill Ramada Inn, a few miles up Indian Head Highway. What they did not know was that they would never spend another day in their new house or in a life they thought was theirs to keep.

• • •

Angie did not get home until after two on Saturday morning. The Bacardis with Coke she had downed at the birthday celebration produced a definite buzz, but midnight supper at a restaurant around the corner from the motel had cleared her head, and she was cold sober now as she parked her gold Camaro in the driveway.

She emerged from the car, gathered the mail, and entered the house, greeting Bandit and B.J., who responded with barks and whines. There were no signs of Cliff, so she headed for the master bedroom to see whether he had left her a message on the answering machine.

At the bedroom door, she stopped. Cliff's glasses were on the dresser. Driving was a blur without his glasses; he never left them home. And an open bottle of Michelob stood by the phone. Cliff hated beer.

Where was Cliff? Maybe the spare room; maybe he'd gone in to watch something on the Betamax. Angie turned back to the hallway, started, and cried out.

The intruder came out of the bathroom: a slender black man wearing a blue tank top, jeans, white mesh slip-on shoes. A mask cut from a pair of panty hose, its amputated legs tied together at the top, hid his face. His eyes fixed on her through two holes in the dark beige fabric. And he carried a gun—the .22-caliber Bernardelli semiautomatic pistol she and Cliff kept in the house.

Her first struggle was with disbelief. *This had to be a practical joke.*

"Where's Cliff?" she asked aloud and tried to grab the gun.

But the man wasn't kidding. Angie called to Bandit, and the little poodle tried valiantly to defend her, growling and sinking his teeth into the intruder's trouser leg. But the man roughly shook the dog off and kicked him into the bathroom. Then he wrestled Angie to the floor and struck her on the chin. One hand clamped on her throat; the other shoved the pistol in her face.

Then he spoke: Unless she obeyed him, he would "bust her up." Stricken now, she followed orders to get up and go into the bedroom. He forced her to her knees, then used ties from a dress to bind her hands behind her back, a shirt to blindfold her eyes. The terror taking hold, she realized what was coming. Please, she pleaded—*she was begging like a little kid, but what else could she do?*—please don't rape me.

His response was a gruff, "That's not my style, baby. I'm just here to do the job of delivering your man to some people." In fact, he said, a "partner" had already dealt with Cliff.

What the hell? It all sounded phony. Nobody was out to get Cliff; that was nonsense. And anyway, this guy didn't seem like a gangster. He hadn't even brought his own gun. But then what did she know?

And now he got down to business. Where were her cards for bank cash machines? He rifled her purse and found one, then flew into a new rage. Where did she keep her other card, for her account at a second bank, he wanted to know, putting the gun to her head for emphasis. *How did he know about her bank accounts? How could she satisfy him? She hadn't seen that second card for days.* Confusion deepening her terror, Angie told him she didn't know where it was. The man stormed out into the hall and returned with the card. *How did he do that?* All she could figure was that he'd ripped through the mail she had dropped as they struggled and found the card, the bank having mailed it back after recovering it from a machine that swallowed it by mistake.

The man moved on to jewelry, pulling her engagement ring from her finger, slipping off the two gold chains she wore around her neck and another from her wrist. Then he yanked her up and made her lie on the bed. Continuing his threats to "bust her up," he demanded the access code numbers for the cash cards. *Give them to him. No problem. Maybe that would get him to leave.* And when she repeated the numbers, he did leave the room for a while. But then he returned. His "partner," he said, had taken the cards to get money.

And then he grew silent. Bound and blindfolded, her brain numb, her body churning with fear, Angie lay still. She thought she could hear him nearby, drinking from a bottle of beer. She found that by tilting her head back and rolling her eyes down, she could see a thin line of light through the bottom of the blindfold.

Time passed. He drank more beer. Then he moved over and sat on the bed. And then the blade of a knife flashed across her sliver of vision.

Something tugged at her blouse, and she realized he was cutting it open. He continued to cut—her jeans, her underwear. Sickening embarrassment mixed with fresh panic. She pleaded with him again: Hadn't he promised not to rape her? But he was done with the honorable gangster bit. He silenced her with a simple "Shut up or else."

Where was Cliff? she wondered again as the stranger went to work. *Where the hell was Cliff?*

• • •

In fact, Cliff was close by, within agonizing earshot of Angie's ordeal. But he might as well have been on the moon. He, too, was blindfolded and bound, held like the prey of a garden spider in a web of telephone cord laced about the two-by-fours that supported the cellar stairs.

He had arrived at the house around seven-thirty in a red Z28 Camaro he had test-driven home from work. He had gone into the bedroom to get ready for his evening out, removed his shirt and tie, then headed for the bathroom. He heard footsteps—*why was Angie home when she was supposed to be celebrating with her girlfriends?*—and he called her name.

That was when the masked man burst in on him. "Lay the fuck down! You don't know who you're messing with," the man shouted, pushing Cliff to the floor. He was too surprised to fight, then too scared: He spotted his .22 in the man's hand. But the bathroom wasn't big enough for a person to lie down in. The man held the gun to his head, cocked it, and pushed him out the door to the hall. There he removed a wallet and checkbook from Cliff's back pant pocket.

Cliff said what sprang to mind: "I don't have much money."

"You think I'm a fucking thief," the man replied. "I'm not here to rob you. You don't know who you're fucking with. Somebody paid me to do this. You've been fucking with the wrong people." *Paid him to do it? The wrong people? The guy acted like some sort of hit man. What weird mix-up was this?* Now, though, there was no trying to explain anything. The hooded stranger was pushing him back into the bedroom, where he tied Cliff's hands behind his back with a belt and neckties, then found one of Angela's sweaters to use as a blindfold.

He walked Cliff down to the basement and used more neckties and belts to tie him to one of the stair supports. "You know what's going on here," he kept saying. "You don't know who you've been fucking with." *I guess I don't, and I sure wish I knew.* But now Cliff resisted saying what came to mind.

The weirdness got weirder as the stranger tried to make Cliff think another man had come downstairs as well. "Watch him. If he moves, kill him," he said, then squeaked "OK" in a different voice. *Some ventriloquist; you almost had to laugh.* And then Cliff realized the stranger had left.

Eyes blinded, ears muffled as well by the sweater, Cliff felt time passing but had no idea how much time. Working his hands behind him, he managed to free one from its ties, but before he could use it to free the other one or remove the blindfold, he heard footsteps on the stairs. *The guy was coming down again. Shit.* Cliff quickly put his free hand behind his back.

Interrogation time: The intruder began with questions about Cliff's paycheck, his bank accounts, when Angie would be home. Then he got rough. He cut Cliff's pant pocket, cursing him when he found a roll of cash there, and struck him with the gun barrel. As Cliff's face stung and shivered with the pain, the stranger continued to curse, then began a playful torture. Cliff felt the point of a knife tracing skin-deep scratches back and forth across his chest. *What was the idea? Who was this guy, and what did he want? Or was this just another form of cursing, meanness expressed in blood.*

When he discovered that Cliff had freed a hand, the intruder seized a mass of telephone cord that hung on the wall. The installers had left it behind in case someone might one day finish the basement and order more phones. The man wove the cord back and forth across the two-by-fours under the stairs and around Cliff's body, securing his arms and his legs.

Over the next few hours, Cliff's tormentor left and returned to the basement a number of times, keeping up the stream of questions.

"Who lives in the second bedroom?"

Cliff explained about the two VCRs.

"Who drives the blue pickup truck?"

Now where did that one come from? Cliff had put the blue pickup—they called the battered '73 Chevy the U.T. for Ugly Truck—in shape to haul his boat around. *How on earth did this guy know about the U.T.? It usually stayed at the shop. It hadn't been parked in the driveway for a week or so. Had he been watching the house for that long?*

Now the intruder was upstairs again, and the sound of the front door opening sent a new jolt of adrenaline to Cliff's exhausted nerves. He heard Angie greeting the dogs—"Hi, Bandit. Hi, B.J."—then footsteps toward the bedroom, and then she cried out.

Thumping. Scuffling. Shouting. Then quiet. Then Angela asked, "Where's Cliff?"

He couldn't make out the reply. Footsteps moved around upstairs, Angie and the stranger doing God knew what. Drawers and doors opened and closed. It sounded bad, so bad now, and a dark, hot wave of impotent rage swept over Cliff as he worked furiously to free his hands.

Still blindfolded, Angela sat on the toilet in the bathroom. Her hands and feet were bound, and her hands were tied to the towel rack. After the forced sex, her assailant's mood had taken a benign turn. He found another pair of jeans to replace the ones he had cut off and pulled them on her before leading her into the bathroom. After tying her up, he had brought a pillow for her head. He even apologized for the rape and said he wouldn't do it again.

What a jerk. What a pathetic jerk—he actually wanted to make friends. But don't think about him. Think about Cliff. She still had no idea where he was. She pictured his face and his mustache. He had a wide mustache that balanced a face otherwise defined by a high forehead and aviator glasses. The mustache needed trimming, and several weeks back she had bought him a little pair of mustache scissors to trim it with, and he kept it here in the bathroom. In the toothbrush holder.

The intruder hadn't tied her hands that well. Working one free, she groped for the toothbrush holder. Her fingers closed around the scissors.

Moving fast, she cut off the blindfold, then the ties on her hands and feet. When she started for the little window to the outside, she heard him coming back. *God damn!* As he burst through the door, she dropped the scissors beside the toilet bowl and sat back down.

He switched on the bathroom lights, and she quickly averted her eyes—he had pushed the mask up on top of his head, revealing his face. No, she hadn't seen it, she insisted. She couldn't see a thing without her glasses. But of course she had seen enough quite suddenly to turn anonymous menace into an individual person: the longish, oval face, a regular face that would not seem threatening in other circumstances, the close-trimmed beard that covered his chin and connected to a thin mustache.

He quickly pulled down the mask and put the gun to her head. "You messed up real bad," he said.

"Are you going to kill me?"

"No, I ain't. I should, but I ain't." And then he began a conversation. *Great. He still wants to be friends.* "I know you hate me," he was saying with a petulance that made her sick. "If you had the gun, you'd shoot me."

"No, no," she responded, all she wanted was for him to leave them alone and let her and Cliff get back to normal.

Right. You want to be friends. Good. Let's be friends. She was gaining an advantage now. Why not press it? Hey, look, she said. Couldn't he leave her untied and unblindfolded so that she could watch some TV? She wasn't going to try anything. And could he let her put on another shirt? The one she had on was all torn up. And she was thirsty. Could he find a bottle of beer for her?

She was scoring now. The man left for a few moments and returned with the beer. He said he'd leave her blindfold off so long as she stayed in front of him and didn't try to look back. Then he walked her into the bedroom, gun pressed to her neck. She found another shirt to put on before they sat on the bed. The clock on the VCR read 4:00 A.M.

They watched TV for more than half an hour, a bizarre tableau: the frazzled woman, her curls a mess, her face puffed with stress and abuse, the man with the hood and gun, sitting

together like Mr. and Mrs. America by the light of the flicker-
ing tube. But then his mood shifted once more. He put a new
blindfold on her—*no more Mr. Nice Guy*—then stood her up
and marched her into the living room, where he made her sit
on the couch while he turned on the stereo. She didn't like
the feel of this at all. *The son of a bitch.*

Another few minutes passed before she felt him sit down
beside her. And then his hands were on her for the second
time, removing the blouse, fumbling with the jeans.

The bastard. The rotten bastard. Exhausted and disgusted,
she pleaded with him once more—you said you wouldn't do it
again. He silenced her with a fierce "shut up."

Numb with the stress, the pain, and the tightness of his
bonds, Cliff grew disoriented, and then the intruder came
downstairs for another visit and an escalation of torture.

Cliff felt a cord tightening on his neck. *My God, I'm going
to die.* And though he had never been a particularly religious
man, he found himself in a state of elemental human prayer,
his soul mounting an appeal for some kind of relief, any kind
of relief, his mind sorting through what he had known in life
that he would miss: his mother, his brother, his sisters, and
Angie, of course, who was by now not just a person but a part
of himself.

He continued to pray. *We like the same toppings on our
pizza. That's the point. On one of our first dates, we went for
pizza and found ourselves ordering exactly the same thing, a
pan pie with sausage, pepperoni, green peppers, and onions.
That was the beauty of it: We liked the same toppings on our
pizza. . . .* And then his prayer was answered as he blacked out.

An unknowable period of time passed before the intruder's voice, familiar now, jolted him awake, asking him again about access codes for the cash machines and the location of the nearest twenty-four-hour tellers. He was growing impatient, he said, because upstairs Angie had not been telling him the truth. If she continued to lie, he said, he would bring her downstairs and cut her ears off in front of Cliff.

Cut her ears off? "Bring her down here," Cliff said. "I'll get her to tell you what you want to know if she's not telling the truth." *If only he would do it. If only he could see her.* The intruder disappeared then, and more time passed—how much more Cliff could no longer determine—punctuated now and then with more sounds of commotion upstairs. When the stranger returned a final time, he had not brought Angie with him. Instead, he told Cliff his partner would be going off to the cash machine and that if the machine produced for him, they would leave him and Angie alone. Their long night, he said, was almost over.

Yeah, right.

Then the man left once more, and this time when Cliff heard more noise upstairs, it drove him down through depths of numbness and confusion to a decision that it was time, at last, to fight back. Writhing in the cords that bound him, he focused all his energy on his wrists.

Flesh on his arm bruised and tore as a hand finally came free. He pushed off the blindfold, blinked, and looked about. No, there was no one else around. Damaged hands managed to loosen the cord that secured his neck to the stair support, and then they undid the bonds that encircled his waist.

But the tight knots that lashed his heavy boots to the two-by-fours refused to budge. Cliff clawed at them—*shit!*—aware that the stranger could return at any minute, and he began to panic. Then reason counterattacked. *Who needs boots to walk? Feet work fine by themselves.* He quickly undid the laces and wriggled one foot loose, then the other. Bleeding, bruised, and barefoot, he was again a free man.

He stumbled to the foot of the stairs and pondered whether to go up and confront the armed man in order to rescue Angie. But his head was clearing. *Don't be a fool. You could both wind up dead.* It was no time for heroics.

So he headed outside, his bare feet avoiding shards of glass where the intruder had apparently broken a pane in the basement door. The ranch house had long windows set only a few feet from the ground, so Cliff crawled along beneath them, through the wet grass, to avoid being seen.

When he reached the first house, no one answered his knock. At the next, a wary man appeared but claimed his phone was disconnected. A teenage girl came to the door at the third house, opened it a crack, and peered out at the distraught, disheveled stranger, barefoot, naked to the waist, his skin scratched, his arms still trailing lengths of telephone cord. Terrified, she slammed the door shut just as her brother appeared behind her.

"Can't you see that man is hurt?" he said and then helped Cliff inside.

After the second assault, the stranger had led Angela back to the bedroom. In the hallway, he stopped briefly, apologized again for raping her, and tried to give her a hug.

As the rage and revulsion welled up, she tried to grab the gun tucked into his waistband. *The son of a bitch.* She would shoot him if she could. But his vulnerability lasted no more than a moment. Cursing, he seized her hands and pushed her away; then he dragged her into the bedroom, tied her hands behind her, and tied her hands to her feet. He placed her hog-tied on the bed and left the room.

Angela had had it. She knew he still might catch her and kill her, but she also knew that humoring him wouldn't gain her anything more. For better or worse, it was time to act. Straightening her legs, she was able to break the binding that tied her hands to her feet. Then she rubbed her head on the bed and shuffled off the blindfold. She swung her feet to the floor, stood, and hopped into the bathroom. Squatting by the toilet, she found the mustache scissors just where she had dropped them an hour or so before.

After she snipped through the rest of her bonds, she slid open the bathroom window and climbed through, emerging to the gloom of a damp, early dawn. She ran across the lawn toward the street, in her freedom now finally engulfed by sobs of rage and relief. Then she heard Cliff calling her name, and there he was, standing in the street, his chest scarred, his pants torn, his feet bare.

"My God," she said, "he raped me," and shaking uncontrollably, she collapsed in Cliff's embrace.

Cliff Barnes's frantic call to 911 alerted police officers cruising the neighborhood to the getaway car, the red Z28 Camaro.

Shortly after 6:00 A.M., Officer Hubert Farrell spotted the car stopped behind another at a red light at the intersection of

Old Fort Road and Indian Head Highway, about two and a half miles north of the house on Proxmire Drive. Farrell switched on his roof lights and radioed to the other cars in the area that he had found the Z28. Be careful, the radio crackled back; the suspect could be armed.

Farrell opened the door of his cruiser, leveled his gun through the window toward the Camaro, and flicked on his car's public-address system. His amplified voice ordered the driver of the Z28 to open his door and stick his hand out. The man complied, but when Farrell ordered him to get out of his car, the hand disappeared, and the door swung shut.

The suspect threw the Z28 into gear, spun the wheel to get around the car ahead, then turned north on a southbound lane of the highway. As he floored the accelerator, the car fish-tailed for a moment on the wet pavement, then roared the wrong way up the road—toward a confrontation with two police cruisers now heading south in response to Farrell's call.

In the first was Corporal David McCamley, who began weaving back and forth as he closed with the Z28, hoping to force it onto the median strip. At the last moment, he swerved right to avoid a head-on collision. Then he saw the driver, a slender black man, up close, and the gun in his hand. As the cars passed, left door to left door with inches to spare, McCamley leaned to the right across his front seat to avoid being shot.

He heard a crash then and looked back as the Camaro plowed into the cruiser behind his, driven by Officer Paul Lopez. McCamley wheeled his car around and headed back up the southbound lane in pursuit of the Camaro, now speed-ing away from the collision. Lopez managed to turn his car around as well, and joined the chase. Farrell and another offi-cer, Joseph Bell, fell in behind.

Just before the Z28 reached Kerby Hill Road, its right front tire, damaged in the collision, went flat. The driver pulled over to the median strip as the police slammed on their brakes. The suspect emerged from the car, and at that point, the police would say later, pointed the gun as if to shoot at the officers scrambling out of their cars. But he fired no shots. Instead, the police claimed, he jerked and squeezed the trig-ger, apparently unable to release the safety catch, trying to make the gun work.

The cops began shooting as soon as they saw the gun, Lopez using a shotgun he had hauled out of his car. As the suspect whirled about, an officer's bullet caught him. He fell to the ground, then got to his feet, dropped his gun, and fled again, across the road and up a brush-covered hill toward a housing development.

As the other officers clambered over a guardrail on the median strip, McCamley emptied his gun in the suspect's direction. Farrell, Lopez, and Bell resumed firing as the man dodged into a wooded area at the edge of the housing proj-ect. There he fell again as another bullet struck. Then he struggled to his feet and ran, his wounds now spilling blood on the ground.

Adrenaline could not sustain such a flight for long. Bell was the first to reach him, slumped to his knees under a bush beside a house, and he should consider himself lucky, per-haps, that the cop did not blow his brains out then and there. Instead, Bell kept his professional cool, took cover behind a tree, held his gun on the suspect, and ordered him to raise his hands. The others converged on the scene, then, swarming in to secure their panting, injured prey, who finally lay still.

Several miles away, a dazed Angela Miller rode in a patrol car headed for Prince George's Hospital Center, where she faced yet another ordeal—a probing examination for evidence at the Sexual Assault Center. Cliff wasn't in the car. The police had immediately separated the couple in order to "protect the case," they said. They did not want to give a defense attorney any reason to suggest that Cliff and Angie might have colluded to falsify their stories. Sensing her fragility, the young officer at the wheel kept up a stream of small talk, studiously avoiding any mention of the trauma she had just experienced, protecting her for precious minutes from the towering waves poised to crash around her, waves of rage and pain and a fear that had no focus.

Dramatic and terrible as they were, the crimes committed on Proxmire Drive through the night of April 3 and 4, 1987, were hardly unusual. That year, some 5.7 million American households were burglarized, 1.6 million Americans were victims of aggravated assault, 1 million were robbed, 1.5 million had their cars stolen, and 148,000 were raped. These nearly 10 million crimes constituted a bit less than a third of all crimes committed that year.

That was a lot of crime, though it actually was part of a subsiding crime wave. During the decade, the rate of violent crimes per thousand people declined, from 33.3 in 1980 to 29.6 in 1990. But this gradual decrease wasn't all that perceptible to anyone except the researchers who compiled the statistics. And the rate still compared horribly with the rates of the sixties and early seventies. The rate for murder and manslaughter, for example, rose from 5.1 per one hundred thousand persons in 1965 to 9.4 per one hundred thousand in 1990. Much of the population could still recall a time when no one worried much about crime, when people did not think they were putting themselves at serious risk simply by going out on the street after a certain hour, going for a walk in the park, or using public transportation. Parents assumed children were safe playing on the streets near home, walking to the store, or going to school by themselves.

Now, however, the sense of security once taken for granted seemed to have collapsed. This fact of life was not one that could easily be avoided. For tens of millions of Americans, the new fear of crime meant a new set of inconveniences and aggravations, if not actual humiliation, loss, or injury. People shelled out money for locks, gates, alarms, parking garages, private guards, and increased insurance premiums. Especially in cities, they limited their social lives and recreation, venturing out less often in the evening, avoiding neighborhoods, parks, and other public areas considered too dangerous to visit. The need to arrange transportation and security for children consumed parents' precious time and energy.

Furthermore, two events of the 1980s gave crime a new, more menacing edge. One was the invention of crack cocaine by South American drug organizations eager to dispose of bumper coca crops. Pellets of the concentrated drug can be smoked to produce a rush that is more intense than the one achieved by sniffing cocaine powder—and is followed by a crash that makes the user desperate for another puff. It was a stroke of marketing genius. A rock of crack sold for ten dollars or less, compared with hundreds or thousands for an ounce of cocaine powder. This innovation opened up a huge ghetto clientele for a drug that had once been limited to the rich.

The second crime-related event of the eighties was the rise of manufacturers willing to sell relatively cheap handguns without much concern for who bought them or how they might be used. These American producers sprang up after federal law banned importation of Saturday-night specials from abroad; the handful of American manufacturers seemed to take a much more aggressive approach to marketing than had the foreigners. By the mid-1980s, guns suddenly were everywhere, especially in the hands of teenagers; some were even found in the backpacks of elementary school kids. The market spiraled as youngsters fearful of other youngsters with guns rushed to get guns for themselves.

Complementing each other, the trends grew like cancer. The crack trade spawned new urban gangs to market the drug; the gang members needed firearms to make war over territory. Drug profits gave them the means to arm themselves. As they did, they encouraged new entrepreneurs, who got rich smuggling guns from states with lenient gun laws and selling them at a big markup in cities with strict gun laws. They worked hard to find new customers on the streets, who now included not just drug dealers but drug users, who needed guns to commit crimes to get more cash for drugs. Meanwhile, the National Rifle Association and its political supporters managed to fend off laws that might have broken the cycle. The whole business was a model of unfettered enterprise in an era when conservative Republicans, devoted to free enterprise, ruled America.

The result was a new urban subculture, an underclass made up of youngsters abandoned in large numbers by failing inner-city schools and their own families to a life based on drug use, drug money, and guns.

This contributed in a big way to the rest of America's new, uncomfortable sense of physical insecurity. From 1979 to 1989, the rate of teenage firearm homicide deaths soared by a shocking 61 percent, with most of the increase occurring in the second half of the decade. During the same period, the rate of non-gun teenage homicides declined. The drive-by shooting and the stray bullet victim entered the vocabulary of urban life; both terms starkly dramatize the extent to which the increase in guns heightened the risk of random death.

The rise of crack and street guns undermined deeper aspects of national identity, character, and confidence as they made once unthinkable depravity seem routine. In crack houses, women freely traded sex for the drug, producing a new epidemic of syphilis and accelerating the spread of AIDS. Hospital obstetric units filled up with babies born to crack-using mothers. These infants' prospects for a stable, nurturing upbringing were grim enough; in addition, they would start out life underweight and mentally handicapped. Mothers desperate for crack abandoned their children; children addicted to it beat and robbed their parents; teenage gang members transfixed by it moved into apartment houses, brutally subjugating or evicting helpless elderly tenants.

As a result of the gun epidemic, armed addicts shot victims dead while robbing them of a few dollars for drugs. Kids shot one another to obtain leather jackets and high-end sneakers or in disputes over romantic triangles and street-corner insults. They fought pitched battles on busy streets in broad daylight; they even staged showdowns and shootouts in school corridors.

As the drug and gun subculture metastasized in urban communities, it contributed to a new racism: Crime news in America's cities portrayed an apparently endless parade of young black men under arrest, on trial, or headed for prison; it did not take long for the automatic, barely conscious association of blacks with crime to become an assumption of urban life. Statistics confirmed that black men were committing crimes at a disproportionate rate. In 1986, for example, a federal study found that blacks had committed 24 percent of violent crimes during the year though they made up only about 12 percent of the general population. Few people took the trouble to learn, or to point out, that even so, the number of blacks committing crimes remained such a tiny percentage of all blacks that the assumption of dangerousness wasn't rational.

All this developed in the larger context of a decade that was the best of times and the worst of times: Tax cuts, lax regulation, and easy credit liberated billions of dollars to subsidize upscale careers in finance, real estate, and law. Yet tides of government money began to ebb, reducing the funds available for both the social services that once secured the basics of life for the poor and the criminal justice agencies that were supposed to keep order. In big cities, the two Americas jostled uncomfortably against each other. Young urban professionals, having spent $100 per person for a meal, encountered hungry or rudely aggressive panhandlers on the sidewalks outside the upscale restaurants. Parents delivering children to $10,000-a-year elementary schools hustled past filth-encrusted people living out of cardboard boxes in the doorways nearby. The jogger decked out in $600 worth of Gore-Tex for her daily turn through the park learned to sidestep crack vials, AIDS-infected needles, and piles of human shit.

What was happening to America? What kind of country had it become, and where was it headed? The news media might have played a constructive role in helping people find answers to these upsetting questions, or at least in helping them understand that a better quality of life in general and more public safety in particular could not be had without more money, which had to come from somewhere. But instead, the daily diet of crime coverage only increased the general sense of fear and confusion.

Daily journalists had for years looked to police blotters and court dockets for raw material, but according to long-standing tradition, the stories they produced served mostly to entertain, not to enlighten or lead. As the crime-control issue intensified, newspaper and television journalism continued to focus on sensational, high-profile crime stories rather than examining the reasons more mundane crimes had become a source of daily anxiety.

In part this course of events reflected nothing more than the institutional racism of the mainstream news business. The collapse of public safety occurred first and most severely in inner-city ghettos populated by blacks and Hispanics whose troubles of any sort rarely received much media attention. And however urgent it had become, however acutely millions of Americans felt its effects, the national crime-control crisis emerged too gradually for daily journalism to handle it with any coherence. Occasionally *Time* or *Newsweek* might devote a cover story to the rising crime rate. But then, their duty done, they would ignore the subject for years.

In its gradualness, the decline of public safety in the 1970s and '80s was like some other large-scale national events: the immigration from the farms of the South to the cities of the North and the West in an earlier period or the progress of the baby boom demographic bulge through its constituents' life stages. These events and trends changed America, profoundly and dramatically, yet for the most part, they were left for the sociologists, historians, filmmakers, and novelists to explain, not for the morning paper or the evening news.

Especially not for the evening news. Television journalism needs to present a story more visually than verbally and to do so in no more than a minute or two. That makes the complexities of criminal justice all the harder to explain, even as it magnifies the emotional force of a victim's anguish or a neighborhood's fear. The chances for serious debate and public education on the criminal justice issue faded as Americans made the tube their basic source of news. More than they liked to admit, even highbrow newspapers found themselves held hostage by television. Fearing lost readers and swallowing their better judgment, they joined in the coverage of crimes that television sensationalized, lending more legitimacy to the fear and anger these stories inspired.

On the few occasions when editors would assign reporters to examine systemic problems of criminal justice, the reporters typically would probe deep enough to uncover outrage but not deep enough to permit a fair assessment of the reasons for it. An investigative report, headlined something like JUNK JUSTICE, would point with indignation to the apparent scandalous laxity of the courts: huge portions of criminal cases settled by plea bargains, with the convict quickly released as the judge sentenced him to the time he had already served in jail while awaiting trial; homicidal felons supposedly sentenced to long terms actually spending an average of six to seven years behind bars.

Too often, such reporting focused on the viciousness of the criminals and the apparent appalling laxity of the system that deals with them. Rarely would stories include a full discussion of how corners were being cut for lack of resources or a realistic estimate of how many tax dollars it would cost to provide more rigorous justice. Readers were left with the impression that the problem had mostly to do with incompetent, cynical, or corrupt public officials.

It was against this background that the media began to discover the new American crime story—random violence against innocent middle-class victims, committed by criminals the system might have controlled better. Such cases dropped like crystals into a solution supersaturated with fear, causing sudden, intense, and often grotesquely disproportionate reactions.

The night of terror on Proxmire Drive was another such crystal and would eventually provoke as potent a reaction as America had seen. That was because the man the Prince George's police found near collapse under a bush in the housing project off Indian Head Highway was yet another criminal who might have been behind bars but for the discretionary judgments of public officials. Ten months before, he had

55

failed to return from a weekend furlough he had been granted from the Northeastern Correctional Center in West Concord, Massachusetts. He had been in prison since 1975, when he was convicted of murder and sentenced to life without parole.

He carried documents that identified him as Tony Franklin. But when the Prince George's detectives sent his fingerprints to the Federal Bureau of Investigation, technicians who discovered that he was an escapee from Massachusetts also reported that the name was an alias. His real name was William Robert Horton. Within two years, it would be a household word.

Lawrence

1 9 7 4

The pounding on the door started sometime after five in the morning, and it woke the dog first. Barking furiously to defend the house, he quickly roused everyone else except little Tara, sleeping soundly in her crib.

Catherine went to the door and opened it to a police officer, who asked if William Horton was there. Yes he was, Catherine said but begged a moment to put the dog away, for she couldn't be sure what he might do to an unfamiliar visitor. Having got the door open, the cop wasn't about to let it close again, so he held it and stood there while Catherine dealt with the dog.

Then she went into the bedroom. She wanted to get Tara out of there, should things get worse. The cop followed her in, his gun drawn now. Catherine asked him to put it away; it terrified her. But he paid no attention. Now Cheryl and little Caroline had appeared in the kitchen, the younger child weeping in fright.

When the cop came into the room, William was in bed with his hands still under the covers. That made the cop nervous. His gun up, he told William to take his hands out slowly; when he saw they held nothing, he relaxed a bit and said, "Come on. You're wanted down at the station." Then with his free hand, he pulled out a little card and read from it the Miranda rights.

"What's it all about?" William asked.

"Come on. Just come on. We're going down to the station," the cop replied; the hint of impatience combined with the gun once again electrified the air. William asked once more what was going on, but the cop gave up no information. "Put your clothes on," he said. "Let's go."

William got up slowly, still shaking off sleep, put on some clothes, and looked for his shoes. But that made the cop more nervous still. "Just put your slippers on and come on," he said. So William obeyed and followed him into the kitchen.

There he confronted Catherine and her girls, ashen faced and disbelieving. "Where are my cigarettes?" he asked the mother of his child. She looked around and found a pack to give him, then watched the officer lead him out, not knowing that he would not return until many years had passed and everything had changed.

The chain of events that landed William Horton in a Prince George's County hospital in police custody began years before, a few hundred miles away, in the state of South Carolina. He grew up there in the 1950s and '60s, near Chesterfield, a country town of some fourteen hundred souls, not far from the North Carolina border. Along with William, there were two sisters and a brother, Charles, a dozen years older, who left town when William was still a little boy. William Senior worked as a trash collector for the city, and his wife, Sara, did domestic work for families in town.

Describing the Horton household, a South Carolina corrections official would write that "income was poor, supervision and discipline was lacking and home had little structure." This was an understatement. According to prison records in Massachusetts and South Carolina, William Senior harbored a vicious temper that grew meaner when he had too much to drink, and he often did. One day in 1956, when William Junior was four, the records show, William Senior argued with Sara and wound up firing a gun at her. Several years later, an accident left him blind and unable to work, so he went on welfare. Idleness combined with an evil temper didn't make things any better at home.

William Junior entered first grade at the Edwards Elementary School and got promoted each year, his work only average to poor. By the time he reached the seventh grade, he had begun skipping days of school. The truancy continued as he moved on to Gary High School. By now, he was growing into adolescence—a tall, muscular kid with a serious attitude problem.

Meanwhile, William's big brother, Charles, had sought his fortune in the North, ending up in Lawrence, Massachusetts, one of several blue-collar towns along the Merrimack River some thirty miles above Boston. There he found work in the defense and automotive factories that supported the region's economy, and he settled down with a local woman named Helen Mays.

Helen had a nephew, her sister Evelyn Cecil's son Lloyd, whom everyone called Dougie. As the boy approached adolescence, Evelyn began sending him down to Chesterfield during summer vacations to keep him off the streets of Lawrence. The first year he went, William was about eleven. The two boys got along well, pursuing an easy summer routine. They lay around William's grandparents' house, located on a small piece of property a few miles outside Chesterfield. Or they headed into town to hang out at a local candy store that doubled as a dance hall. Sometimes William's grandfather took them fishing.

But Dougie also remembers a teenager harboring a lot of unfocused anger. "William had a bad temper then," he says. "He would get into fights over nothing; he would start them." When Dougie went to Chesterfield in the summer of 1964, William wasn't around; he'd been arrested for breaking and entering and had been sent off to a state reformatory in Columbia for six months. When he came out, he went to work, claiming he no longer had any use for school. He found a job as a laborer and then another in a laundry before he got arrested for another B & E. This time he stayed at the reformatory a year.

About then Sara, understandably fed up, decided to take the girls and move to New York, where she had family, leaving her husband and son behind. When young William came out again, he lived with his grandparents until a night in January 1968 when the volatile temper ignited once more. William and a friend had taken a taxi to a nightclub outside town. As they arrived, they got into a dispute with the driver. William pulled a knife, and the hapless driver fell beneath it. This time, the charge was assault with intent to kill, and William served nearly two years in a state penitentiary for adults.

Free again at the end of 1969, he made what seemed like a sensible decision to get out of Chesterfield. Like his brother before him, he headed north in hopes of rejoining his mother and sisters in New York, but the reunion lasted only a year. Horton would say later he couldn't handle his mother's having found a new husband. Others suggest he got into trouble with the law as well. Whatever the reason, he left New York in 1971 for the only other place he might find a welcome, Lawrence, Massachusetts.

And there, for a time, he began to build a life. Dougie was glad to see him, as were Charles and Helen. He was by now an attractive, slender young man with a bushy Afro haircut that made him seem even taller than six feet, three inches. He found a job as a machine operator for a company that made brake linings, and he held it for more than a year. And he started going out with Helen's sister Catherine.

The relationship was rocky at times. Catherine Mays was about eight years older than William, already the mother of two daughters. Even so, in 1973, William moved into her place on Acton Street, becoming the man of the house for Cheryl Elizabeth, sixteen, and Caroline, six. In January 1974, he shifted jobs, signing on as a solderer in the big Raytheon plant where Dougie, Helen, and Catherine all worked on the lines that produced guided missiles and other military hardware. Horton stayed only until April, however, when he left to take a construction job. That May, Catherine gave birth to Horton's child, a little girl they named Tara. Catherine still remembers William's fatherly pride, how he took the baby out to show her around the day she came home from the hospital.

But in other ways, Horton, now all of twenty-three and still tasting the angry residue of a rotten childhood, found the role of solid citizen an uncomfortable fit. For one thing, despite his new family, he still had trouble connecting with others in positive ways. "[Horton] has had many associations during his lifetime but very few friends," a prison social worker would observe a bit later. "He has usually hung around with small groups but has also maintained an aloof position. This is a protective device that has kept [him] from being hurt." Law-enforcement people who eventually dealt with him would recall his coldness, his affectless calm in circumstances that normally call for some emotion.

Furthermore, like his father before him, he had acquired a taste for strong vodka; enough of it could take the lid off his violent temper. "When he was drinking, he was an evil man," Dougie says of him in those years. His baptism in crime down in South Carolina, reinforced by exposure to more criminals at the reformatory and penitentiary, hadn't helped.

"William would do any kind of shit to get money," Dougie recalls. He was not above muggings and burglaries. "William was good at it because he didn't care. He didn't worry about people hurting him because he was so big and strong. He didn't worry about going to prison because he'd already been there. It was like he had a death wish."

He also dabbled in drugs. Later on he would admit to having used marijuana, heroin, and cocaine during his years in Lawrence but insisted that he never became an addict. He also learned the ropes of dealing, earning enough to supplement his paychecks by a few hundred dollars per week. But he couldn't hold on to money for long. After Dougie Cecil and his father opened a weekend after-hours club, William became a regular at the poker and crap games.

Police records reinforce the portrait of a man who managed to combine the respectability of steady work and family life with a self-destructive streak, if not a death wish. In June 1971, for example, a judge fined him $175 for driving without a license, registration, or insurance. He would be arrested again several times in 1972, 1973, and 1974 for more motor vehicle violations, drunkenness, assault and battery, and low-level drug dealing, though none of the charges resulted in more than a small fine.

Whatever commitment he felt to Catherine and Tara did not keep him from taking a night out from time to time with people he knew from the streets, and that is what he decided to do on the evening of October 26, 1974, a Saturday. One of his partners that night was Alvin Wideman, a short guy with a wild reputation who stayed at a place on Hannigan Street with his friend Jesse James (J.J.) Thomas, Jesse's wife, Thelma, and five of their six kids. Horton's other companion was Roosevelt Pickett, who had appeared in the neighborhood within the last couple of months. Pickett had a wife, a white woman, down in Cambridge. But recently he'd been staying at a place on Park Street while working in the shipping department of an Andover plant.

The three took off in Pickett's blue and white '63 Chevy, heading for a party they'd heard about in Lowell, nine miles up the river to the west. Drink flowed, and drugs were injected, smoked, or snorted, but Horton and his friends decided not to linger there. Sometime after 8:00 P.M., they got into Pickett's car and drove back toward Lawrence. The night was still young, they realized, and they needed money to keep it alive.

A few hours before Horton, Pickett, and Wideman had taken off for Lowell in Pickett's Chevy, a young man named Joseph Fournier reported for work at Marston Street Mobil. The gas station stood near a ramp onto Route 495, the big expressway running through the valley, just before it crosses the Merrimack River on the O'Reilly Bridge. At five feet, ten inches and 120 pounds, Joey was hardly an imposing seventeen-year-old—his family had reason to worry about him pumping gas alone on the evening shift. But Joey loved cars and needed the money. Besides, his friend Joe McComiskey also worked at the station, and Joey was living with the McComiskeys that fall. His parents had moved up to Londonderry, New Hampshire, and Joey wanted to stay in town so he could continue at Greater Lawrence Regional Vocational Technical High School, known as the Voc.

That Saturday, McComiskey had worked until three in the afternoon, until Fournier arrived for the evening shift. The late-October day was turning cool, and Joey wasn't wearing a jacket, so McComiskey left his, a red one with white stripes at the shoulders.

About nine-fifteen that night, McComiskey returned to Marston Street Mobil with his friends Paul Noone and the Smith brothers, Scott and Randolph. The Smiths had borrowed their mother's Pontiac to go bowling at Lawrence Rec, and the car needed gas. McComiskey also wanted his red jacket back. The only other one he had found to put on that night was an ugly brown color with a big rip in one side, and he didn't feel like wearing it to the Rec. So after putting some gas in the car, he asked Joey to exchange the red jacket for the brown one.

Joey decided to give him a hard time. He took the brown jacket, but before surrendering the red one, he asked McComiskey to go and get him something to eat. McComiskey refused: There wasn't time; Mrs. Smith had said she wanted the boys home early with her car. So Joey took off with both jackets, heading around the side of the station.

McComiskey knew how to get back at his friend: He went over to a rack of tires and tossed them to the ground. Then he chased Joey all the way around the back of the station so that he would see the tires as he returned to the front. When he saw them, Joey flew into a rage and came after McComiskey; the two boys moved into one of the service bays, scuffling and throwing punches. At one point, Joey picked up a wooden measuring stick and broke it across McComiskey's shoulder.

Just then a yellow Mustang rolled up to the gas pumps, ringing a bell in the service bays, and the boys came to their senses. McComiskey backed off and told Joey he'd replace the tires if Joey would give him the red jacket. Joey agreed, and McComiskey asked Randy Smith to handle the customer at the pumps while he stacked the tires.

So Randy pumped gas, McComiskey stacked tires, and Joey cooled down, then went out to take the money from the Mustang's driver. Moments later, the Mustang departed, and McComiskey, wearing his red jacket, piled into the Pontiac with his friends and drove off to Lawrence Rec.

The fight over the coat and the tires was nothing more than adolescent horseplay, but soon enough it would intrigue the Lawrence police and cause Joe McComiskey a measure of guilt. For Joey Fournier never came home that night. McComiskey was the last of his friends to see him alive.

Customers driving into Marston Street Mobil a short while later found no one to pump their gas. James Scuderi arrived in his brother's car from a house nearby, hoping to purchase a can of fuel for his own car, which had run out. He waited a few minutes at the pumps, then went into the station, all the way into the back office, where he found nothing but a wastebasket covered with rags. So he went back outside.

In the meantime, two young women, Denise Cote and Eleanor Montgomery, had pulled up in a white Mustang, followed a few moments later by John MacKenzie and two friends in a blue Buick. MacKenzie and his buddies were spending their Saturday night driving around, looking for Methuen Mall. But they'd been taking their time, chugging beer and sipping wine as they drove. And now they were lost.

Driving past Marston Street Mobil, MacKenzie thought he recognized the girls in the Mustang, so he pulled in to say hello. It turned out he didn't know them at all, but that didn't stop him from walking over to their car, a beer in one hand, a wine bottle in the other, to introduce himself. They allowed him into the backseat of their car for a few minutes before sending him on his way and driving off.

When he returned to the Buick, he found his friends talking with Scuderi, who had wandered over. MacKenzie invited him into his car for a drink. The four discussed the fact that no one seemed to be around, and MacKenzie suggested making off with a few free cans of oil; he even backed the Buick up to a rack of them. But another car's arrival squelched that idea.

The driver of this car was Michael Byron, a student at the Voc and a friend of Joey Fournier. Byron was in the habit of pumping his own gas when Joey was on duty, then finding Joey to pay him. He was followed by two friends, Stephen Beaulieu and John Baggett, who pulled up in a Ford Falcon. Byron put five dollars worth of gas in his tank and went into the station to pay. Moments later, as the men in MacKenzie's car watched, Byron rushed out, called to his friends in the Falcon, jumped in his own car, and sped off toward Lawrence General Hospital, a few blocks away.

Seeing this, MacKenzie decided it was time to split; he let Scuderi out and headed for Marston Street. Scuderi went into the station and entered the back office again. There was something odd about the pile of rags over the wastebasket. Looking more closely, he saw a head of hair. Scared now, he approached what was undeniably a person. Then he saw the blood on the floor. He pushed on the corpse's left shoulder and saw more blood. He reeled back, collected himself, then rushed out to the pay phone and called the police. At the hospital, nurses dealing with the panicked Byron had done the same.

The crime outraged the whole Merrimack Valley. Whoever attacked Joey Fournier had stabbed him nineteen times— apparently for the sake of about $250, the cash from gas sales that he kept in a roll in his pant pocket.

With the case on page 1 of the local papers, police mounted a determined investigation, focusing at first on the blond young man in a ski mask who had held up a gas station in another part of town earlier that same evening. Within a few days, however, detectives began to pick up another story from informants in the community.

One Lawrence cop, Bill Pedrick, even learned the names from a young marijuana dealer who was willing to trade information for small favors. Word on the street, he said, was that three men were involved: Alvin Wideman, the little guy who lived with Jesse and Thelma Thomas; William Horton, the tall kid who had taken up with Helen Mays's sister Catherine; and a smoother fellow named Roosevelt Pickett, new to the neighborhood, said to be still married to a white girl down in Cambridge.

But so far, this was just rumor and no basis for arrests. The crime scene had yielded no solid clues to speak of; none of the people who had gone to the station for gas that night looked like a suspect, nor had any of them seen anyone hanging around who might.

Despite all the spent shoe leather and massaging of informants, the break that solved the case came by chance, courtesy of Wideman's landlords, the Thomases.

J. J. Thomas considered himself a tough dude. He had grown up in the Deep South—born in Magnolia, Mississippi; raised in Hammond, Louisiana—and had arrived in Massachusetts in 1969 while still in the army: When he finished his year in Vietnam, they had sent him up to Fort Devens, located in the center of the state, about forty miles southwest of Lawrence.

After his discharge, he decided to settle in Lawrence, finding work at Raytheon and other plants in the area to support his wife, Thelma, and their six kids. The Thomases lived in a third-floor apartment in the house on Hannigan Street. Alvin Wideman would say that J.J. fooled around with drugs to augment his income, using space in the basement of the house to cut big bags of heroin into little ones for sale on the street. But J.J. denied all that.

He did not deny, however, that like his namesake, he had an abiding interest in guns. He'd learned how to use them over in Vietnam, where combat duty had inflicted a chronic case of nerves, for which he still collected disability. He claimed to own several firearms: some hunting rifles along with .22-caliber and 9-millimeter pistols. And according to Wideman, he didn't mind his reputation as a gunslinger. "He plays with them a lot," Wideman would say of J.J. and his guns. If you passed him on the street and said a word to him, Alvin recalled, he might pull out one of his guns and point it at you.

The two men had known each other for about five years before Wideman's final arrest, in 1974, ever since Thomas had moved up to Massachusetts. During that time, as Thomas strived however he could to support his big family, Wideman became a neighborhood ne'er-do-well. He claimed that a heart condition limited his career options. "He's about thirty years old, and he's got the heart of a seventy-two-year-old man," Thomas would say when people asked why Wideman never seemed able to find a job. So Wideman became something of a fixture on the block, playing with kids, hanging out. "Everyone around here knows Alvin," Thomas would say. "Everybody knows he's all right."

But not quite everyone. For Wideman was also known to have a mean and violent streak, especially when it came to women. In 1971, he was convicted of assault and battery for beating up Irene Moore, a woman he'd been dating who lived next door to the Thomases. A judge let him off on probation when he agreed to pay her hospital costs. Later that summer, Jesse Thomas said he'd actually had to pull a gun and fire it at Wideman in order to calm him down after a fight with Irene on the Thomases' back porch. At first, J.J. said, he didn't want to get involved, but then he heard Alvin threaten Thelma's sister, Rosalie, when she objected to his hitting Irene. As J.J. walked onto the porch, gun in hand, Alvin cursed him out— "Nigger, I will fuck you up, too"—and came at him. J.J. fired once, and the bullet grazed Alvin's temple. Wideman later acknowledged that Thomas had shot at him (the incident never came to the attention of police) but insisted that no women were present.

Even so, the two remained friends. J.J. continued to say that Alvin "was like a brother." In 1973, a few weeks after J.J. quit a job he had taken with the local community action council, he and Alvin drove down to Louisiana together, just the two of them, to visit J.J.'s family and old friends. The next year, Alvin got in trouble with the law again. He was indicted for selling heroin in January and again in May for assaulting and robbing a man named George Bruce. Alvin went to jail, and stayed there until the Bruce case went to a trial that ended in acquittal. J.J. came to visit from time to time, and when Alvin walked out of court a free man on October 8, the Thomases were glad to take him in.

At home with J.J., Thelma, and all those kids that fall, Wideman found himself in the middle of a tense scene. The Thomases weren't getting along, and when J.J. leaned on

Thelma, she sometimes appealed to Wideman for help. Given his own problems with women, Alvin knew enough to keep his distance. One night, he sat playing chess with one of J.J.'s friends from the Raytheon plant when they overheard the Thomases fighting in the bedroom. At one point, Thelma began calling to Alvin to "come and make J.J. stop."

"Aren't you going back there?" his chess partner asked.

"No, it ain't my problem," Wideman responded, and as soon as they finished their game, he left the house. He didn't even mention the matter to J.J. until a week or so later, after Thelma had moved out for a few days.

On the evening of Saturday, October 26, J.J. decided to go across the street by himself to play cards with some neighbors. The game broke up a little after ten, and J.J. walked back to his house, where he found Thelma and a couple of the kids in the living room, watching television. He plopped himself down in front of the tube and watched it with them for an hour or so, until they heard Alvin come in.

Wideman was agitated and wanted to talk. J.J. was annoyed; by now, the news was on, and a sportscaster was about to tell him whether Alabama or Ohio State was number one in the nation. But here was Alvin, maybe a little drunk, blurting out something wild.

"He told me he killed somebody," J.J. testified later. "I told him he was lying. And he said, 'No, man, I'm telling the truth.' . . . He told me that he wasn't kidding. . . . He told me he don't know what happened. He said it just happened, he stabbed him, he couldn't stop stabbing him. And I still didn't believe him. I just told him he was lying."

J.J. turned back to the television. It was impossible to believe some of the things Alvin said.

Thelma was more inclined to listen. "He said that he went in this place and asked the fellow to give him all his money," she would testify. "He said the fellow gave him his money and asked him please not to hurt him. And he said he don't know what happened, he got mad, and he started stabbing him, and he couldn't stop. . . . He told us that we'd probably read it in the paper the next day, because he didn't know whether the fellow was dead or not."

But the Thomases didn't see a newspaper the next day, a Sunday, because they had *The Lawrence Eagle-Tribune* delivered only during the week. Alvin went out in the morning and came back in the afternoon. He rummaged around and found one of J.J.'s handguns, but before he could get out of the house with it, one of the kids spotted the gun and told J.J.

J.J. confronted his friend: What did he think he was doing?

Borrowing a gun, Alvin said.

"Hell, no," J.J. declared, grabbed the gun away, and went into the kitchen, where Thelma was sitting with some of the kids.

Alvin came into the kitchen to plead with J.J. He needed the gun to shoot William Horton and Roosevelt Pickett because they had burned him when he was drunk, he explained. He had done all the work; he had killed a person to get the money, got all the money by himself, he told J.J. and Thelma, and then William and Roosevelt had stolen his share. It made him feel bad, he said, because he'd wanted to give some of the stolen money to J.J. to help cover his room and board.

J.J. still didn't know whether to believe Alvin or not. That afternoon, William and Roosevelt showed up at the house, spoke to Alvin for a few moments, then left. The Thomases never learned what was said, but no one got shot, for J.J. remained adamant about not lending Alvin a gun.

The next day, Monday, J.J. had the day off and slept late. The paper arrived early, and there on page 1 was a story about the robbery of Marston Street Mobil and the murder of Joey Fournier. Thelma brought the paper into the bedroom to show her husband, then called Alvin in and handed the paper to him. Is this what he was talking about? she asked.

Yes it was, Alvin said, paying close attention to the words confirming that the stabbing victim had died.

"You know Alvin lies," J.J. said.

But Alvin said he did it, Thelma responded.

"You know he lies," J.J. insisted, "just like I know he lies."

Alvin had the last word that morning: He sure hoped everybody would react just the way J.J. had, he said, that everyone would think he was lying, that everyone would think he didn't do it.

J.J. might have preferred to put the whole business out of his mind, but as days passed and publicity about the crime and the search for the killer continued, he found he couldn't. What if Alvin had told the truth? Here he had the murderer, the man everyone was looking for, living in his own house! He knew he didn't have to worry about Alvin around Thelma or the kids. But what if his friend got arrested? Could he and Thelma then get in trouble for not having gone to the cops with what they knew?

The anxiety was too much for J.J. to contain. The first to notice something amiss was Fred Sciuto, his foreman at

Raytheon. Eleven days had passed since the murder; J.J. was at his desk on the evening of November 6—he worked a four-to-midnight shift—when Sciuto walked up and told him he seemed distracted. Was there a problem?

Yeah, J.J. said, there was a problem.

"Is there something I can do to help you?" Fred asked.

"I don't know," J.J. responded. "I don't know if nobody can help me."

So Fred took J.J. into a little room, a photo lab, where they could talk privately, and J.J. told him the whole story. He still didn't know whether to believe Alvin or not, he said, but he was worried about himself now, whether he might have to go to prison if Alvin turned out to be telling the truth.

Sciuto said he didn't know how much trouble J.J. might be in, but he certainly knew how to find out: His cousin Stephen was a captain with the Lawrence police.

By the next night, J.J.'s anxiety had deepened. The last thing he wanted to do was turn his friend in to the police. When he had talked to Fred, he had only wanted to find out a bit more about the law so that he could consider his options. But as it turned out, he had lost control of them.

When Fred came by that night, J.J. recalled, "I told him that I really didn't want to go to the police about it, you know, I just want to find out what could be done to me, and he told me that he felt that I was already involved and that since I had told him, *he* was involved and that we would have to go to the police. It wouldn't be no other choice, you know, either I was going or he was going."

So after midnight, when the shift ended, J.J. went to Fred's house in Methuen, and Fred called his cousin Stephen to invite him over for a chat. When the captain arrived, "I told him who I was," J.J. recalled, "and he told me, 'I understand you got a problem.' I say, 'Yeah,' and he says, 'Well, you know, tell me what it is,' and I told him, and he told me, 'Yes, you can be charged. . . . You can be charged as an accessory.' "

The sentence for a person convicted of being an accessory to murder after the fact, the captain explained, was seven years.

J.J. swallowed hard and began to backpedal. He couldn't really swear to all that much, he said, because he'd been watching television when Alvin blurted out his confession; he hadn't paid much attention to what Alvin was saying.

Was anyone else there? the captain asked.

"Yeah," J.J. replied. "My wife was there."

And would she be willing to tell the police what Alvin had said to her?

Not unless she had a good reason, J.J. told the Sciutos.

A reason? "Like what?" the captain asked.

"Like if you had me, she would tell," J.J. said.

And that became the basis for a little scheme. Fred drove J.J. home, where he went to bed without a word to Thelma about his conversation with the Sciutos. A short while later, Captain Sciuto and two more officers arrived from the Lawrence Police Department and woke the Thomases up. They were arresting J.J. as a prime suspect in the murder of Joey Fournier, they said, and as Thelma watched, they read him his rights and handcuffed him.

Don't take him, she told them, because he didn't do it. But she didn't tell them that she knew who did.

After they had left, Thelma woke Alvin and told him that the police had just arrested J.J. for the Fournier murder. She had to go down to the police station herself, she said—the cruiser would be coming back for her—and she told him to watch the kids.

"Oh, God," Alvin moaned as Thelma rushed out.

So the scheme worked. At the police station, Thelma willingly gave Captain Sciuto a full statement about Alvin's confession, grateful that she could straighten things out that simply. Sciuto dispatched more cops to Hannigan Street to bring Wideman in, and they gave the Thomases a few minutes alone in a room with Alvin, perhaps hoping they'd persuade him to repeat his confession for the police.

The scheme didn't work that well. J.J. said he wasn't going to take the rap for the murder or for knowing about it and that Alvin should tell what he knew to the police. But Alvin said he couldn't do it.

Meanwhile, Sciuto sent a car for Horton and rode to Pickett's place on Park Street. The police rousted Horton from bed at gunpoint as Catherine and her older daughters, stricken with fear, watched from the kitchen. And they stopped Pickett just as he left his house to catch a ride for an early shift at work, carrying a bag of kielbasa sandwiches for lunch. They also found the blue and white Chevy parked in the yard at Pickett's house. Sciuto reached under the front seat and retrieved a knife.

Lawyers for all three men would argue later that the suspects had not been read their Miranda rights, but the judges weren't impressed. Wideman and Pickett also claimed that Sciuto, feeling his oats, had been less than professional.

Shortly after his arrest, Wideman claimed, Sciuto had told him to wait in a room where a police officer sat before a radio console. "He said to the officer," Wideman testified, ". . . you going to have some company for a while, . . . and the other officer say okay, and Captain ask him if he had his hand-gun . . . and he didn't have it on at the time. The officer didn't. So he say, yeah, he say, well put it on and if this bastard moves empty it in his fucking head."

Pickett claimed that after his arrest, the cops put him into the back of a cruiser and that Sciuto climbed in beside him. "When Captain Sciuto got in the car," Pickett testified, "he asked me was I going to tell him what happened. I told him I don't know what he is talking about. He pulled his gun out . . . and put it in my face, and told me to open my mouth. I just looked at him at first, and he asked me, was I going to open it, so I opened my mouth, and he stuck the gun in my mouth and told me he was going to blow my damn brains out."

But Sciuto denied both incidents of intimidation, and the defendants' complaints never advanced beyond early hearings.

With all three back at police headquarters—by now, it was close to six in the morning—Sciuto took Horton aside, heard his story, and decided to make a deal. If the kid would testify against the others, he'd be charged only with robbery, leaving the others to stand trial for murder as well. But then Sergeant Patrick Schiavone, the detective who had led the investigation since the night of the crime, came in, Sciuto finally having remembered to call him. Schiavone had a right to be around for the interrogation, Sciuto thought, even though it was he who had cracked the case.

Once he learned what the captain was about to do, Schiavone sensed trouble. Though he outranked Schiavone,

Sciuto had less experience with interrogations like this. The deal with Horton, Schiavone immediately understood, could put the whole prosecution at risk. Should Horton, once charged with robbery, decide to back out, the case would collapse. Sciuto would be able to testify only to what Horton had said about himself; what he had told Sciuto about the others, out of their presence, would be hearsay, inadmissible as evidence.

And there was a good chance Horton would have second thoughts once he had spoken with a lawyer. For under Massachusetts's felony murder law, everyone who participates in a robbery that results in murder can be held responsible for the murder. Unless the court agreed to grant him immunity—not likely—Horton would expose himself to punishment for murder simply by admitting to the robbery. Therefore, the only safe way to proceed, Schiavone figured, was to take each man's statement in the presence of the other two.

So Schiavone waded in, and an annoyed Sciuto agreed to defer to the detective's expertise. Schiavone ordered Pickett and Wideman brought back to the booking room and sat them down across the table from Horton. Then he read them all their Miranda rights. And then he asked Horton to repeat his version of the crime.

Horton said the three had started out the evening of October 26 drinking at a party in Lowell. They left early in Pickett's car with Horton at the wheel. When they got back to Lawrence, they decided to rob a gas station. Horton parked the car on a hill above Marston Street Mobil. He stayed in the car, he said, while Wideman and Pickett took knives and walked down to the station. Wideman came back first, Horton said, then Pickett. Horton asked Pickett what happened. Pickett said they had to get rid of evidence, Horton stated, and "there's another dead honky." Then, Horton said, the three divided the take, about seventy dollars apiece, in the car.

Now Pickett spoke up, imploring Wideman to "tell them what happened, tell them the truth." But Wideman remained silent. So Pickett then said it was he who was driving the car back from Lowell. It was he who parked it on the hill above the gas station; it was Horton who went with Wideman to rob the place. Wideman, Pickett said, came back first, then Horton. They drove on to a club called the Tangerine in Haverhill, where they divided the money.

At that point, Sciuto turned to Wideman and asked if he had anything to say. At first he said no, but Pickett kept pleading with Wideman to "tell them what happened." Finally, Wideman made his statement: They had been drinking in Lowell; as they drove back to Lawrence, Horton had suggested holding up a gas station. Wideman admitted going into the station and robbing the attendant at knifepoint, but when he left, he said, the boy was still alive.

"Well, will you tell them it wasn't me that was there?" Pickett implored. "Will you tell them it wasn't me?" Wideman, the captain stated, then said, "If you wasn't there, Roosevelt, there is only one other fellow that was there." But he refused to say Horton's name. Horton jumped up, shouting, "They're framing me! I have a daughter to protect, and they're framing me!" He stayed in the car, he insisted, while the other two went to do the robbery.

Sciuto then produced the knife he had found under the front seat of Pickett's car and placed it on the table. That was one of the knives they used, Horton said, and when the captain asked him, Pickett admitted the knife belonged to him.

"I then pleaded with Wideman," Captain Sciuto testified later. "I says, 'Look, Wideman, why don't you tell me the truth? Who did the stabbing?' And from here he stated to me, 'Why don't you take the prints off that knife,' he said, 'and you will find out.' "

But there were no incriminating fingerprints on the knife or, for that matter, anywhere else. Even so, in the minds of the police and prosecutors, there could be little question that the three had caused the death of Joey Fournier in the course of robbing Marston Street Mobil. The crime lab eventually would find traces of human blood in Pickett's car, and the Thomases could be brought in to testify about Alvin Wideman's confession to the actual stabbing. The big murder case was solved less than two weeks after it occurred, and there was evidence enough to prosecute.

The following April, Horton, Wideman, and Pickett went on trial together. The proceeding went on for more than three weeks as the three defense attorneys entered their objections and cross-examined witnesses at length. The joint trial frustrated Horton's attorney, James Murphy, from the start. In truth, there wasn't that much of a case against William for the actual murder, and Murphy had hoped to separate him from the other two, perhaps cut a deal to get him tried on a lesser charge. Sciuto, after all, had been inclined to do that after Horton's arrest, before Schiavone showed up.

But given Wideman's reluctance to repeat his confession to the police, the two prosecutors, Michael Stella and Robert O'Sullivan, felt on safer ground presenting the jury with a robbery and murder in which three men took part. The law allowed "joint venture" prosecutions. As the judge would explain it to the jury, "if more than one person join together intent upon committing a particular crime, working as a joint venture or as a team, helping each other, and the crime is actually committed physically by only one of the team, the law doesn't stop to distinguish between the members of the team. . . . They are all criminally responsible."

This was reinforced by another law that defined felony murder. "The theory of the law is this," the judge explained. "If a felony punishable by life imprisonment is taking place and any one of the persons involved in the commission of that felony kills the person upon whom the felony is being committed, all participants in the felony are responsible under the law for the first-degree murder."

Since the law allowed the punishment of life in prison for robbery, the prosecutors could win conviction of murder in the first degree for all three men once they had proved that they had participated in a robbery that resulted in the murder of Joey Fournier. They would not need to prove who actually did the killing.

So in addition to documenting the murder—with an autopsy physician's clinical testimony about the wounds to Joey Fournier's neck, chest, abdomen, and left arm—Stella and O'Sullivan also went to some lengths to document the robbery. With no eyewitnesses, this was not so easy. The prosecutors had to rely on the testimony of James Yarwood, the station's owner, that gas sales exceeded the cash receipts deposited in a floor safe, which was undisturbed. And Joe McComiskey, in answer to the prosecutors' questions, recalled seeing Joey put a wad of bills from gas sales into his pant pocket, money that had disappeared by the time the body was found.

At the heart of the prosecution's case were the statements taken by police from the three defendants, all basically admitting to the robbery but leaving actual responsibility for the murder unclear. The prosecutors also brought the Thomases in to tell their story once more: Wideman had come home and said, "I killed somebody." When J.J. accused him of lying, he said, "No, man, I am not lying." According to the Thomases, Wideman volunteered that when he had demanded money at knifepoint, the victim turned it over and then pleaded for his life. The victim's pleading, Wideman had told them, caused him to fly into a rage so that he started stabbing him and couldn't stop.

Stella and O'Sullivan also put on the stand crime-lab chemists who had identified human blood smears on swatches of vinyl retrieved from the interior of Pickett's car. They had discovered invisible traces on other parts of the car, but they were so faint that it could not be determined if they were human blood.

And the prosecutors produced a man named John Greenwood, who had been working at Marston Street Mobil since Joey Fournier's death and lived nearby, on Woodland Street, just one house away from the gas station. The evening of October 26, he had started out at his house with a buddy and a couple of girls they knew. Sometime after eight-thirty, Greenwood testified, he had noticed a four-door '63 Chevy,

blue on the bottom, white on top, prowling the neighborhood. He'd seen it again when he and his friends left the
house to drive to North Andover and had seen it a third time
when they returned to the house a short while later. Three
black men were in the car, Greenwood said, and the one at
the wheel had a bushy Afro haircut.

Vague as it might be, this was crucial testimony. It was the
only evidence suggesting that Pickett's car and the three
defendants were anywhere near the scene of the crime. (It
also corroborated Horton's claim that he had been driving the
car that night: He had the bushiest Afro and because of his
height—he was the tallest of the three—it would have been
clearly visible.)

The prosecution's case left plenty of room for a vigorous
defense, and the defendants' attorneys—Murphy, who represented Horton; Peter Brady, who represented Pickett; and
James Fleming, who represented Wideman—made the most
of it. They pointed out that no eyewitnesses placed any of
their clients on the premises of Marston Street Mobil, and
there was no forensic evidence other than the blood on
Pickett's car, which could not be positively typed or linked in
any other way to Joey Fournier. And there were no fingerprints, palm prints, footprints, bloodstained clothing, or anything else that might conclusively place Horton, Pickett, or
Wideman at the scene of the crime.

The Thomases, they hinted, might have fabricated their
story about Alvin Wideman because they wanted to get him
out of the house. And the defense lawyers made much of the
fact that though the police swore to their accounts of what the
defendants had said, none of the defendants had signed or

dictated his statement, and the police had no notes or tapes to document the interrogation. Everything depended on the credibility of police officers who were under heavy pressure to find the murderer.

The defense attorneys also argued that the testimony of people who came to Marston Street Mobil between nine and ten on the night of the murder, none of whom ever saw a black person, made it impossible to believe a black person had committed the crime. Their recollections of the times at which they came and went seemed to leave no gaps long enough for the murderer or murderers to enter the gas station, commit the crime, and depart unseen.

James Murphy, Horton's attorney, went so far as to bring in Catherine Mays, who offered an alibi for the man in her life: On the night of October 26, she said, he had been playing with their baby, Tara, then got up and said he was going out for a while without saying where—"he comes and goes as he pleases," she testified. That was about 6:00 P.M. Soon after, she left to do the weekly grocery shopping with her sister and the kids, then stopped by her mother's place, several blocks from her house, for a visit.

William knew she was likely to be there; she shopped and visited like that every week. So she wasn't surprised when he knocked on the door after she had been at her mother's for a while—it was about eight-thirty by now, she said—and she went outside and talked with him on the steps. He wanted to know when supper would be ready, then asked her for money so he could go and get a drink. She gave him a few dollars, she said, and went home to start supper, the hot dogs and beans she served every Saturday night.

He came home about nine-thirty, she testified, ate his supper, and they moved into the living room to watch television. Then he asked her to go out with him to have another drink. She didn't feel like it, she said, so they stayed home the rest of the evening. But the incident stuck in her mind, she said, because he so rarely asked her to go out.

If all this were true, of course, there was no way Horton could have been over at Marston Street Mobil between nine-thirty and ten, participating in the robbery and murder of Joey Fournier. In his instructions to the jury, the judge made a point of including cautionary words about alibis: "Alibi evidence should be scrutinized by the jury with care. It is easily fabricated. It is difficult to disprove, and it is often attested to by friends or relatives of the accused. On the other hand, you must bear in mind that an alibi may be the only refuge of an innocent person."

It provided no refuge for Horton, however. The jury deliberated for only three hours and ten minutes, surprising even those who harbored no doubts about the defendants' guilt. All three were convicted of armed robbery and first-degree murder. The maximum punishment possible was life in prison with no chance for parole, and the judge imposed that sentence immediately after the verdict.

Horton, Pickett, and Wideman listened stoically, leaving the displays of emotion to the women in their lives, according to an account in *The Lawrence Eagle-Tribune*. Pickett's wife, up from Cambridge for the trial, fought back tears, while a girlfriend of Wideman's began to sob. And Catherine Mays rose from her seat, exited the courtroom, and fainted dead away at the foot of the courthouse steps.

Horton, Pickett, and Wideman would pursue a number of appeals, but only one advanced to the stage of actual hearings. The issue was "new evidence"—knowledge of the fact that J.J. Thomas had once fired a gun at Alvin Wideman, injuring him slightly. Wideman also alleged that J.J. had poured ammonia or lye on him as he slept in the basement of the house on Hannigan Street. Didn't these incidents suggest a level of animosity that might explain J.J.'s concocting a story about Wideman's confession to the murder of Joey Fournier?

It was not a particularly persuasive point. If J.J. disliked Alvin so much, why had he invited him to live in his house? And if he had wanted to incriminate Alvin in order to get rid of him, why hadn't he simply gone to the police himself? In fact, he had revealed Alvin's confession rather reluctantly, first under pressure from his boss, Fred Sciuto, and then when told by Stephen Sciuto that he might be prosecuted as an accessory after the fact.

Even so, J.J., Thelma, Alvin, and Stephen Sciuto all went back into court. There, lawyers for the defendants tried to suggest that J.J. was up to no good, drug dealing out of his basement, that he wanted Alvin out of the house because he didn't pay his way, and that, yes, back in 1971, J.J. had fired a shot at Alvin on the porch after Alvin fought with Irene Moore.

The judge wasn't impressed. He denied the motion for a new trial after finding that although J.J. had fired the shot (he didn't believe the story about an attack with ammonia or lye), the incident mattered little to the murder case because J.J. and Alvin continued their friendship for a few years afterward. In a ruling sustained by the state's supreme judicial court, he held that the shooting "would have no real weight or materiality for possible use to impeach the credibility of Thomas."

So ended the significant court activity concerning the murder of Joey Fournier, with no hint at all that William Horton would become the subject of a surprising sequel. Before it played out, another drama took place in Lawrence involving two other members of the cast, the police officers Stephen Sciuto and Patrick Schiavone. Their roles in the Fournier case—Schiavone using his superior knowledge of interrogation and the law to salvage Sciuto's big arrest—foreshadowed a startling climax.

Both were ambitious cops who competed for promotions. In 1981, Schiavone finally bested his rival, winning appointment as chief of the 130-officer Lawrence Police Department. Schiavone's ascendancy deeply angered Sciuto, and he joined another captain, Joseph Tylus, in a lawsuit challenging the appointment. Sciuto and Tylus had scored higher on the civil service exam than Schiavone had. They also charged nepotism: Schiavone, they said, was a captain only because his brother, Terrence, who served as a Lawrence alderman and director of public safety, had approved his promotions.

The lawsuit took more than two years to settle. A supreme judicial court ruling that the promotions violated a conflict-of-interest law forced Schiavone to step down in December of 1983. He eventually left law enforcement; by 1994, he was working as the night manager of a resort hotel in Naples, Florida.

Sciuto, however, did not live to taste victory. He and his wife, Mary, had a house in Salisbury, Massachusetts, several miles to the east of Lawrence, where the Merrimack River empties into the Atlantic. One morning in March 1983, before the supreme judicial court had ruled, Sciuto returned from a jog on the beach and got into a fight with his wife that ended when she seized his service revolver and shot him to death. Mary Sciuto told the police that her husband attacked her when she criticized him for disciplining two officers under his command, one a family friend.

In court, the tearful widow testified that she and her husband had had a wonderful marriage for twenty-five years but that when he was denied promotion to chief of police, he turned abusive. The jury acquitted her of manslaughter.

Walpole, Norfolk, Concord

1 9 7 5 – 1 9 8 6

Sometime after three in the morning, Dougie gave William the keys to the Cadillac. He could see that William was drunk. For much of the night, he'd been knocking back shots of vodka, undiluted, his favorite drink. And the car was Beth's pride and joy. But Dougie barely hesitated. They had been friends for years, since those summers in South Carolina when they were teenagers. If William needed the car and thought he could handle it, Dougie wasn't about to turn him down.

Besides, William had a big roll of cash in his pocket—at least a few thousand, Dougie figured. Where it came from, he wasn't sure. He might have hit the lottery, though the cash seemed like a lot to collect over the counter. In any case, the money was real: William peeled off a couple hundred dollars and gave them to Dougie before he left.

What neither of them anticipated were the cops who pulled William over two hours later, after he had picked up the

Hispanic prostitute. He gave a phony name and told the offi-cers that he'd borrowed the car and left his driver's license at home. The cops returned to their cruiser to run the name and license plate number through the computer. When they approached the Cadillac again, William floored the accelera-tor and sped away.

In the rough chase that followed, he bounced the car off a median divider, punching a hole in the oil pan. But he man-aged to shake the cops. He ditched Beth's car in a housing project, ran on, and found the answer to his prayers: a blue delivery van parked outside a convenience store, its motor still running as the driver darted inside to make a purchase. William jumped into the driver's seat, roared off toward the expressway, and headed south toward New York City, a place to check in with his sisters, score some dope, make some money, then disappear.

By the early 1970s, prisons in most urban states of America had begun to falter under the weight of crowding and the stress of dealing with inmates who each year seemed to get younger, more violent, more drug involved, and generally more resistant to control. There was nothing really wrong with the prisons, the older guards would say, that couldn't be fixed by sending down a better class of criminal.

Massachusetts was no exception, and the response there as elsewhere was to revise yet again the philosophy of prison administration. The idea, embodied in a Correctional Reform Act passed in 1972 under the administration of the Republican governor Francis Sargent, was to combine incentives for good behavior on the inside with a program to ease inmates' return to free society. This would make for better internal prison management even as it reduced recidivism.

The prison system implemented the approach by adopting two policies. First, prison officials were to assess, or "classify," inmates according to their behavior and assign them to the least restrictive appropriate setting—maximum, medium, or minimum security. Second, inmates were to be granted some time back in the community before their formal release. This "community reintegration" would smooth the transition to life in the free world and give prison and parole officials a chance to monitor a convict's adjustment and gain valuable information on which to base the release decision.

In Massachusetts, a basic tool of community reintegration was outside-under-supervision status, or OUS. Once granted it, an inmate might leave the penitentiary from time to time for classes or community-service assignments, eventually qualifying for furloughs—short visits at home with family or friends. Convicts would come to consider OUS a coveted privilege, a goal that gave shape to their lives inside.

Inmates serving life terms were included in the new approach. For those sentenced never to return to the community, the security levels and opportunity for time on the outside constituted a powerful reward structure, giving a reason to behave in prison and to pursue academic study, work, or job training. Besides, however rarely it might be acknowledged, many sentenced to life would eventually be released.

For the majority, those convicted of second-degree murder and some other violent crimes, the life term was only a theoretical maximum; their sentences allowed for release on parole after they had served a minimum number of years. But those serving life without parole, the penalty for first-degree murder, could also be released if they could win a commutation of their sentence to life with parole.

Simple economics motivated prison administrators, with the quiet approval of governors, to make a practice of releasing lifers after they had passed middle age. By that time in their lives, even the wildest young criminals are likely to have calmed down; often their physical health has begun to fail, so that it is hard to imagine them posing a danger to anyone. Meanwhile, if they remain incarcerated, the potential cost of their medical care looms ominously.

Medicare and Medicaid, the big federal health insurance programs, will not cover inmates in state penitentiaries. Rather than shoulder the full financial responsibility for Alzheimer's, Parkinson's, cancer, heart disease, strokes, and other health problems of old age, states let many of their older inmates go free. In the vast majority of cases, the authorities chose well, and the released convicts caused no new trouble. But because they had been in prison for so long, these inmates more than any could benefit from community reintegration.

"Offenders have traditionally been taken out of our society and placed in another social system, the prison, that in no way constructively resembles the society to which they will eventually return," explained Michael Fair, Massachusetts's commissioner of correction in the 1980s. "Family ties, heterosexual relationships, economic roles, and political participation are severed. In short, the individual enters the prison society and gradually loses touch with some of the most basic aspects of normal societal life. . . . It is no wonder, then, that after a period of incarceration, a tremendous shock is faced upon reentry to society."

On the day in May 1975 that William Horton entered the maximum-security prison at Walpole, community reintegration was still a relatively fresh enthusiasm in the Massachusetts Department of Correction. The new inmate was twenty-three years old; his long, full-featured face stared into the mug-shot camera with alertness and pride, if not defiance. But as it turned out, he was not defiant enough to impress his keepers. His prison career was wholly unremarkable. Horton, observed Commissioner Fair, "was a nothing. . . . Nobody ever heard of him."

Horton stayed in touch with Wideman and Pickett, their relationships now somewhat strained by their mutual betrayal during interrogation by the Lawrence police. But Horton appears to have made no other close friends among the inmates. The hundreds of records that accumulated in his file over his eleven years in the Massachusetts prison system portray a convict who kept to himself, participated well enough in prison life, and for the most part managed to hide his most serious misconduct from official scrutiny.

Having had a taste of prison routine in South Carolina, Horton settled in with relative ease, records show, working in the metal shop and attending classes to prepare for a high-school-diploma equivalency test. He earned generally good reports from his supervisors at work and on his housing unit. Though he was cited four times for disciplinary infractions, the infractions appeared to be routine.

"Inmate Horton reluctantly started to work this afternoon and worked for about one hour and then he left for a drink," one reporting officer wrote. "He returned to his work assignment and lit up a cigarette and stood doing nothing. A few minutes later I approached him about going to work, he told me he would return to work when he was ready to. I told him that [sic] the results of this kind of attitude and he replied that he did not care one way or the other. I told him to go to work immediately or he would suffer the consequences. He still refused to go to work." For this moment of obduracy, Horton was made to serve five days of room detention.

Another time, the officer wrote, Horton "went out of the block. I then ordered him back to the block but he kept on walking to the chow hall." Another five days in his room. Refusing an order to help clean up the cellblock earned him five days in an isolation cell, as did a fight with another inmate. "A number of punches were thrown by both inmates, at each other," the reporting officer wrote.

In general, however, Horton had bought into the community-reintegration strategy. It gave him reason to hope for elevation out of maximum security, with the eventual possibility of OUS. That and a solid record of participation in prison programs might document his responsible behavior and support a request for commutation.

Billy Doucette, another Massachusetts murderer sentenced to life without parole, recalls how inmates in those years got the message. At Walpole, he met some men he had known from the streets "who told me, Billy, . . . this is what you have to do to get out. You have to give up the drugs, go to school, keep your nose clean, do the right thing, and that's the only way to get out."

In November of 1976, the department's Inter-Institutional Classification Committee reviewed Horton's record and found that he "has shown good adjustment" and was "not considered a management problem." The committee therefore unanimously approved his transfer to the medium-security prison at Norfolk, where Horton would spend the bulk of his years in the Massachusetts prison system. This was a big step up, if only in terms of quality of life.

Outwardly the Norfolk prison looks forbidding enough: a cluster of dingy stone cell halls surrounded by a gray concrete wall some twenty feet high that is topped with barbed wire strung along metal posts. Yet for a time during the seventies and eighties, Norfolk, like some other American prisons, had evolved into a community affording inmates certain comforts that don't usually come to mind when one thinks of prison.

Many convicts had access to substantial money, whether from legitimate institutional job assignments, trafficking in contraband, or gifts and allowances from relatives on the outside. Medium security meant inmates had freedom to move about the prison for much of the day. It was also an era when guards on some units took a live-and-let-live attitude, ignoring seemingly inappropriate conduct or outright violations of rules so long as they did not flagrantly disrupt daily life.

As a result, more than a few Norfolk inmates were able to "do their own bit"—shape individual styles of life by preparing their own meals and furnishing their cells with the trappings of the middle class. Nothing prevented their ordering small appliances—coffeemakers, hot plates, stereos, televisions—by mail. And the prison canteen, in other places a source of little more than toothpaste and canned soups, responded to inmate demand by stocking fresh meats and produce, baked goods, pantry staples, and on some days, Doucette claims, even lobster and shrimp. Units of the prison were equipped with kitchenettes, and inmates filled idle time by using the available groceries to produce sumptuous feasts. Italian gangsters in particular were noted for their memorable pasta dishes.

Doucette, who now resides at the Bay State Correctional Center, next door to Norfolk, recalls with some longing the food and freedom, along with the mail-ordered fifty-gallon fish tank he set up in his cell, complete with angelfish. And his cat. Where did he get a cat? In those days, cats were part of the scene at Norfolk, Doucette says, after a few that had been living in the prison started breeding. After one had kittens, its owner sought good homes for them. "He said, 'Bill you want a cat?' I said, 'Yeah, I'll take this one with the big paws.' I named it Bear." The guards, living and letting live, ignored the cats for a few years, until the sad day they brought in agents of a humane society to scoop them up and take them away. In the meantime, the canteen filled orders for Tender Vittles and Kitty Litter.

In short, the transfer to Norfolk from Walpole, where activities were restricted, many more doors were locked, and life moved according to whistles and clanging gates, handed the inmate a pleasant surprise. "You can't imagine what that was like," Doucette recalls. "When I first got there, I just walked around saying, 'This is prison?' . . . It was more like a city. It was like being set free."

But if Doucette would go on to make constructive use of new freedom and amenities, serving on inmate committees and participating in a drama group, the environment appears to have reawakened the self-destructive inclinations that haunted Horton's life. His commitment to the community-reintegration track began to flag. The backsliding may also have had to do with a health problem: He developed a worrisome swollen gland on his neck that by April 1977 had grown to the size of an egg. A prison doctor put Horton in the hospital for a week in order to treat it with hot packs and antibiotics. Absences and distraction that year cost him a number of prison jobs and resulted in poor evaluations.

Though his record was turning negative, Horton applied for OUS, a privilege that, combined with the existing routine at Norfolk, would make life tolerable indeed. That August, the Inter-Institutional Classification Committee turned down Horton's application, citing "lack of program involvement, his poor work record and short time he has served on his sentence."

His health and demeanor apparently got better the following year. In October 1978, he again applied for OUS, and his request again was denied. But the committee referred to "significant improvements in his behavior, attitude and work evaluations." He had been employed steadily on the prison's utility crew; he also had developed an interest in music, learning to play the electric bass and enrolling in a course in music theory.

Horton continued to apply for OUS, finally winning the committee's approval in September of 1979, only to be turned down by the prison's superintendent, who noted that Horton had accumulated a few more disciplinary reports.

Two of these resulted in minor penalties for disobeying orders: At dinner, Horton had taken a second helping of meat out of turn and refused to put it back; he also had refused to sweep and mop an office floor. The third, in July, was more serious: Guards had caught him smoking marijuana in his room—the disciplinary committee gave him five days in isolation.

Then in October, disaster struck. "While conducting a routine shakedown," an officer wrote, "myself and other officers entered Unit 3-1. Several other officers and myself went to room #206 which belonged to inmate William Horton; there were two other inmates in his room. C.O. Grundy asked the inmates to step out of the room. We then entered the room and started to shakedown. As I was searching the waste basket I noticed something wrapped in tissue paper. I unwrapped it and found it to be a syringe set."

The evidence of hard-drug use following the write-up for marijuana smoking was a serious matter. It didn't help that two days later, another guard searching Horton's desk drawer came across a betting slip for making wagers on horse races, an unauthorized activity.

Horton admitted that the betting slip was his, "from last season." But he said he couldn't recall where it came from and denied any involvement in bookmaking. As for the syringe charge, he offered a defense, insisting that a visiting inmate had dropped the works in his wastebasket. But the disciplinary board sided with the officers and found Horton guilty. Not only did they sentence him to fifteen days in an isolation cell; they also recommended his reclassification to higher security.

Alarmed, Horton tried to appeal the decision to the Norfolk superintendent. "I . . . have been in this camp for three and a half years and this is the first time that I have been involved in anything of this nature," Horton pleaded. "I didn't put the paraphernalia in my trash can were [sic] they was found. As you will see in your copy of the report the officers testified that my trash can was empty except for what was found in it. It wasn't like I was trying to hide anything. Thank you kindly."

But the superintendent and ultimately the commissioner's office, which had to sign off on the issue, were unmoved. They bounced Horton back to Walpole that November.

The shock of returning to Walpole's harsher environment had a salutary effect, as far as prison officials were concerned. According to their reports, Horton showed a generally positive attitude for the next several months. Supervisors praised his work in the metal shop and his conduct in his housing unit. He added leatherworking to his list of interests. He was cited for only one disciplinary infraction: failure to present himself for one of the countings of inmates that occur throughout the prison day. Horton admitted that he had overslept and accepted a weekend of isolation.

Because of his overall good record, the classification board agreed to return him to Norfolk in September 1981. Once there, Horton settled in for a prolonged period of apparent commitment to the community-reintegration system, resuming his quest for OUS approval and transfer to even lower security.

For nearly two years, then, he performed well at prison jobs and in his housing unit and incurred no "tickets" for disciplinary violations. In August of 1983, the board and the superintendent finally granted him OUS but not a transfer to minimum security. Horton went to work in the prison shop that produced furniture and other items for government agencies. His supervisors gave him "excellent" reports.

But then the following March, Horton stumbled again. "At 8:05 A.M. on the above date," the report said, "this reporting officer conducted a routine search of room 317 belonging to William Horton. During this search this officer found (2) marijuana roaches under a towell [sic] located on top of inmate Horton's desk."

An abashed Horton threw himself on the mercy of the disciplinary board. "The inmate stated he was guilty of the charge," the board wrote in its report. "He agrees with the charge and the report. He stated he will not smoke any marijuana in the future."

The board sentenced him to five days of isolation and suspended his OUS for thirty days. They accompanied the sentence with a stern warning that any further evidence of illegal drug use could result in complete loss of his OUS privilege and another dose of Walpole.

Horton got the message. When his thirty-day suspension of OUS expired, he was assigned to the prison's farm crew and set to work to restore his reputation. The effort succeeded. In September of that year, 1984, he won reclassification for minimum security and transfer to the Northeast Correctional Center at Concord.

There he appeared to flourish, at least according to prison records. He would incur no more disciplinary tickets. Instead, he immersed himself in a culinary arts program, learning institutional food preparation. In April 1985, the correction department awarded him a Certificate of Completion. Shortly thereafter, he gained approval to participate in the Concord Achievement Rehabilitation Volunteer Experience Program, known as CARVE, which placed inmates at the Massachusetts Mental Health Center, where they helped care for patients or worked as laboratory assistants and janitors.

CARVE was another element of the correction department's effort to help prepare inmates for reintegration and gauge their readiness for release. It functioned on the honor system. Inmates were subject to little supervision while working at the hospital and were even allowed to walk across the street to a public park during their breaks.

The state's Department of Mental Health considered the program a valuable asset. "The CARVE volunteers help improve the quality of care that a patient receives through their one-on-one involvement with the patients," a mental health official testified. "Although we have had several instances of problems, they were far outweighed by the long and overall solid performance of the program in contributing to the care of patients."

Horton received positive evaluations for his CARVE work, though critics of the correction department's handling of him would later wonder whether he had been able to purchase drugs while visiting the public park on his breaks. Corrections officials never found any evidence that he had, however. His successful CARVE record finally established his bona fides. For nearly a year, he demonstrated that he could be trusted to work on his own in the community, to behave himself, and not to seize the opportunity to escape. It was entirely reasonable, then, that the Massachusetts Department of Correction would also consider him for furloughs.

Section 90A of the Massachusetts Correctional Reform Act empowered the state correction commissioner to "extend the limits of the place of confinement of a committed offender . . . under prescribed conditions to be away from such correctional facility but within the Commonwealth for a specified period of time." In other words, it authorized furloughs.

A convict might be granted temporary freedom to visit a critically ill relative or attend one's funeral, receive medical treatment or social services not available in prison, or look for work and a place to live after release. In addition, a furlough might be granted "for any other reason consistent with reintegration of a committed offender into the community."

Along with the broader concept of community reintegration, furloughs were fast becoming a common feature of American prisons. By 1975, a survey conducted by *Corrections Magazine* found that prison systems in forty-four states and the District of Columbia would allow a qualifying adult convict out on a furlough, which might also be called a home visit, a temporary leave, or a temporary community release. Nationally, adult furloughs were occurring at a rate of more than 250,000 per year.

The magazine observed that the rapid expansion of furlough programs "represents a veritable revolution in correctional thinking around the country," since the practice was virtually nonexistent as recently as 1969. States with the largest furlough programs, the magazine found, released inmates for no more specific a reason than family visiting, as opposed to attending a funeral or going on an interview for a post-release job. In addition to helping with community reintegration, these states found, the furloughs improved morale within the prison and gave parole boards more information on which to base their decisions about release.

The Massachusetts law limited an inmate's furlough to a total of fourteen days per year and required that those convicted of violent crimes be approved by the superintendent of their prison as well as by the corrections commissioner. The correction department added further eligibility rules and set up a procedure for furlough approvals. A furlough committee at the inmate's institution would pass on the initial application, after which bureaucrats in the correction department's central office and the commissioner's office would have to sign off.

The rules also required that prisons notify the police in the community where the furloughed inmate would stay and declared that any inmate who failed to return more than two hours after the official end of the furlough would be declared an escapee, even if he or she had called in with a reason for the delay.

The arguments for extending the furlough privilege to first-degree lifers, even those serving with no chance for parole, reflect those for involving them in the other aspects of community reintegration. There is a purely human benefit, as lifers' family members, especially their children, gain periodic access to their convicted relatives outside the confines of the penitentiary visiting room. And prison administrators came to consider furloughs an especially important management tool, the sweetest plum of all to dangle before long-term inmates in order to motivate good conduct. "To remain on positive furlough status, all inmates, but especially first degree lifers,

must continue to receive positive evaluations at their facility,"
Michael W. Forcier and Linda K. Holt, two correction department researchers, wrote in a position paper on furloughs.
"The receipt of any major disciplinary reports would result
both in a return to higher custody and exclusion from eligibility for the furlough program."

Furthermore, peer pressure could insure against escapes or
other misconduct while inmates were out on temporary
release. All lifers recognized that a single individual's misbe-
havior could result in restriction or cancellation of the program for everyone. They therefore strove mightily to impress
upon one another the importance of exemplary conduct.
"The furlough program . . . has created an internal system of
social control among inmates conducive to successful completion of furloughs since the inmate who escapes on furlough places the entire program in jeopardy for other
inmates," Forcier and Holt wrote.

In Massachusetts, lifers themselves would eventually make
an impassioned—and respectable—case for their access to
the furlough privilege. A position paper on furloughs for lifers
issued by the Lifers' Group at Norfolk prison made the familiar points that furloughs help lifers maintain relationships
with their children and other relatives and prepare them for
release, which was by no means unobtainable.

It went on to argue that the whole prison had an interest
in a program that boosts the morale of inmates serving life
terms. "Lifers as a whole," the paper stated, "provide significant stabilizing influences in daily prison life. This is true
mainly because lifers generally are older, more mature and
do not possess an extensive criminal background or history."

Prison wardens confirm that observation. Many lifers are not habitually violent criminals but people who committed one horrible crime for peculiar reasons and would be unlikely to commit another. And even those with extensive records tend after a few years to accept the fact that as long-term inmates, they have far more to gain from cooperating with the prison regime than they have from trying to defy or outmaneuver it.

The Lifers' Group met weekly to provide support for convicts serving life terms, to improve their image with the public, and to pursue a number of programs. These included a staff that produced a newsletter for lifers, drama and poetry groups, a runners club, and groups that made toys for distribution to hospitalized children and volunteered to renovate the prison auditorium, chapel, and library. Outreach groups met with college students interested in learning about prison life and lobbied the legislature on corrections issues.

Why shouldn't inmates involved in such constructive activities be given a bit of encouragement? the lifers wanted to know. "If an inmate successfully meets his or her prison related responsibilities and has shown a significant development regarding accepting and living out the responsibilities of citizenship, then that behavior needs to be rewarded," the Lifers' Group wrote. "The most significant and positive motivator for responsible behavior is the furlough program."

Shortly after Massachusetts enacted its Correctional Reform Act, furloughs and prisons in general became entangled in state politics. Disturbances erupted at the maximum-security Walpole prison during 1973. As conditions at the prison deteriorated to the point where it had to be taken over by state police, newspapers critical of the Sargent administration attacked the governor's corrections commissioner, John Boone, for his management of the prison system and the furlough program.

It didn't help that in March of that year, Joseph Subilosky, serving life for first-degree murder, escaped while on furlough. He did not return to prison until five months later, when he was arrested for robbing a bank. By June, Sargent had fired Boone and replaced him with Frank Hall, a young prison administrator from North Carolina. Despite the uproar over furloughs, Hall declared his adamant support for them but issued new rules intended to mollify critics. They required first-degree lifers to serve five years before they could apply, second-degree lifers to serve three years.

That drew attacks from the state's Democratic attorney general, Robert Quinn, who hoped to challenge Sargent in the gubernatorial election the following year. Quinn issued a ruling that barred furloughs for inmates serving life without parole, citing the inappropriateness of a community-reintegration program for inmates who apparently could never be released. Furloughs for such lifers ended in September 1973.

A group of inmates led by Arthur Devlin filed suit, and in December they won a ruling from the supreme judicial court that settled the issue as a matter of law. The court ruled that the language of the Correctional Reform Act referred explicitly to the participation of lifers in the furlough program and that it permitted furloughs "for any reason consistent with . . . reintegration. There is no requirement . . . that integration into the community be imminent or certain."

In addition, the court acknowledged that inmates serving life without parole might still look forward to release. "We know that life sentences for murder in the first degree are from time to time commuted," the court continued.

The fact that a committed offender who is serving a life sentence for murder in the first degree has an additional legal barrier to clear before he may be paroled may have a bearing on the reasonableness of the granting of a particular furlough. However, because that barrier is not insurmountable, we see no justification for concluding that the temporary release of a "first degree lifer" can never be "consistent with . . . [his] reintegration into the community." In fact a furlough may produce information, not otherwise obtainable, about the capacity of such an offender to become a law abiding, effective member of the community.

Some state legislators that year sought to amend the Correctional Reform Act to eliminate first-degree lifers from the furlough program. They succeeded in the house, but after Commissioner Hall mounted a lobbying campaign against the amendment, the measure died in the senate in May 1974.

Over the years, however, state corrections officials did tinker with the program to limit the furlough privilege for first-degree lifers. In 1975, they barred furloughs for lifers who had not won promotion to the nonwalled minimum-security prisons. And in 1981, to fend off legislative attack after another highly publicized furlough escape, they tightened the rules, increasing the minimum time for eligibility from five years to ten and excluding inmates who had received major disciplinary reports. They also required that the inmate remain with a sponsor at all times during the furlough, and they authorized random telephone checks to make sure the inmate was following the prescribed schedule.

Though the Massachusetts prison furlough program was one of the more liberal in the nation, statistics over the years suggested that it functioned relatively well, especially after the rules were tightened up. Between November 1972 and March 1987, Massachusetts prisons granted 117,786 furloughs to 10,553 inmates. During that time, only 426 escaped, and another 218 returned more than two hours late. Most of these escapes occurred in the earliest years. In 1972 and 1973, the escape rate was 1.9 percent, but by 1985 it had declined to 0.2 percent.

The lifers were some of the most successful participants. Between 1972 and 1975, lifers went out on 756 furloughs that resulted in 8 escapes. But from 1976 to 1980, after lifers' furloughs were limited to those lifers in minimum-security prisons or pre-release centers, only 2 escapes resulted from 2,328 furloughs. And from 1981 to 1986, after lifers were required to serve ten years before applying for furloughs, 2,434 furloughs resulted in only 3 escapes, for a rate of 0.012 percent.

Critics of the furlough program would point out that since lifers typically went out on many furloughs, it was misleading to compare numbers of furloughs with numbers of escapes. The more meaningful figure, they insisted, was the number of lifers granted furloughs compared with the number of escapes. The number of lifers who went out on the 2,434 furloughs granted between 1981 and 1986, for example, was 112. On that basis, the escape rate was 2.7 percent.

Is even one escape too many? The question gets to the heart of much confusion over furloughs and criminal justice in general. To the victim of a crime committed by a convict who escaped while on furlough, the escape appears to document an egregious failure of the system, dangerously incompetent prison management, a genuine menace. Yet prison administrators have a powerful argument in response. To the extent that the program achieves its goal of easing culture shock for thousands of convicts—including scores of lifers who do eventually get released—it surely prevents hundreds more crimes than those committed by furlough escapees. Ending furloughs would likely result in a net *increase* in crime rather than in a reduction of it.

In 1991, Daniel P. LeClair and Susan Guarino-Ghezzi lent strong support to this idea with a study of convicts released from prisons in Massachusetts from 1971 to 1983. Comparing those who had gone out on furloughs and participated in other pre-release programs with those who had not, they found that the programs substantially and consistently contributed to reduced recidivism. The finding survived an elaborate set of calculations designed to correct for possible built-in bias of the selection process—that prison officials might approve for the furlough and pre-release programs only those prisoners who would do well after release from prison anyway.

Specifically, the researchers found that for 1,393 male prisoners released from 1973 through 1976, participation in furlough programs reduced recidivism to 17 percent from an expected rate of 25.2 percent. Participation in both furlough and pre-release programs reduced recidivism of another 769 prisoners from an expected 22.2 percent to 9 percent. Using these figures, it is possible to estimate that the furlough and pre-release programs averted at least 216 crimes over the four-year period—more than 50 crimes per year.

Meanwhile, 426 inmates escaped from the furlough program from 1972 to 1987, for an average of 28 per year. In other words, the Massachusetts furlough program appeared to produce a net reduction of more than 20 crimes per year, on average, over the fifteen years, assuming that all the escapees committed crimes. The net reduction grew in the later years of the program as the management of furloughs improved.

From the potential victim's point of view, a crime prevented is a crime prevented, whether by allowing furloughs or banning them, and there seems to be no question that more are prevented by allowing them. Yet understanding this requires a mathematical calculation and a bit of psychological work—willful separation from sympathy for the victim immediately at hand in favor of the more abstract concept of public safety. It is much easier for the news media or politicians to fan outrage over victimizations that occur than to stir public emotion in favor of those that are prevented, especially when the prevention, however real, appears on the surface to transgress common sense.

Early in the history of prison furloughs, a furloughed California inmate shot a police officer to death, and in New York, an inmate convicted of hurling his two daughters out of a two-story window went home on furlough and threw the same two daughters off a roof four stories high. Such events appear to document failure, however spuriously, far better than any statistics can document genuine success.

"It is often said by corrections officials that the worst thing that can happen to a furlough program is for the media to find out about it," *Corrections Magazine* declared in 1975, hardly aware how prophetic those words might be.

To go out on a furlough, Horton needed a sponsor. The regulations issued in 1981 to tighten up the program required that first-degree lifers on furlough remain with the sponsor at all times, a policy to be enforced with random telephone calls by prison officials. The sponsor, proposed by the inmate, had to survive a background check by the probation department and an interview by officials of the prison that housed the applicant. He or she also had to sign a furlough-sponsorship agreement that outlined the conditions of the furlough and the sponsor's responsibilities.

Substantive as these conditions were, Horton had no trouble coming up with a suitable candidate. Her name remains undisclosed to the public, but her existence, along with glimpses of her character and her relationship with Horton, would later be revealed in a report on the Horton case prepared by investigators for the Massachusetts Executive Office of Human Services. The investigators called her Sponsor A, to distinguish her from her eventual replacement, Sponsor B.

They introduce A as a person who has no criminal record and no family relationship with Horton. She apparently got to know him by exchanging letters with him when he was still at Walpole. Their correspondence developed into an ongoing relationship, and she soon became one of Horton's regular visitors at Walpole and Norfolk. By the time he had moved up to the minimum-security Northeast Correctional Center, the visits were occurring almost weekly.

Horton shamelessly exploited Sponsor A's naïveté. Despite their extensive correspondence, visits, and furlough time together, she never learned that Horton was one of the notorious trio convicted in the murder of Joey Fournier, nor any other specifics of his criminal record.

Getting a furlough required the approval of a Northeast Correctional Center Furlough Panel, a Central Office Furlough Panel, and the commissioner of correction. The NCC group approved Horton's first request, submitted in October 1984, for eight-hour furlough visits with Sponsor A on the coming Thanksgiving Day and Christmas Day. But the Central Office turned him down "based on the short time at minimum security."

Horton filed his next request the following June, for a twelve-hour visit to A's home on August 4, 1985. Corrections officials, noting that Horton was "doing well," granted this request, stipulating that Horton remain at home with A for the full twelve hours. They approved a similar furlough, on the same condition, for the following September 8. When Horton had completed these furloughs successfully, they granted him his first twenty-four-hour furlough with A, on October 5–6.

Again he returned on time, apparently having behaved himself, so they approved his request for three more furloughs, on Thanksgiving (twenty-four hours), Christmas (forty-eight hours) and New Year's (twenty-four hours). With these furloughs, they also relaxed the rules: On Thanksgiving, Horton could go from A's house to Lawrence to visit his daughter; on the Christmas visit, he was allowed not only to visit his daughter but to take her out to a movie. On the first visit, A drove him to Lawrence, waiting outside in the car while he went in to see Tara. On the second, she accompanied them to the movies. Though all went well, corrections officials insisted that Horton remain at home with A for New Year's Eve.

Horton requested, and completed, another twenty-four-hour furlough on February 15–16, 1986. But this would be his last with A, for his conduct had begun to concern her. As a result, she refused to sponsor any more furloughs. Later on, she explained to investigators that whereas Horton had behaved well on the earlier furloughs, she had had a difficult time over the holidays and in February getting him to stick to the itinerary approved by prison officials. Instead, he wanted to party with his friends or hang out on the beach late at night. Though she had dissuaded him from doing so, she worried that she might not be able to keep him under control on future visits.

"Sponsor A stated that she sensed Horton was becoming 'more desirous of his freedom' to pursue such activities when on furlough and he knew that random telephone spot checks would not be made during normal sleeping hours after he made his final telephone call for the evening," the investigators wrote. As a result, A told Horton in February that she would put off sponsoring any more furloughs for him until he had "calmed down."

And this, in hindsight, is the fateful point at which the furlough program miscarried. Had corrections officials learned of the problem, they could have reimposed stricter conditions or curtailed Horton's furlough privilege altogether. Yet

Sponsor A, still committed to her friendship with Horton, never communicated her misgivings about his furlough behavior to prison officials.

Thus did Horton become the inmate who discovered and exploited a soft spot in the furlough process. Investigators found "that no NCC employee had ever specifically informed [sponsors] of their responsibilities . . . either verbally or by providing a list of duties. None of the NCC employees interviewed indicated that such a briefing or instructional session was institutional practice." In retrospect, this looks like a serious lapse, but at the time, with hundreds of inmates going out on successful furloughs and sponsors effectively enforcing the rules, there seemed no need for better orientation and training.

In any event, the news of Horton's restlessness never got back to prison. When A picked him up or dropped him off, no guards or counselors asked her specifically about his behavior. And why should she volunteer the information? So far as she knew, they had handled the matter between themselves, and Horton took no more furloughs. On her weekly visits, which continued, he seemed to consider the matter closed. What she never reckoned with was Horton's capacity for manipulation.

After his last furlough with A, he moved quickly to preempt any report she might make by telling his counselors and guards at NCC that a problem had developed. Catherine Mays, he explained, had grown jealous of his new relationship with A and didn't like him coming to see their daughter, Tara, in her company. Horton therefore requested permission to shift to sponsor B. This turned out to be Catherine's sister, Helen.

In retrospect, especially given the real problem with Sponsor A, Helen Mays was a terrible choice. Release to her care assured Horton contact with his old friends from Lawrence, especially Dougie Cecil, who was living in a house on Bunker Hill Street with his girlfriend, Beth Henderson. And Helen, by now separated from Charles and working two jobs to make ends meet, was not in a good position to lay down the law to Horton about respecting schedules and curfews. But Helen was also family and had a relatively clean record herself. On paper, she looked as good as Sponsor A, if not better.

In March 1986 and again the following May, Horton was granted twenty-four-hour furloughs, with the panels citing his "positive status" to justify their approval. His prison-approved itinerary permitted him to go to movies and shop at malls with his daughter and to visit relatives in Dorchester, on the south side of Boston. His sponsor was to accompany him at all times.

Yet Horton would take gross advantage of his relationship with Helen and her apparently casual attitude toward her role as sponsor. "Sponsor B stated that she was not aware that Horton was to remain with her at all times or required to follow an approved itinerary when on furloughs" the investigators' report states. "Sponsor B stated that she never went with Horton to the movies, shopping malls or church as scheduled on his itinerary for furloughs with her. Sponsor B stated that she was surprised Horton had listed on his itineraries trips to Boston to visit a cousin because such visits did not occur and the individual to be visited was not Horton's cousin, but Sponsor B's friend."

Horton submitted an application for his tenth and last furlough on May 8, 1986. The furlough, to begin Friday evening, June 6, would last forty-eight hours; the itinerary included a shopping trip to Methuen and a movie in Woburn on Saturday, followed by church services with his daughter on Sunday.

Helen picked him up at NCC at about six Friday evening, dropped him off at her house, and went off to her part-time job in a bar. She returned at 2:00 A.M. Saturday to find Horton in his room. An hour or so later, she heard him leave but did not attempt to follow him, nor did she report his departure to prison officials. Dougie recalls William coming to him in the night and begging to borrow the used Cadillac his girlfriend, Beth, had purchased recently. Much to her subsequent annoyance, Dougie handed William the keys, at which point William produced a roll of cash and pressed two hundred dollars into his old friend's hand. Dougie, of course, was even less likely than Helen to report William's violation of the furlough rules.

At 5:22 A.M., Methuen police stopped a car for running a red light on Route 110. The driver, accompanied by a young woman, said his name was William Crawford. He didn't have a license with him and said he had borrowed the car from a friend. The officers returned to their cruiser to call for a records check on the car and on William Crawford. As they emerged to question the driver again, the car roared away.

Police pursued the car through side streets, but the driver managed to elude them. Much later, they would find the car by a Lawrence housing project, its driver long gone. Motor vehicle records confirmed its owner: Beth Henderson. Prison officials produced photographs of William Horton, declared an escapee after he had failed to call in on Saturday morning to verify his whereabouts. Yes, the Methuen cops said, that was the man they had stopped as dawn was breaking.

It was the last police would see of him for nearly ten months.

In the wake of Horton's escape, embarrassed prison administrators rushed to bad-mouth him, as did inmates worried about the future of the furlough program. In hindsight, it suddenly seemed clear to everyone that Horton was no good and never should have been granted furloughs, whatever the prison records showed. There was no arguing with this point after Horton's escape, of course; the more germane question was whether those who approved his furloughs could have known the truth. Was his escape really the result of incompetence or corruption? Or was it an accident that occurred despite basically sound management of a useful program? It would take some time for this issue to be examined in detail, with results that were hardly obvious. A more immediate question, in June of 1986, was why Horton sought to take off when he did.

The roll of money Horton flashed at Dougie Cecil on the morning of June 7 provided one reason for him to leave and a source of speculation about others. Horton would later tell people that he had won the money, playing either the numbers or the state lottery. But that was hard to believe. There seemed too little time to place and collect on either sort of bet between his arrival in Lawrence on Friday evening and his departure before dawn the next day. The more likely explanation was that Horton had accumulated the money from drug deals in prison. He had been disciplined for drug offenses and would later admit to both drug use and dealing.

"I *did* sell drugs," he told an interviewer some years later. "My motive was a simple one: money. I was in a situation where I needed money. So I did what I had to do. I had needs. And my family had needs. I'm not saying it was right, and I'm not looking for sympathy. But that's the way it was."

Dougie Cecil claims to have been Horton's outside source. He says he supplied the goods to a woman who worked on the prison staff. She had befriended Horton and was in a position to deliver the contraband to him undetected. Horton confirmed as much in his interview but denied that the prison employee who served as his conduit was a woman.

Dangers inherent in the drug trade—dissatisfied customers, rivals who depend on violence to protect their market share— could well have provided an additional motive for Horton's decision to bolt when he did. If in fact he had involved a member of the prison staff in drug dealing, he might also have come to worry about the relationship going sour.

In the end, though, the best explanation looks far less dramatic. Dougie Cecil asserts that William took off simply because when stopped by the police that morning, he was still sober enough to understand that if he surrendered, he would never see the outside of a prison again. Horton himself, far better than anyone else, understood how borderline a candidate for furloughs he had been in the first place, how in prison he had continued to live on the edge, combining the wholesome with the illicit just as he had back in Lawrence, how he had manipulated the system to keep his furloughs going when they should have been cut off, how very lucky he had been so far.

Now that part of the game was over. The hour, the car, the vodka, the woman—any one of them was enough to kill his chance for any more furloughs, not to mention commutation and release. Should he have submitted to arrest, he would no doubt have been busted all the way back to Walpole. The wad of cash in his pocket left him with some options. What, then, did he have to lose?

Horton fled to New York, where he stayed only a short while; then he took a bus to Washington, D.C. There, by his account, he befriended a "white dude," with whom he traveled down to Fort Lauderdale. He found a room in a motel, where he lived for several months. When his roll of cash ran out, he says, he found work as a carpenter's apprentice and "took other short-term jobs—let's just say I kept my head above water." The vague euphemism may refer to more drug dealing, for which Florida certainly provides opportunities.

Eventually he met "three black ladies," apparently down for vacation, and began dating one of them. She was from a place in Maryland called Oxon Hill. When it was time for her to go back, she brought Horton along; her sister and brother-in-law gave him a basement room in their house on Shelfar Place, right around the corner from Proxmire Drive.

There he found construction work, odd jobs, and whatever else to support himself as he had in Florida. And while he led a marginal life by most measures, he had also realized a huge achievement: He had made good his escape from prison.

Massachusetts corrections officials did not have the faintest idea where he might be, nor did any other law-enforcement agents. Indeed, had he not decided to burglarize the house of Angela Miller and Clifford Barnes, he might have remained free for the rest of his life.

Upper Marlboro

1 9 8 7

"Did you get a good look at him?" McManus asked.
"Pretty good look, yes," Angela replied.
"Mrs. Barnes, do you see that person in the courtroom today?"
"Yes, I do."
"Where is he?"
"Sitting right over there."

At the Prince George's County Courthouse, the Horton file landed on the desk of Tom McManus, a sandy-haired, baby-faced man with a lawyer's gift for choosing his words carefully and never quite looking a questioner in the eye. McManus had by that time been working in the county prosecutor's office long enough to know his way around felony cases; if not quite a slam dunk, this one looked hard to lose.

Police searching the Z28 found a number of items removed from the Barnes-Miller house, including binoculars, cameras, a calculator, cologne, and jewelry. They found Angela Miller's coin collection—nickels, dimes, and hundreds of pennies she had been squirreling away for the past three and a half years in a watercooler jug. And they found her bank cash cards, usable at automatic teller machines near the intersection of Indian Head Highway and Old Fort Road, where the police had discovered Horton in the Camaro.

They also found phony identification documents for Tony Franklin and a number of items apparently stolen from other houses in the area. McManus speculated, plausibly, that sometime during the night, Horton had taken the Z28 from the driveway and returned to his own place nearby to collect loot he had stored there from other burglaries.

Searching Horton's pant pockets, police found Angela's engagement ring, bracelet, and necklaces along with Cliff's keys and cash. They also found a panty-hose mask, gathered at the top with two cutouts for eyeholes. A doctor who examined Angela on the morning of the crime found bruises consistent with sexual assault. Photographs recorded the scratches on Cliff's chest.

And the victims, respectable middle-class folks, made fine witnesses. They gave articulate accounts of the crime, citing many specifics, and their stories jibed. McManus could also count on police to describe the chase along Indian Head Highway and Horton's desperate attempts to fire Cliff Barnes's handgun at the officers in pursuit.

The indictment, filed on April 28, charged Horton with forty-four counts that included the burglary of the Proxmire Drive house; theft of cameras, jewelry, cash, and ATM cards; the assault and rape of Angela Miller; the assault and malicious cutting of Clifford Barnes "with intent to disable"; their false imprisonment and kidnapping; the theft of the Z28 Camaro; and the assault and attempted murder of police officers.

Horton's attorney, a Prince George's County public defender named F. Anthony McCarthy, conferred with his client and apparently sold him on a realistic strategy: Concede the burglary, rape, and assaults in the Barnes-Miller house but fight the assaults and the attempted murder of the police officers. Horton, after all, had never fired the gun. To be sure, according to the police, it was not for want of trying. But the bottom line remained compelling enough: Though there had been considerable shooting, the bullets flew in only one direction.

There followed the usual fencing over a plea bargain, though the case seemed to afford little chance of one. Criminal defendants usually plead guilty to avoid exposing themselves to a long prison term or perhaps to avoid prison altogether. But Horton was headed for decades more of prison no matter what. Even if acquitted in Maryland, he remained subject to the life sentence in Massachusetts, and his escape had erased the years of credit he had built toward eventual commutation and release. If nothing else, a trial offered Horton another round of public drama and diversion before return to dismal anonymity in prison.

Even so, McManus and McCarthy believed they were making progress as spring gave way to summer. The court finally scheduled an appearance for August 21, in the expectation that Horton would plead guilty to seven counts, including rape, kidnapping, assault with intent to murder, and assault on a police officer.

In the courtroom, however, Horton balked. He told the judge he wanted more time to study legal texts on the subject of guilty pleas. McCarthy explained that Horton still objected strongly to the assault charges stemming from the police chase and shootout. "He was feeling slightly put upon because he was the one shot at and not the police," McCarthy said.

"I'm not going to offer anything to make it more attractive," a frustrated McManus declared. With a shrug, the judge, Vincent J. Femia, set a trial date for October 13.

McCarthy saw his job as a matter of damage control. Given the compelling evidence, it would be difficult, if not impossible, to present any credible defenses against charges of housebreaking, theft, rape, and assault. But the forty-four-count indictment still left the public defender with plenty of ways to cut the inevitable conviction down to size.

The kidnapping charges, for example, required proof that Horton not only had imprisoned his victims but had transported them from one place to another; the prosecution had based the charges only on Horton's taking Cliff from the bathroom to the basement and shifting Angela among different rooms in the house.

And the charge of malicious cutting with intent to disable left a lot of room for argument. True, Horton had used a knife to score Cliff's torso. Police photographs plainly showed the scratches. But had the intent been to disable? Horton might have wanted to torment Cliff, but it was hard to see how the shallow wounds he inflicted had disabled him much or why Horton would need to disable him with a knife when he had already immobilized him by tying him to the stair supports.

As for the charges arising from the police chase, there was no evidence whatsoever that Horton had fired a single shot, and the assertion that he had tried to shoot depended on the testimony of officers who might face discipline for shooting at Horton if he had not attempted to fire at them. In any case, his brandishing the gun more plausibly reflected a desire to cover his flight than an intent to commit murder.

With relatively few witnesses, the case took only five days to try. Angela and Cliff, now married, went first. McManus conducted them through accounts of their ordeals. And he had them identify the powerfully incriminating exhibits— Angela's engagement ring, Cliff's set of keys, the coin collection, jewelry, and other items found on Horton's person or in the Camaro.

Angela told how she had used the mustache scissors to free herself and remove her blindfold after having been tied in the bathroom and how her assailant had burst in on her with the mask pushed up, revealing his face. Despite her nearsightedness, she said she harbored no doubts about what she saw.

McCarthy cross-examined the Barneses gently and courteously, well aware of the sympathy their story evoked, and he did little to sow much doubt about it in the minds of jurors. But he made an aggressive pitch for acquittal on the charge of malicious cutting with intent to disable. It was a classic appeal for jurors to put their heads above their hearts, to remember the letter of the law, however repugnant the victim's conduct might have appeared.

"Was the intention that night to disable this person, the person who's already tied up, bound hand and foot and bound by his neck as well to an upright?" he asked. "Was that the intention, to further disable him, or was it simply to frighten him into complete and total obedience?"

McCarthy reserved most of his energy for the charges arising from the police chase.

McManus put four officers—McCamley, Farrell, Lopez, and Bell—on the stand to say Horton had pointed his gun at them and attempted to fire it. But however certainly the officers might have portrayed Horton's menacing actions in earlier interviews, the case for attempted murder of the police officers began to crumble as the prosecution witnesses testified under oath. Only Lopez, who had been closest to Horton after he got out of his car, would swear with conviction that the defendant had pointed the gun directly at him.

In a final dramatic flourish, McCarthy had Horton stand before the jurors and lift his shirt to display scars from the wounds he had suffered from bullets and buckshot fired at him by the police. The sight would balance the emotional impact left by photos of the scratches on Cliff Barnes's chest.

The testimony forced McManus to retreat. After resting his case, he agreed to nolle prosequi—drop—all the charges based on Horton's alleged menacing of Bell and Farrell with the gun. That and the dropping of some lesser charges reduced the forty-four counts in the original indictment to eighteen.

The jury consisted of seven women and five men, most of them black. They began deliberating just before noon and had reached a verdict by seven-fifty that evening. McCarthy had controlled the damage well: Of the surviving eighteen counts, the jurors found Horton guilty of only ten. They included the rapes of Angela and the assault of Cliff, false imprisonment, theft of property, and housebreaking. They also included an attempt to discharge a firearm at Paul Lopez and an assault on Paul Lopez to avoid apprehension. The jury spared Horton conviction on the charges of attempted murder, kidnapping, and malicious cutting with intent to disable.

Judge Femia congratulated the jury for "your obviously well-thought-out deliberations, amazingly well-thought-out, if you want my honest opinion." Interviewed by a news reporter outside the court, the foreman, Joseph Bradley, gave a glimpse of the jurors' thinking. There was little disagreement over the rape convictions, he said, and he added an explanation for the acquittal of malicious cutting: "We believed he did not do major damage when he had the opportunity to do so to Mr. Barnes. He could have made knife cuts two inches deep."

Both McManus and McCarthy expressed satisfaction. The verdict would "insure that Horton will be sentenced in a way he will never get out again," the prosecutor said. The public defender declared that "the jury was scrupulously fair."

But the Barneses were hardly pleased. "There's no relief or anything," Cliff said. "He got off easy, too easy."

"All of it," Angela added. "They should have convicted him of all of it. But it's over now. What can you say?"

If McCarthy's arguments had impressed the jurors, they hadn't impressed the judge. Something about the case and the defendant got under his skin. How old was this guy? Thirty-six the record showed—a lot older than the messed-up kids who committed a lot of the stupider crimes in the area and wound up in his court, old enough to know better. And there was his general demeanor, the apparent total lack of feeling as he sat in court.

Then there were the victims. They hadn't done anything wrong; Horton attacked them in their own house. Now the judge worried about the woman. On the witness stand, Angela Barnes had spoken in a monotone, her face a dull mask. Clearly she was having a hard time with it—who wouldn't? Why did things like this have to happen to good people like that?

After pondering the case overnight, Judge Femia's enthusiasm for the "well-thought-out" deliberation faded fast.

At the sentencing the day after the verdict, the lawyers each had their final say. McCarthy told the judge that Horton had "indicated to me from the beginning that he had not been involved in any attempt to kill anyone, at least [not] the four police officers." McManus stated only that "Mr. Horton is a profoundly evil human being. If Mr. Barnes had not gotten away, from the Court's evidence, he would have killed him and he would have killed Angela Miller if she had not been able to escape."

After that, it was Horton's turn. Instead of expressing remorse or pleading for mercy, he uttered a single request: "If the state would agree I could go back to Massachusetts. That's all."

Then Judge Femia let him have it. "I must say that this case had more chilling implications to me personally than most any case that I've ever heard," he declared. He expressed his shock at "the almost detached manner" in which Horton had raped Angela and tortured Cliff. "I too am convinced that had Mr. Barnes and Miss Miller not escaped from that situation, they would have been dead. . . . I'm equally convinced that had you been able to release the safeties on that automatic, Officers Lopez and McCamley would have suffered death or severe injury from that gun."

With that, he sentenced Horton to two life sentences for the rapes and sentences of ten, fifteen, or twenty years for the various other counts. Most of them would run consecutively so that Horton would have to serve eighty-five years in prison before he might be eligible for parole in Maryland.

The judge contemptuously dismissed Horton's request that he be allowed back to Massachusetts to serve some of his time: "I'm not prepared to take the chance that Mr. Horton might again be furloughed or otherwise released. . . . I would strongly urge the people of Massachusetts to not wait up for Mr. Horton. In fact, I would ask them not to bother to put a light out for him because he won't be coming home. He now belongs to the state of Maryland."

The massive sentence included a final grace note. Given space on his sentencing work sheet to state his views of the convict to parole and probation officials, Judge Femia did "something that I've never as a judge done before." He warned against any temptation toward leniency. "This man should never draw a breath of free air again," he wrote. "He's devoid of conscience and should die in prison."

A few days later, the judge would get one more chance to express his disgust. Angela Barnes had requested that Horton be tested for AIDS, but he had refused to give a blood sample. His jailers called the judge for a ruling on how much force they might use.

"Do whatever it takes," the judge told them. Twenty minutes later, they called him back to say they had the blood, having used a stun gun to subdue the reluctant donor. But they still seemed worried about future liability. What if you're reversed? they asked. "In that case," Femia responded, "you can put the blood back in."

Trials resolve official issues of guilt and punishment, but they often leave unanswered questions. A big one in Horton's case was what *he* had to say about the night of April 3 and the morning of April 4, 1987.

No court transcript documents his version of the events that led to his conviction because McCarthy wouldn't put his client on the witness stand. This was for a reason apparent to any lawyer: So long as Horton remained silent, the jury would never have to know about his criminal record and his escape from Massachusetts. Had McManus been able to cross-examine the defendant, he could have quickly forced Horton to reveal these facts, which were devastating enough to over-power the whole case, virtually guaranteeing conviction even with less compelling evidence of the current crimes. But until Horton testified, the judge would scrupulously protect the jury's ignorance. Indeed, at one point in the trial, Judge Femia dismissed a juror because she confessed that she had inadvertently spied a headline in a local newspaper, *The Prince George's Journal,* that said CONVICTED KILLER'S TRIAL OPENS WITH ACCOUNT OF BEATING, RAPE.

But Horton's silence did not mean that he lacked a story—or stories—to tell. At the time of his arrest, he told police that he had been visiting Cliff, drinking with him. He said Cliff had given him the keys to the Z28 when he offered to go to the liquor store. Instead of doing that, Horton said, he had stolen jewelry from the house and taken off.

After his trial and sentencing, he told a somewhat different story. A friend of his, he explained to a reporter, had actually burglarized the house, bound and scratched Cliff, and raped Angela. He was in the Z28 himself on the morning of April 4 simply because the friend who had stolen it from Barnes and Miller's driveway had offered him a lift. He especially protested the rape conviction. "Being charged with it [rape] is just disgusting. I've never had a problem with women in my life."

He had agreed to take the rap for his friend, he said, because of the trouble waiting for him back in Massachusetts no matter what the outcome of the Maryland trial. "I knew I was going back to Boston," Horton said. "And so rather than put someone else in jail, I kept quiet. I didn't think the judge would keep me from going back to Boston."

"I was convicted because I refused to tell them what they wanted to know about the other individual," he said at another point. "I don't want to finger anyone else so I'll have to deal with it the best I can."

But if he were so innocent, why had he almost pleaded guilty during the summer? He did so out of concern for his former fellow inmates back in Massachusetts, he said. He claimed to have worried, with good reason as it turned out, that all the publicity about him would kill the Massachusetts prison furlough program. "I was tired of the whole bit. Tired of everyone saying, 'He did this.' And my attorney told me it would take the pressure off the inmates and the furlough system."

A year and a half later, two attorneys from Massachusetts, Anthony DiFruscia and Charles Capace, visited him at the Maryland Penitentiary, seeking to interview him in connection with a lawsuit the Barneses wanted to file against the state of Massachusetts. Assuming they could get him to cooperate, what better witness could there be to the failures of the furlough program than the infamous Willie Horton himself? Their venture would bear no fruit, but in the process, DiFruscia and Capace collected another Horton account of the Maryland case.

While living in Oxon Hill, Horton told them, he had been working in a junkyard; there he befriended Cliff Barnes, who visited the yard in search of auto parts. Cliff and Angela turned out to be neighbors. Horton told the attorneys he had partied with the couple frequently. On the night of April 3, he said, extended festivities began at the Barnes-Miller house, at which drugs and liquor were consumed in quantity. At one point during the long night, a man and a woman began to fight. When one of them produced a knife, Horton said, he worried police would be called. He decided to leave in a hurry, fearing any involvement with police because of his fugitive status.

He took off in the Z28, he suggested, taking with him a number of items from the house, which he claimed was full of stolen property accumulated by Cliff Barnes. He said he had no knowledge of any rape of Angela Miller. The marks on Cliff's body, he suggested, were fingernail scratches.

Later that year, Horton granted his friend Jeffrey Elliot an interview that appeared in *Playboy* magazine. At the outset, Horton boldly stated his "wish . . . that the public possessed the common sense to understand that there's two sides to every story—and that they should suspend judgment until they've heard both sides." Then he made an extravagant statement: "I have the evidence—which is readily available to anyone who wishes to examine the trial transcripts—that I did not commit the crimes I was convicted of."

But to substantiate such a claim, he did no more than question Angela's identification of him and point out that the prosecution had no fingerprints to place him in the house on the night of April 3, no blood or semen analysis tying him to the rape, no eyewitnesses. Because he had been convicted on only ten of the forty-four counts in the original indictment, he declared, "the entire trial—from start to finish—was bullshit."

He made no mention of a party that had got out of hand or of taking the rap for a friend. Instead, he simply insisted that Clifford and Angela were liars, saying, "I seriously doubt if she was raped."

As he had in the newspaper interview immediately after his trial, Horton went out of his way to declare himself incapable of committing rape. "I've never had a problem with women; in fact, I've experienced considerable success with women. If I had my choice, I'd much rather be in the company of women than of men. That's why the rape charge is so ridiculous. I've never been at a loss for women. In fact, I suppose I've had too many women in my life. Sex has always been easy to come by. . . . In my mind, any man who commits rape must be sick."

At the same time, he acknowledged a sizable measure of guilt. "They tied me to the gun—which they said I stole from Barnes. And they testified that when I was arrested, I was found with some of the property that had been in Barnes's car, which I admit I stole."

And he confessed freely to Elliot that he began using drugs at the age of "eighteen or nineteen." He had had a sheltered childhood, he said. "Nobody ever discussed drugs. But I

wanted to experience life—and drugs were a part of life. They
certainly were a part of the world where I grew up."

He insisted that he had "never let drugs take over my
life. . . . I wasn't a dope fiend or a drug addict." But he soon
learned that he could "make good money—really good
money—selling drugs. Back then, the streets were wide
open—you didn't have to search the back alleys for customers.
Once the word spread that you had some good stuff, they
found you. You didn't have to knock down anybody's door."

In 1993, the enterprising Elliot conducted a twelve-hour
interview with Horton at the Maryland Penitentiary and sold
pieces of it to *The Nation* and *Emerge,* a magazine of current
affairs with an upscale black readership. Both articles
included Horton's account of the crime, which by now omit-
ted any mention of the gun or the other property stolen from
the house.

"At the time I was living in Upper Marlboro, Md.," Horton
said confidently in the *Emerge* interview, apparently having
forgotten that he had actually been living in Oxon Hill, some
fifteen miles away; Upper Marlboro is where his trial took
place.

I decided to take a short, impromtu [*sic*] trip to
Washington, D.C., after which I planned to go to New
York to spend a few days with a friend. However, I did not
own a car. I called a Yellow Cab, only to discover that the
driver wanted to charge me for coming to my house to
pick me up. Needless to say, I got mad. And once again,
without thinking about the consequences, I decided to
steal a car.

I saw this car which, as it turned out, belonged to Clifford Barnes. . . . Barnes had left his keys inside the car. So, I decided to steal the car. After doing so, I made a quick stop at a local market to buy some beer and cigarettes for the trip. Moments later, I passed a police officer, with whom I exchanged glances.

When I pulled up at the intersection, I looked back at him and thought to myself, "I'm going to have to take a different route." Unfortunately, I wasn't very familiar with the area. Soon thereafter, I spotted six or seven police cruisers. I stopped at a red light, only to see the police officer do a U-turn, turn on his flashing red light, and pull up behind me. . . . He exited his vehicle and said, "Get out of the car." Very politely, I opened my door, at which point I saw that he had a gun aimed at me. He appeared to be very shaky. I thought to myself, "The guy is nuts." When he turned around, I jumped back in the car, ran a red light, and tried to get away.

Horton's inconsistent and implausible denials reveal a manipulative person with an active, if somewhat limited intelligence and a desperate imagination. It is true that the police had not asked Angela to pick him out of a lineup, nor had they found his fingerprints in the house or produced other forensic evidence.

But McManus didn't need that sort of proof to make his case. A medical expert documented that rape had occurred. Police photographs and reports portrayed a crime scene with no evidence of a party—just a vodka bottle and beer bottles Horton had apparently emptied himself—and much to corroborate Barnes and Miller's story: a bruise on Angela's cheek, the knife scratches on Cliff's chest, the phone wires that had bound Cliff wrapped around studs beneath the basement stairs. The gun and the car full of Barnes and Miller's stolen property, not to mention the mask, linked Horton to the house.

If Horton had only taken items from the house and had not assaulted Barnes and Miller, how had he wound up with the engagement ring from Angela's finger? And if Horton actually had so many good reasons to challenge Barnes and Miller's testimony, why had he allowed his lawyer to concede the bulk of it?

A second question the trial failed to answer is perhaps more interesting than that of Horton's story: Why did he decide to commit the burglary in the first place? Why do anything that might call attention to himself or incur new legal risk when he might have continued to live in freedom indefinitely?

In the aftermath of the trial, local crime buffs would advance a speculative theory: Horton believed that the Barnes-Miller house was a center of drug dealing and that Cliff and Angela had access to a large amount of cash. He committed the crime, they suggested, in hopes of finding that money and retiring for life in the style of a drug baron.

Proponents of this theory point out that Cliff Barnes frequently drove different cars home from his shop in order to road test them. Horton might well have noticed the variety of cars turning up in the driveway on Proxmire Drive and assumed they belonged to drug dealers or their customers. The presence of continual drug selling, he knew too well, could also mean the presence of a lot of money.

The assumption that he hoped to find such a stash would explain much of his behavior on the day of the crime. After turning up only jewelry, cameras, and a jug full of change, he decided to wait in the house for Cliff to come home in order to get him to reveal where the real money and drugs were hidden. He kept referring to fictitious partners and pretending to have a confederate in order to intimidate Cliff, who he assumed was part of a drug organization.

He brought up the blue truck in order to make sure Cliff knew he had been watching the house and understood what had been going on in it. He bound and tortured Cliff in hopes he would offer to buy his freedom with drugs or money. He raped Angela in order to increase the pressure on Cliff even more.

The Barneses and Tom McManus consider this theory far too elegant, however. The Z28 was the only flashy car Cliff had driven home recently. The Ugly Truck—the only vehicle Horton mentioned specifically—was an unlikely reflection of drug dealing. "With suburban drug houses, you do get a lot of vehicular traffic," McManus says. "But this was a quiet neighborhood; a strange car in the driveway shouldn't have suggested that much."

Cliff believes Horton, living in the neighborhood, had become obsessed with Angela and broke into the house in order to commit the rape even more than the burglary. She recalls encountering someone who fit his description acting suspiciously around their house in the weeks before the crime, once even staring in one of their windows. Another time, she says, a man who looked like Horton drove by her as she walked the dogs, never taking his eyes off her as he drove past.

But even this relatively simple thought may be too complex. "Why does any criminal personality decide at any time to commit a crime?" asks McManus, who has seen plenty of felons. "People have antisocial impulses they can't control. They get restless." Dougie Cecil, who conversed with Horton after his arrest in Maryland, says he quietly admitted to the crimes for which he was convicted. "William was one of those people who would go in spurts with his drinking," Dougie observes. "He could do some real bloody shit without thinking." When Dougie asked him about the burglary and rape, "He said he had to do what he had to do."

Perhaps the best answer is that Horton, after living in Oxon Hill for a few months, simply felt it was time to move on. He burglarized some houses in the neighborhood to assemble a grubstake, then decided to burglarize one more before finally leaving town. Once inside the Barnes-Miller house, he could not resist the vodka and beer he found there, wound up staying too long, drinking too much, indulging his meaner impulses, and botching the job.

Despite its eventual notoriety, Horton's crime remains banal, an act of generic evil.

Boston

1 9 8 7

After the hearing, Maureen Donovan and her friends joined a delegation led by State Representative Kevin Blanchette, Donna Cuomo, and Ron Fournier to confront Governor Dukakis at the statehouse. Told he was away campaigning for the presidential primaries, Blanchette wrote out a letter for the group to sign and leave with the governor's receptionist.

It read: "Dear Governor Dukakis: While you were away campaigning, we the undersigned came to speak to you about the furlough of William Horton, who after conviction of first degree murder and a sentence of life without parole, was released and then escaped, only to commit another heinous crime in Maryland. Governor, we want answers. We want justice. We want to believe in the system again."

Dukakis aides accepted the letter, and as one helped to ease the group on its way, he suggested they might want to get a petition going to present to the governor when he returned. So *that's what they did. Joan Bamford wrote it up. It said: "We the undersigned would like to have the furlough program for 1st degree murder, abolished. Too many of these murderers are put back on the street only to rape and/or murder again. When a person is sentenced to life imprisonment, without parole, he should spend the rest of his life in prison. Please vote in favor of House Bill #5342."*

Donovan gave copies to relatives and took some to the senior citizens center where she worked, handing them out to co-workers and seniors who came in for the lunch served each day. On their free afternoons, the women took more petitions out to shopping malls and street corners.

Within days, they began to get a little scared as evidence mounted that their local protest had set off something much bigger and beyond their control—as if by innocently shoveling away at a little pile of snow, they had started an avalanche. More and more of the petitions they distributed began coming back bearing hundreds of signatures. Within two weeks, the total reached several thousand, and there was no indication that the surge was about to abate. Reporters sought interviews with Donovan and her friends. Crime victims called to express gratitude and unload pent-up anger with the criminal justice system.

All of which left the normally voluble Donovan at a loss for words. She called Joe Hermann, the state representative from North Andover.

"Joe," she said, "what are we supposed to do now?"

In the first week of April 1987, as news of Horton's capture reached Lawrence, the Merrimack River, swollen by torrential rains, climbed over its banks and flooded the valley. On the day she first heard about the case, Susan Forrest, a reporter for *The Lawrence Eagle-Tribune*, had spent several hours knee-deep in water, following police who were trying to evacuate reluctant residents from their homes. A lieutenant she knew called her name. Had she heard? he wanted to know. They caught Willie Horton!

"Who," she replied, "is Willie Horton?"

Forrest was twenty-seven. She had been working at *The Eagle-Tribune* for three years, after journalism school and a series of jobs on weeklies in the area. But at the time of the Fournier trial, she was a thirteen-year-old growing up in Brookline, where the case hadn't made news. Eleven years later, when Horton hadn't returned from his last furlough, *The Eagle-Tribune* had run a small story, but Forrest hadn't been involved; she barely remembered it.

Horton was serving life without parole, the cop told her, when he walked out on a furlough.

Walked out on a furlough? Forrest responded. If he was serving life without parole, how could he get a furlough?

"Fuck if I know," the cop answered, and Forrest registered a twinge of regret that so pithy a quote could never appear in *The Eagle-Tribune*.

She went back to her office and made some calls. The Horton capture turned out to offer some drama: the night of terror at the Barnes-Miller house, the chase and shooting on Indian Head Highway. Her piece ran the following day.

Other editors might have considered that the end of it; why should the miserable punk's capture be more than a one-day story? But Forrest's boss, Dan Warner, had other ideas. After running her original account of Horton's arrest, Warner called Forrest in for what would be the first of almost daily discussions about where to take the story. "He looked at me," Forrest recalls, "and he said, 'I want you to find out how a cold-blooded killer ever got out in the first place.' " Forrest looked up to the soft-spoken, silver-haired Warner as "my mentor, the father I never had." His order would launch her on what she considered a crusade for truth.

Later on, Warner and Forrest would be accused of consciously using the case to pursue a political agenda—a conservative-minded paper out to embarrass a liberal Democratic governor. And Forrest admits that the political ramifications caused her some discomfort. She was a Democrat, and beyond that, she had even met the governor in private life. Back in Brookline, she had attended high school with Dukakis's son, once even played opposite him in a school drama production. The night of the performance, she recalls, her parents had sat proudly in the audience—right next to Michael and Kitty Dukakis.

But with Warner's active encouragement, she managed to overcome any misgivings. The lead of an early story echoed her mentor almost word for word. "The question everyone wants answered is how a cold-blooded murderer ever got out in the first place," the article began, and then went on to quote heavily from local prosecutors and police.

"The whole system here is really a joke because one state agency spends thousands of dollars in murder trials trying to get the Hortons behind bars for good and then another state agency turns around and furloughs them," a state police lieutenant told the paper. "People like Horton are cold-blooded murderers and nothing will ever change them."

Next to that, the explanations of a spokesman for the correction department sounded pathetically lame: "Clearly a regrettable and tragic mistake has been made . . . but William Horton is an exception to the rule."

It hardly helped the Department of Correction that for a few weeks, its commissioner, Michael Fair, seemed to be in hiding. *The Eagle-Tribune* made gleeful sport with his failure to return Forrest's calls.

Last night, the fifth and final call of the day was placed:

"He is not available," correction department spokesperson Mary McGowen said.

"Do you know when he will be available?" reporter Susan Forrest asked.

"No I don't."

"Will he be available tomorrow?"

"Nope."

"The day after tomorrow?"

"No."

"Next week?"

"No."

"Will he ever be available for me?"

"No, he will never be available."

"Can you answer how many other murderers furloughed by your department have gone on to commit violent crimes while out on passes like Horton?"

"I don't know."

Larry Giordano and Joseph Hermann, two state representatives from the valley, succeeded in meeting with Fair but said they found him hopelessly unhelpful. Fair would not divulge details of Horton's furlough approval, they said, because of the state's Criminal Offenders Records Information Act, or CORI, which protects the privacy of prison inmates.

Giordano filed a new bill to bar first-degree murderers from the furlough program and sought support from Donna Cuomo, Joey Fournier's sister. At first, she refused, saying she didn't want to get involved, but a week later she called to say she had changed her mind. "What happened with Horton in Maryland just brought all the pain and hurt back," she told reporters. "The Department of Correction should come clean."

The tone of shocked reproach and incredulity seemed appropriate. The simple fact of a furlough program for murderers serving life without parole apparently defied common sense. *Eagle-Tribune* stories read like aggressive investigative exposés. THERE IS NO GUARANTEE KILLERS WILL STAY JAILED, shouted one headline over three columns of page 1. It discussed the furlough process and quoted a local prosecutor as saying he was unaware that furloughs were available to murderers.

Forrest recalls being genuinely perplexed. "It was such a nightmare, that story." She felt she had "this incredible story, but there were pieces of the puzzle missing. . . . I just wanted somebody to explain to me in their way how this whole thing transpired." Yet no state officials seemed either able or willing to help her understand.

Even so, the outraged news coverage betrayed a gaping ignorance of recent history. At the time, Massachusetts's furlough policy had been in place for fifteen years and resembled prison-release programs operating in many other states.

It had been the subject of political maneuvers and legislative debate in the early seventies, and the rules for furlough release had been tightened in 1975 and 1981. As long ago as 1973, the Devlin case had established the right of first-degree lifers to participate.

Fair and Philip Johnston, the state's secretary of human services, whose responsibilities included the Department of Correction, understood these points well enough. Why didn't they try to get out in front of their critics and rein in *The Eagle-Tribune*'s runaway coverage?

Apparently neither man believed, until it was way too late, that the Horton flap would last more than a few days or would attract much attention outside the valley. They found Forrest unprofessional, to say the least, in her approach. Fair, she recalls, "was so rude to me. He called me names. He called me a flake." Still relatively inexperienced as a daily journalist, she had never been involved in anything like this before. She admits now to a certain immaturity. High-strung by nature, she recalls losing her cool, begging and pleading for interviews or comments from officials who felt under attack. In general, Johnston looked on *The Eagle-Tribune* as "a rag. It's not taken seriously as a newspaper," whereas "*The [Boston] Globe* is the name of the game in Massachusetts." And *The Globe* hardly considered the Horton story worth daily coverage.

In fact, *The Globe* had reported the only other recent furlough incident with an even hand, giving state officials a fair hearing. The previous September, a lifer named Bradford Boyd, who had completed a dozen furloughs without any problems, suddenly went berserk while in the company of his sponsor, a family friend named Norman Foster. Brandishing a gun he had somehow managed to acquire, Boyd tied up Foster and Foster's niece, abducted the niece's roommate, raped her, and then committed suicide. The press devoted no more than a day or two to that story. But then, it had happened down in Boston, not up in the Merrimack Valley.

Fair had worked as a corrections administrator in Ohio, Pennsylvania, and Illinois before coming to Massachusetts; he did not lack experience at crisis management or media relations. As he saw it, hunkering down for criticism was part of the job. "None of us ever cried about the fact that we would get whaled on from time to time," he would say. After the Horton story broke, sympathetic prison officials around the country sent him clips of similar incidents in their states, most of which drew only cursory media coverage.

Furlough programs, he observed, are one more example of the "risk management" that characterizes all of corrections and criminal justice. And risk management "by definition means that you're not always going to bat one thousand."

When you don't, he believed, too much explanation could be dangerous. "You can't go out in the fury and the emotion of a tragic incident . . . and try to defend the program." If you do, it "appears like you're defending the inmate. Willie Horton was no good. I can't defend and I won't defend anything that he's done in his life." The Horton flap, Fair believed, was just "a case of taking our lumps."

Furthermore, the CORI law did in fact tie his hands, in effect forcing him to stonewall what looked like perfectly legitimate questions about the decisions that led to Horton's having been granted furloughs. The law, passed in 1972, was intended to prevent a criminal's record from following him or

her for life, barring employment and limiting other constructive activities after release from prison. But it also prohibited
any release of information about an inmate's experience in the
prison system.

Fair grew to hate CORI as much as any reporter or state
legislator did. The law, he says, "put the administrator in a
totally no-win situation. You looked like you were hiding
information, you looked like you were unwilling to share
information with the public, and yet if you had shared, you
were liable for fines and imprisonment." If a reporter wanted
to know if someone had broken rules, been disciplined, suffered injury, or experienced virtually anything else in a prison,
the only permissible response from the staff was "I'm not at
liberty to say." And in the spring of 1987, that had to be the
response to all questions about William Horton.

To an extent, Fair's protestations were disingenuous.
Forrest points out that other state officials seemed willing
to violate the spirit, if not the letter of CORI by providing
information about criminal records on background "law
enforcement sources said so and so had this or that . . . [on his
criminal record]."

In any event, by the end of April, Philip Johnston realized
that he had miscalculated. The Horton story, along with the
issues it raised and the confusion it stirred, wasn't going to
fade. He met with Fair and the Merrimack Valley legislators,
then announced an investigation of the Horton furlough. He
promised that "heads might roll" if the inquiry showed it had
been improperly approved.

Meanwhile, *The Eagle-Tribune* kept going. It was a great
ride for Forrest, exhilarating and nervous-making all at once.

For no other newspapers seemed to care. "Even after I did stories, nobody else was doing stories," she says. "I was concerned. . . . It scared me. Was I doing something wrong? Was this not a story? Was I fooling myself? . . . I wouldn't have minded some help. I thought if *The Globe* had jumped on it, they would get some answers for me."

But there wasn't time to think too much about the larger picture as Giordano and Hermann kept up the pressure. "Joe and I were feeding *The Eagle-Tribune* every day," Giordano recalls. "They were calling all the time," Forrest agrees. " 'Suzie, don't let the story die'; that's all they kept saying to me. 'Don't let it die before we get to the truth.' " Today, Forrest acknowledges, she might have been more skeptical. But at the time, she lacked that kind of judgment. "This was my first involvement with any kind of state reps. I was naive. . . . I felt in hindsight that I was used. . . . They were getting a lot of publicity, but at the time, I didn't think about it."

The paper mounted a campaign for access to Horton's prison records on the assumption that they would document the inappropriateness of his furloughs and reveal the identities of individual bureaucrats who might be hung out to dry for approving them. Such access was possible under a 1977 amendment to the CORI law, passed at the behest of news organizations. The amendment permitted release of an inmate's records if two groups, the Massachusetts Security and Privacy Council and the Criminal History Systems Board, found that a compelling public interest in the information outweighed the inmate's right to privacy.

On its editorial page, the paper also began printing a form for readers to clip and send to Governor Dukakis. It read:

Governor Dukakis, please tell me
WHY: Killers go free on furlough.
       Killers are paroled.
       The state lies when it says killers are
       jailed for life.

On May 24, an editorial above the form denounced the
CORI law for aiding and abetting "the Department of
Correction's continuing refusal to answer any questions on
the Horton case. . . . As long as the CORI Act exists, the
Department of Correction may release a virtual army of crim
inals and no one can do a thing about it. No newspaper, no citizen, no politician can prevent it."

On June 11, representatives of *The Eagle-Tribune* appeared
at a Security and Privacy Council hearing to press their
request. Peter Caruso, an attorney for the paper, gave gruesome descriptions of Horton's crimes and declared that "there
must be a balance between the privacy of an individual and
the public's right to know."

William Plante, executive director of the Massachusetts
Newspaper Publishers Association, argued that because of
the confidentiality law, "the bureaucracy of the system has in
effect generated a kind of self-attained benign arrogance
which excludes itself from the public at large; . . . and excuse
me if someone says cover-up, but if this doesn't read like a
bureaucratic curtain, I don't know what does."

And Daniel Warner, editor of *The Eagle-Tribune,* explained
simply that "the reason we brought this to you is because
when we try to talk to corrections officials, they repeatedly
cite CORI as their reason for not speaking with us."

But most members of the council remained unmoved. Granting the request would have set a precedent—it would have been the first release of evaluative information on a prisoner to a newspaper for publication. They pointed out that there still appeared to be much information about Horton that remained unprotected by CORI, and they encouraged *The Eagle-Tribune* to press the agency harder for it. The council turned down *The Eagle-Tribune*'s request by a vote of four to one.

At that point, *The Boston Globe* and the legislature's Joint Committee on Human Services and Elder Affairs joined *The Eagle-Tribune* in seeking release of the Horton records. And with that, Fair went public with his own feelings of frustration with CORI and began stating that the Department of Correction would also support release of the Horton files.

"In my personal opinion, Willie Horton breached any trust we had in him when he escaped," said Dennis Humphrey, a corrections official. "I have no interest in protecting Willie Horton."

Andrew Klein, chief probation officer for the Quincy district court, pointed out that CORI was designed to enhance the constructive possibilities for offenders *after* release from prison. Those who were still in had a much weaker claim to privacy. "Those inside don't have the same rights as those outside," Klein declared. "There is no right to privacy for a guy on furlough or in an institution."

New support and new arguments for release turned the council around. In July, by a unanimous vote, it recommended that the Criminal History Systems Board approve the opening of Horton's records. A few days later, the board complied.

Horton's file contains nearly six hundred pages covering transfers and other status changes, furlough applications, disciplinary records, medical reports, and other administrative documents. Even so, it denied furlough critics the devastating climax they had anticipated. Search as they might through the files, they found no smoking gun, no conclusive evidence that Horton's furloughs were illegal or improper, no identification of prison officials whose gross incompetence had allowed a predictable tragedy.

And given the facts, that was hardly surprising. Horton's escape would eventually be traced properly enough to a systemic lapse—a failure to prepare furlough sponsors better for their role and to maintain adequate communication with them, along with the specific misstep of turning Horton's furloughs over to Helen Mays. But this point remained far too obscure to stand out in the pile of miscellaneous records, and even if it had been noticeable, it did not make possible the quick identification of a bureaucrat on whom to heap the blame.

Susan Forrest "pulled all-nighters just going through it," but wound up disappointed. Under a headline declaring HORTON FILE: MANY PAGES, FEW ANSWERS, FURLOUGH RATIONALE STILL MYSTERY, she reported that the hard-won battle for the documents had produced "no clear explanation of why he was approved for monthly weekend furloughs from his life sentence for first-degree murder, except that he apparently learned to follow prison rules."

In addition to its CORI campaign, *The Eagle-Tribune* also became a willing conduit for Cliff Barnes's and Angela Miller's anger and frustration. Forrest's access to them began with a spooky coincidence.

Six weeks after the crimes on Proxmire Drive, Cliff took Angela to Cancún. Cliff's boss at the auto dealership, a sympathetic man appalled by what had happened to the couple, paid their way. He thought the trip might be a kind of honeymoon, a way to make a new start.

Relaxing by the pool at their hotel, Angela and Cliff fell into conversation with some people from New Hampshire named Beauchesne. They had lived in Lawrence in the 1970s, they said, and remembered a family named Fournier. It was a terrible thing that happened to the Fourniers' son Joey they recalled.

"Small world," Cliff replied, and told them he and Angela were Horton's victims, too. The Beauchesnes, astonished, promised to send newspaper clippings from Lawrence about local reaction to their case.

The more he read, the more Cliff appreciated *The Eagle-Tribune*'s coverage. One day in August, he picked up the phone and called Susan Forrest. She had been frustrated by Maryland police, who refused to divulge the couple's names or address in order to protect Angela's privacy as a rape victim. Now Cliff was prepared to give her the scoop that would inject *The Eagle-Tribune*'s campaign with a powerful dose of human emotion. "I've been looking for you," Cliff said. "Someone in your area has been sending us all your articles on William Horton. We like your stories. We feel like we know you."

Forrest hurried down to La Plata, Maryland, where Cliff and Angela had found a place to rent while they looked for a new house. She visited with them for three days, interviewing them over restaurant meals, going out on their boat, driving with them back to Oxon Hill, to the scene of the crime.

Her first subsequent story, published on August 11, announced that the couple planned to sue the state of Massachusetts. Quotes from Angela, whose name wasn't used, were bitter. "Why do monsters exist and why do civilized correction officials let monsters out? This man stole my spirit. He deserves nothing. He is a monster. All the crying and pleading just egged him on more. He had no remorse, no compassion. He is completely without emotion."

Cliff was angry. "We decided that going ahead with a lawsuit is the only way to teach Massachusetts corrections officials a good, hard lesson in accountability."

Five days later, the paper published the full report of Forrest's visit: a twenty-nine-hundred-word story based on her extended interviews, along with the texts of statements Cliff and Angela had given to the police on the morning after the crime.

The main story, under the headline HOW 12 HOURS SHATTERED TWO LIVES, was accompanied by a page-1 photo of Cliff and Angela embracing, his face to the camera, hers hidden. It gave their dramatic accounts of the crime and was studded with angry quotes (Cliff: "I'd love to get this animal alone in a room with me now, one-on-one with no weapons"). It reported that Angela, the child of a father who had deserted his family and a mother who died when she was seventeen, had no real family but Cliff. She was a Catholic, she said, and the ordeal strengthened her belief in God because she had escaped with her life. Cliff, a Baptist, said the crime had shattered his faith.

And the story told how they continued to cope with the aftermath of the crime every day. "I'm afraid of my own shadow," Angela said. "She carries a knife all the time when she's in the house now," Cliff added, "and she won't go to the bathroom until she checks behind the shower stall first." Along with Bandit and B.J., they now relied on five attack dogs to guard their home.

The crime, they said, had disrupted their sex life and caused them to fight. They had tried counseling but found it too upsetting to pursue yet realized that they still needed help. "We keep going over and over in our heads why it happened to us, but we don't understand," Cliff said.

Where was the other side of the story? According to Forrest, its absence from the pages of *The Eagle-Tribune* did not reflect a lack of trying. Warner, she says, kept asking her "over and over again," to "get Dukakis's side, get Dukakis's side." At one point, she recalls, he took her off all other assignments for a week and sent her to stake out the statehouse in hopes of cornering the governor for a response. "I stood there with a tape recorder and a pen and a notebook. I waited outside the governor's office and kept asking could the governor talk to me." She managed to ambush him, finally, as he emerged one day, but he gave her no more than a five-minute interview that yielded little worth reporting.

As for Horton, Forrest soon learned the identities of his relatives in the house on Bunker Hill Street and says she made two dozen attempts to get inside and interview them. But they reacted with hostility. "They were vile to me," Forrest recalls. "They didn't want to be connected with [Horton] at that point." Beyond the basic embarrassment, they no doubt were worried about their jobs at Raytheon. After one fruitless visit, Forrest returned to her car, only to find it settled awkwardly on slashed tires. Then she began receiving anonymous phone calls threatening her life if she continued to approach Horton's family and friends.

Still another attack on the furlough program sprang from grass roots watered and fertilized by the articles in *The Eagle-Tribune*. Maureen Donovan, a housewife from Methuen who worked part-time coordinating a Meals-on-Wheels program for senior citizens, read that on the night Horton escaped, the police had stopped him only a few blocks away from her house.

As she went over the paper's latest account one day with three of her friends from the senior-citizen program—Joan Bamford, Joanne Pekarski and Gert Lavigne—her anger mounted. It was scary enough that the vicious murderer of Joey Fournier had been driving around in the neighborhood, scarier still that the police could pull him over not even knowing who he was or that he was on a prison furlough—and then let him get away. What on earth was going on?

Donovan wasn't much of a political activist. Even if she'd had the inclination, where would she find the time? After work with the nutrition program each morning, she had plenty to do at home, with four of her six kids still living there. Even so, as she talked it over with her friends, the story about Horton got to her. It was a horrible thing, they all agreed, but what could they do about it?

Donovan finally called up Larry Giordano, the Democratic state representative from Methuen, and asked him the same question. He suggested that the four women come down to Boston a few days later for the hearing the Joint

Committee on Human Services would hold on a bill he had sponsored to end prison furloughs for lifers. The show of citizen interest could help the bill. Maybe they would even like to testify, he suggested.

It turned out to be an eye-opening day. At the hearing, Donovan and her friends listened with rising disbelief as state officials explained that, well, a sentence of life doesn't really mean a person actually serves for life. Most got out after seventeen years or so, even those supposedly serving life without parole. In the meantime, many were routinely released on furloughs; they could go home for a weekend for no reason other than to see their families and friends.

Corrections officials tried to defend furloughs for lifers in the face of hostile questioning. Dennis Humphrey explained that "we're operating under the assumption that everyone in our Massachusetts Department of Correction will eventually make parole. People who are originally sentenced to first-degree life do not complete that. They do not die in prison."

Philip Johnston asserted that "most inmates in correctional institutions are going to return to our communities whether we like it or not. It's very, very important that they have an opportunity to do so in a way that allows them to be well prepared for reentry."

But these defenses were overrun by the emotional stories of crime victims. "My daughter Claire was found strangled," said Mary Gravel. ". . . We still do not know who did it. But when he is caught, . . . we will know what he looks like and we will know his name. What do you think it will do to my family when we are walking along the street someday and see this man ten years down the road because he was furloughed? It's going to trigger a very human reaction which will probably end up with us going to jail."

Coincidentally that day, police in New Hampshire arrested John Zukoski for the rape and beating of a Lawrence woman the previous March. Zukoski had been paroled from prison after serving seventeen years for the rape and murder of a New Hampshire woman. That woman's son, George Chaffee, appeared at the hearing "with a cracked voice and tears in his eyes," according to *The Eagle-Tribune*. "This man was fur-loughed seven times before he was paroled last September," Chaffee said. "How many times does a person have to rape and murder other people before they lock him up for good?"

When it was her turn to speak, Donovan told the legislators that as a citizen, she felt it wasn't fair—people paid taxes to be protected, and yet here the prisons were letting people like Horton out on furloughs. There were enough reasons for the seniors she knew to fear the streets. Why did the authorities have to create more?

Donovan and her friends also met Donna Cuomo, Joey Fournier's sister. An impressive woman, she had spoken elo-quently, still carrying the burden of her loss. And no one had even bothered to tell her and other members of her family that Horton was coming out of prison on furloughs. She could have run into her brother's murderer on the street!

The hearing moved Donovan and her friends to begin cir-culating a petition in support of Giordano's bill. It started as just a neighborhood thing. The women distributed copies at the senior centers where they worked and gave them to mem-bers of their families to pass around. They had no trouble get-ting people to sign. Everyone had read the Horton stories.

Too many shared in the general fear and the frustration with crime: It seemed to get worse every year. Now there was an issue on which to focus those feelings. Furloughs for lifers! It made no sense. Whoever allowed such a thing had to be crazy. Here was the way to fight back, to show the people in power they couldn't get away with it any longer. Some people would grab a petition and sign it before the women even finished explaining what it said. Others asked for copies so they could collect names themselves. Within days, the campaign had produced two thousand signatures.

Now Donna Cuomo was calling up, saying she'd like to pass some petitions around herself. After two weeks, the total approached ten thousand names, and the Horton stories in the paper had begun to mention the women from Methuen.

"I am just a housewife, but I am outraged at the Horton case," Donovan would say when reporters called. "We started this out of anger and frustration. We want them to stop the furlough program. It's wrong to have first-degree murderers back out on the streets. It's scary." Before the cameras, she looked and sounded just right: a no-nonsense housewife, comfortably attractive in middle age, with short curls and a square Irish face, sure of herself and willing to explain it all in a broad Merrimack Valley accent.

Even as a mounting wave of public sentiment fed the petitions, however, the legislature's interest, focused by the first hearing at the end of May, began to dissipate. In subsequent sessions, some lawmakers listened sympathetically as Johnston and Fair gave their statistics about the furlough program's overall success, their explanations of how it kept prisons quiet and helped guide decisions on commutation and

parole. Exactly how Giordano's bill might make the long jour-
ney from introduction to final passage remained unclear.

Donovan and her friends, amazed at what they had already
wrought, had no idea what to do next. But Donna Cuomo
wasn't about to let the campaign wind down. A dynamic
woman who had worked as a schoolteacher and a real estate
executive, she spoke to the others with the authority conferred by her family's tragedy.

"We went to the statehouse, and we had all these hearings,
and they were just yessing us to death, and they weren't going
to do a darned thing. We could tell," Cuomo recalls. So she
went to the others with a plan. To get the bill passed, she said,
they could turn the informal petition drive that had caught
fire in the valley into a statewide push for signatures, meeting
all the legal requirements for a ballot initiative. If successful,
such an effort could put the furlough issue before the voters
in the general election the following year. As important, the
prospect of furloughs on the ballot would guarantee more
public debate on the issue all the way to election day. And that
might force the governor and Democrats in the legislature to
get rid of furloughs much sooner.

It didn't help that Michael Dukakis, already preoccupied
with the 1988 presidential primaries and unaware that his
administration had wandered into a political minefield, bob
bled the issue. He had begun his quest for the presidency and
spent many days that summer campaigning in important primary states. He left Johnston and Fair to deal with the brush-
fire over this Horton business in the Merrimack Valley.

When Donovan's group did catch up with him, as it did one
day in Salem, New Hampshire, as he campaigned for that

state's primary at a reception in a private house, they stood outside with signs reading FIRST DEGREE MURDERERS KILL AGAIN and LIFERS ARE IN FOR LIFE. Inside, Dukakis the policy wonk stoutly defended furloughs for lifers as "an important part of any modern and effective correctional system." The Horton incident, he said, "was a tragedy. I regret it very much." But he added that "it's one of the few escapes we've had in administering the program in the ten years since we tightened it up in the mid-1970s." He explained how commutation was possible even for inmates serving life without parole and how the furlough program made an important contribution to the commutation decision process.

At the end of June, when Donovan's group brought thousands more signatures to the governor's office, Dukakis still refused a meeting with them, but a few days later he did receive Giordano, Hermann, Blanchette, and two other Merrimack Valley legislators to discuss the Horton case. He managed to impress them with his concern. "The governor admitted things that people high up in his administration paid to speak for him should have said a long time ago," Hermann said after the session.

That day, the governor made similar remarks to reporters gathered on the statehouse steps. "When someone goes out on furlough and proceeds to rape and try to kill, it's pretty obvious a mistake was made," he declared. He said he would reexamine the furlough program, support an amendment to CORI permitting release of prison records when convicts commit crimes on furlough, and issue an apology to residents of the Merrimack Valley when he visited there the following week.

But when Dukakis did visit Andover to join the chief of police in announcing a computerized fingerprint-identification system, the sympathy seemed to have receded. He offered no apology to the people of the valley, and when reporters questioned him about the issue, he defended the furlough program. Asked if he would apologize to Horton's victims in Maryland, the governor acted annoyed. "No, no, no," he said. "Look, we are running a very tough, strong, well-defined furlough program in this state, which has by and large been very successful."

He referred to the Horton case as "a tragedy and a very, very sad and terrible thing."

"Of course it's a tragedy," Joe Hermann sputtered. "[Dukakis] doesn't have to remind us it's a tragedy."

That day, the governor did agree to meet with Maureen Donovan, Joanne Pekarski, and Mary Gravel, who had joined the petition campaign. Sitting with them in the Andover police chief's office, he continued his defense of furloughs, explaining how useful they were in helping him decide who deserved to have a sentence commuted at Christmastime.

Mary Gravel asked the governor about the murderer of her daughter, Claire. "What if Claire's killer is caught and convicted, then furloughed? What do you think it would do to my family if they were walking down the street and saw this person?"

Dukakis told her he would probably feel the same way she did, but that possibility "is not going to change my mind" about the furlough program. At that point, according to Donovan, Gravel lost her cool. "Your commutations make me sick," she told the governor.

For a remarkable moment, the fundamental issue was joined. It was a footnote, for now, to the developing presidential-primary campaign—but an event that would prove deeply revealing in the larger emerging drama of crime, fear, and official responsibility. Here were anxious citizens and aggrieved victims face-to-face with a technocratic governor, and it was clear that communication between them had utterly collapsed.

The Horton case was escalating the furlough program into a powerful symbol about which citizen and public official could only talk past each other, neither speaking the same language.

That July, to formalize their quest for a ballot initiative on furloughs, Donovan, Cuomo, and the others set themselves up as Citizens Against Unsafe Society, or CAUS. The nonprofit group could raise money to spread the word and collect signatures. Its literature listed five goals:

To abolish the Furlough Program for first degree murderers.

To recognize the need and amend any and all statutes that are in conflict with "truth in sentencing."

To propose, lobby and testify for the above goals.

To raise public awareness of criminal justice issues through educational presentations, seminars, etc.

To make our society safer by reviewing current laws and amending as needed to better protect the citizens of this Commonwealth.

Succeeding with a ballot initiative would require much more than simply working the local senior centers and shopping malls. According to state law, the group would have to collect in excess of fifty thousand signatures, all verified as those of validly registered voters. No more than 25 percent of the names could come from any one county. And the signatures would have to be gathered within a two-month period, between September 18 and November 18.

Through August and the first weeks of September, Donovan, Cuomo, and the rest of the group held meetings to organize signature collection and fund-raising. William Habib, Giordano's former campaign manager, turned up to help with publicity. Donovan and Cuomo appeared on talk radio and television. The campaign attracted other adherents, some of them families of murder victims. They included Vivianne Ruggiero, the widow of a police officer murdered by a convict later given furloughs; George Hanna, a retired police officer whose son George Junior was murdered while on duty as a state trooper; Marion and John Spinney, parents of Karen, who was killed by a furloughed inmate back in 1975, and Jim and Paula Danforth, whose daughter Paula Marie had recently been murdered.

CAUS also made its own TV commercial, which featured interviews with members of Joey Fournier's family, Maureen Donovan, Vivianne Ruggiero, Michael Stella, and Larry Giordano. It presented the furlough issue in the form of a "five-minute quiz" entitled "Judge for Yourself."

When a first-degree murderer is sentenced to life in prison without parole, he may be released on temporary furlough

    a. never
    b. in twenty-five years

    c. in fifteen years

    d. in ten years

    D. Massachusetts law provides for even those convicted of the most brutal murders to be eligible for furlough after serving only ten years in prison.

When a first-degree murderer is released on furlough, the state will notify

    a. the victim's family

    b. the local police chief

    c. the district attorney

    d. all of the above

    e. perhaps none of the above.

    E.

When a first-degree murderer is released on furlough, how strictly enforced is his supervision?

    a. remain handcuffed to parole officer

    b. report to police every eight hours

    c. report to police every twelve hours

    d. may spend weekend without supervision

    D.

It went on like that, with Giordano finally declaring that "it is obvious that the furlough system in Massachusetts is totally out of control" and concluding with Donovan's appeal for signatures and financial support.

CAUS's most potent weapons were Cliff and Angela Barnes, who came north twice in November to testify before the legislature and help with the signature campaign. Did you know, Cliff would say to a prospect at a mall, that a man released on furlough from your prison system raped my wife? Confronted with the startling question, few refused to sign.

Cliff and Angela also performed compellingly on television. On one talk show, they sat grim faced across from Omar Haamid Abdur-Rahim, a murderer serving life without parole who had used prison furloughs to pursue constructive activities.

"When they've proven themselves to be dangerous to society," Angela declared as Abdur-Rahim shifted uncomfortably in his seat, "then they should be kept away from society for life."

With the furlough program, Cliff added, "you're talking about endangering millions of people. We had no ties to Massachusetts prior to this. William Horton ended up in my basement. Would you want him in yours? . . . They're saying that [the furlough program] is a tool for managing the inmates. If they can't manage them when they're in, why the hell put them out on the streets?"

When Abdur-Rahim explained how he had used the furlough program to marry and begin a family, the Barneses allowed him no credit.

"You guys are building lives when you've torn them apart," Cliff said. "You're making babies and getting married."

And Angela offered nothing but scorn. "You can imagine your children have to look up to a father like that," she lectured the murderer. "My child—if my husband murdered someone, I'd have to say I'd disassociate myself [from] him. I really would."

In general, the presence of the Barneses, living proof of the damage Horton's release caused, electrified the issue. "That's when the media started paying attention to it and people knew what the heck we were doing," Donna Cuomo says. The symbolic issue of the furlough program, already concentrating public energy in a big way, now gained human faces, flesh, and blood, specific and irrefutable stories of anger and pain.

Even so, Dukakis, his mind on the presidential-primary states, continued to neglect the issue. When the Barneses arrived in Massachusetts, the governor was campaigning in Iowa. He sent an emissary to offer an apology, but by now it was too late. Horton's victims spurned the overture. "They had seven months to apologize to us," Cliff said. "What took them so long?"

Dukakis would insist that he had appropriately stayed aloof. "Look, I said repeatedly that I regretted it, I was sorry, it was a tragedy, and so on and so forth," he protests, "but to turn this into a television spectacular didn't seem to me to be a particularly constructive thing." He could not have made a more horrible miscalculation, for his detachment, however rational, guaranteed that the two sides would continue to talk past each other, speaking in different tongues.

"Had he met and said, 'We're going to look into this; it's an injustice,' . . . it damn sure would have made a difference about us going public and fighting against him," Cliff would say later. "Our biggest reason for going against him was because he refused to acknowledge that there were victims. . . . I think the whole ball was in his court." And as the ball stayed there, Cliff's anger grew. "You know," he says, "I remember thinking the biggest reason I wanted to do this was because he had no consideration for what Angie went through."

The Dukakis administration's grave underestimation of the crime and fear issues bore abundant fruit for CAUS. Members of the group spent the last days of November rushing around the state, collecting piles of signed petitions from offices of town clerks, who had to certify them in order for them to qualify for the ballot initiative. Finally, on the evening of December 1, they gathered at Joan Bamford's house and counted the grand total: 52,407 certified names, enough to put furloughs on the ballot. One way or another, Dukakis now would have to face some unpleasant music. At the time, few could predict how unpleasant it would be.

The petition drive projected the issues of murder, its punishment, and its victims' trauma with the bold, two-dimensional strokes that would eventually seal the fate of furloughs for lifers. But Maureen Donovan and her friends were not the only ones to pursue these issues. As their political campaign proceeded, the state house of representatives' Post Audit and Oversight Committee probed in depth the questions raised by the Horton case. The inquiry provided a kind of obbligato acknowledging the complexities of themes that sounded so simple to CAUS, *The Lawrence Eagle-Tribune,* and much of the public.

Fearful citizens might turn away from the historic tradition of crime control and rehabilitation in favor of a symbolic campaign that ventilated pent-up emotion: The legislative committee could not do so as easily. The voluntary revolt of the crime-weary made for bold political theater as it humiliated an ivory-tower administration. But when given the chance to state their case fully, the folks from the ivory tower still had plenty to say, and much of it still made sense.

The Post Audit and Oversight Committee spent four months investigating the details of the furlough process and

Horton's escape. Then in October, the committee convened public hearings that would take place over seven sessions. It summoned human services, corrections department, and other state officials, inmates who belonged to the Lifers' Group, crime victims and their families. The hearings climaxed on November 5 with dramatic testimony from Cliff and Angela Barnes, then on their first trip to Massachusetts.

Philip Johnston and Michael Fair stoutly defended the furlough program on the governor's behalf. "It is an important program for both the reintegration of inmates and as a correctional management device," Johnston stated. "The governor feels that the only way he can make a decision as to whether or not a sentence should be commuted is if the person has some kind of track record that he can look to."

When the committee's chairman, Robert Cerasoli, asked Johnston to elaborate, the secretary told an instructive story about "a young man who was eighteen years old when he was involved as an accessory in a holdup of a restaurant on Route 1. He came from a very good family, came from a family where in fact two of his brothers were leading law-enforcement professionals." He had gone joyriding with some friends who decided to hold up a restaurant. When police arrived, another member of the group shot and killed an officer.

"This particular young person, although involved in the holdup, didn't pull a trigger," Johnston pointed out. "He was convicted and served many years at Walpole and had a sterling record." In prison, he earned high school and college degrees, learned trade skills. "And that is the kind of case where I could personally consider, I would certainly consider a furlough, and, I suppose later, a commutation."

Fair, arguably the man with the most explaining to do, handled himself with skill. Well prepared for the committee's grilling about the apparent absurdity of ever releasing a person sentenced to life without parole, he produced a sixteen-year-old study to confirm that despite the existence of a life-without-parole sentence, Massachusetts had never intended people to die of old age in prison. The study counted thirty-seven convicts whose death sentences had been commuted between 1898 and 1971. Seventeen of them had been paroled. "These were individuals who had been sentenced not to life without parole; these are individuals who had been sentenced actually to death," Fair emphasized. And if they were going back to the community, it was hardly illogical to make community-reintegration programs available to them. Doing so, in fact, could enhance public safety.

Representative Paul Kollios, who had chaired the hearings sponsored by the Human Services Committee, appeared before the Post Audit and Oversight Committee to speak in favor of furloughs. His committee's exploration of the issues, he said, had made him a strong supporter of the program, even for first-degree lifers. He testified that "over 60 percent of the lifers are first-time offenders. They have committed no other crimes. This was their first offense. Many lifers are felony murderers. They didn't do the killing. The lifers in an institution are not the guys you hear about who are cutting up all over the street. The typical offender in prison is between the ages of nineteen and twenty-six. He has got a history of crime, a history of drug abuse to a great extent. He is a bad actor. He doesn't get too many rehab programs. . . . The lifer is about ten years older than that. They live in the prison. It is theirs. That is where they are for life, unless they get commuted. . . . They are the best-behaved inmates in the prison."

He described the many constructive programs lifers had started and reminded the committee that especially for inmates in for long terms, rehabilitation remains possible. He expressed concern that without the furlough program, a person who committed first-degree murder when he was nineteen and subsequently rehabilitated himself would go unrewarded. "He is not the same person at age thirty-eight or forty as he was when he was nineteen," Kollios declared.

The Post Audit and Oversight Committee also heard from some first-degree lifers, who testified that while not all such inmates deserve furloughs, they should remain eligible to the extent that they can demonstrate their trustworthiness. Inmates who had been going out on furloughs said they used them to maintain relations with their families. A first-degree lifer named Robert Marshal who had been going out on furloughs turned out to be familiar to some state representatives because he had learned construction skills and had been working with a crew that had recently been remodeling and painting rooms in the statehouse.

A second lifer was the same Omar Haamid Abdur-Rahim who would appear opposite the Barneses on television. He said that in addition to visiting his family, he had spent furlough time speaking to high school groups and to addicts in drug-rehabilitation programs. He also made an instructive revelation: He had participated in a robbery with another man who actually did the shooting. Even so, Abdur-Rahim was charged with first-degree murder under the felony murder law. Prosecutors offered both men the chance to plead guilty to second-degree murder. Abdur-Rahim refused the deal and went to trial, where the jury found him guilty of murder in the first degree and therefore subject to life without parole. But his accomplice had accepted the deal and was sentenced to second-degree murder. Even though it was he, not Abdur-Rahim, who had done the killing, he was already eligible for parole.

Under the committee's intensive questioning, Johnston, Fair, and other officials left openings for their critics. "I have mixed feelings about furloughs for first-degree lifers on a personal level, as I suppose everybody does," Johnston admitted. "These are normally people who . . . have committed very serious, arguably the most serious, and violent offenses that one can imagine, and so . . . I would be inclined, just on the face of it, to deny it."

Fair sought to reassure the committee by pointing to the furlough program's success rate of 99.5 percent. But when his interrogators wanted to know if that meant the Horton case could never happen again, he had to say no. "I don't know that [the furlough program] would be improved in any way, shape, or form where I could honestly look you in the eye and say that if we did these twelve improvements, there could never be another Horton case again."

Persuasive as the officials' arguments might be, the victims' testimony provided heavy emotional counterweight.

Donna Cuomo declared that "when they arrested the three men that murdered Joey, we felt that we had been served by the judicial system and that justice had been served. And what a shock it was to find out, so many years later, that it hadn't. And that's why we have to do something about it. And someone said to me, Are you doing this for your brother? I said, I guess I am doing [it] for my brother because if I didn't do anything, what a shame it would be that he had to die for nothing, because justice has not been served."

She ended her testimony by suggesting that legislators "spend some time at the bimonthly meetings of a group known as the Parents of Murdered Children, where you'll have considerable difficulty listening to their sad, personal tragedies, real stories, real-life stories, hear their voices tremble, and see their haunted eyes. . . . I met most of those people for the first time last Sunday at a rally, and the feeling that you get is . . . The only thing I can liken it to is at the wall of the Vietnam Memorial."

Vivianne Ruggiero, widow of the murdered police officer, complained that her husband's killer had been let out thirty-three times. "Isn't he lucky he can go on with his life?" she said, still tasting the bitterness of her devastated life after many years. "How fortunate for him, and we are not allowed to. I have to live with it every day of my life to the day I die. I wish I could have a furlough . . . one weekend . . . one hour."

Lorraine Cook-DeCosta gave a vivid account of the night fifteen years before when the police informed her that her son Steven had been stabbed to death. "I do not feel he should be a member of a program that allows him to be out of jail, regardless of how short a time it is for," she said of the man convicted of her son's murder. "My son can never be alive again, not for eight hours or even one second. If [the murderer's] punishment is not for life, then where is justice?"

Angela Barnes testified angrily. "It's your job to protect us," she told the committee. "We had nothing to do with any of you; I didn't know any of you people before this, and now I'm up here in a state I've never been before trying to plead with you people to keep my family safe. . . . The next person that's hurt or killed [by a furloughed lifer]—it's going to be on your blood, it's going to be on your soul, every single one of you that let it happen."

Cliff Barnes picked up on Fair's statements about the furlough program's 99.5-percent success rate. "I think when you're dealing with people that are this dangerous and this violent, anything short of 100 percent is not successful. I mean, you can't get any guarantees that they're not going to harm somebody else. They've already given up their rights when they kill someone."

The Barneses were particularly enraged at suggestions that their victimization might be considered tolerable since it apparently resulted from one of a tiny percentage of furlough escapes. They railed against references to the furlough-program statistics.

"Are you saying that some people on this committee think if you use figures and numbers, . . . it's acceptable?" Cliff asked indignantly. "That's acceptable, so we're . . . By that system, we're expendable—is that what they're saying? . . . It obviously angers us both greatly that they're saying that there's an acceptable statistic, an acceptable ratio, for how many lives can be destroyed or damaged by these first-degree convicted murderers."

Even so, the Post Audit and Oversight Committee's report maintained a relatively even hand. It concluded that Horton was eligible for furloughs and that corrections officials had followed procedures for granting them. But it also found a number of procedural flaws in the process, among them inadequate record-keeping to document the reasoning behind furlough decisions, inadequate supervision of inmates on furloughs, and poor screening and training of sponsors.

Its succinct summary of the furlough debate framed it in terms of crime control: "If you believe that only a 100-percent guarantee against a lifer ever committing a crime while on furlough is the only solution—then the furlough program, as it exists for lifers, must be eliminated. However, if you believe that the present 99.5-percent success rate outweighs the potential risk to public safety, then we must seek ways to improve the program as it now stands."

In an appended "Chairman's Report," however, Representative Robert Cerasoli restated the outrage he had expressed more than once in the hearings: "You can take a human life in Massachusetts premeditatedly, with malice aforethought, and it appears that you will serve no more than twenty years in prison. Clearly, a human life in Massachusetts is worth only twenty or less years in prison. Therefore, the question arises, does the criminal justice system in this state dispense justice?"

But despite the emotion with which he wrote about justice, Cerasoli stopped short of calling for a ban on furloughs or doing anything else that would create genuine life without parole. Instead, he endorsed legislation that would substantially tighten the furlough program. He had learned too much, in other words, to join the clamor for a symbolic sacrifice. Appeasement would have to do.

In addition to supporting the release of Horton's prison records and testifying in legislative hearings, Johnston, Fair,

and others made further attempts to protect furloughs for lifers. The Department of Human Services study of Horton's
furlough and escape also found that Horton had been eligible
for furloughs under the rules and that his furloughs had been
granted according to the established procedures. But it, too,
found a lack of documentation in some areas of the furlough
review process, a need for more attention to sponsors, and "a
sense of routine that may, in some cases, reduce the high level
of scrutiny that should be applied to each and every furlough
request by 'first-degree lifers.' "

In May, the Human Services office announced new rules
that in part reflected these findings. The rules tightened eligibility further, gave victims' families a voice in the furlough
process, and subjected sponsors to more rigorous investigation. In September, Representative Kollios introduced a bill
that would codify the new rules, giving legislators concerned
about the issue an alternative to Giordano's bill, which sought
to eliminate furloughs for lifers entirely.

All of this was ambitious damage control, but in the end, it
was not enough to save the program. By December, votes in
the house indicated strong support for Giordano's bill. The
governor's case suffered a powerful blow on December 11,
when Armand Therrien, a former New Hampshire state
police officer serving first-degree life for murdering his business partner, escaped while on a work assignment at a state
hospital. Though Therrien had not been on furlough, the
work program recalled Horton's experience. The escape generated scornful editorials suggesting that the corrections
department had lost all sense of responsibility for keeping
dangerous criminals locked up.

Giordano's bill passed the state house of representatives by a large margin but ran into trouble in the senate, where it landed only three weeks before the session was to end. Though a huge majority of senators seemed ready to support the ban, one of them, Royal Bolling, decided to make a last stand against the return to expressive justice and in support of the old belief in reason, rehabilitation, and crime control. He began a determined campaign to prevent the ban from coming to a vote.

Asserting that "this whole thing has been an emotional thing," Bolling, a black senator who represented the Roxbury district of Boston, warned against a rush to destroy the furlough program. "I think that the legislature is acting impulsively because of several very atrocious incidents," he said. "But when we look at the number of lifers that have been on furlough and have kept their bargains over a period of years, it's an admirable record."

He pointed out that the furlough program had played an important part in helping to stabilize troubled prisons in the 1970s, and he made no apologies for believing that rehabilitation ought to remain a part of corrections. "The furlough program is a necessary thing for the rehabilitation of the people serving these terms," he declared.

Giordano and Hermann charged that Bolling was cynically "carrying the governor's water," hoping to spare Dukakis the embarrassment of having to veto the bill. But Bolling, a courtly, elegant man with flowing gray hair and mustache, seemed to relish the chance to stand up for rational policy against "an emotional tide."

He set out to stall the bill by introducing amendments— one would keep furloughs but further tighten the rules;

another would allow them only for first-degree lifers being considered for commutation—and insisting that they be printed and distributed before the senate considered and voted on them. At other times, he used his power under the rules to defer votes on amendments or bills until another legislative day. He managed to prolong the parliamentary shuffling all the way to January 5, the last day of the session.

"We lost the battle, but we're going to win the war," a disgusted Hermann declared after the senate session ended without a furlough vote. He and other supporters of the ban pointed out that William Bulger, president of the senate and another Dukakis supporter, might have ruled Bolling's parliamentary delays out of order but had failed to do so despite the clear will of the senate.

Speculation that Dukakis was behind the senate maneuvers made some sense. By December, the overwhelming sentiment for the furlough ban in the legislature, backed up by the successful CAUS petition drive, made clear that the governor would have trouble defending the furlough program for long. And that winter he faced his first big presidential primary, in New Hampshire, just over the border from Lawrence and Methuen. *The Lawrence Eagle-Tribune* counted southern New Hampshire as a big circulation area. Why give the paper the satisfaction of rubbing his nose in the issue just then?

Indeed, as soon as the drama in the senate had played out, Dukakis moved to take the initiative. With handwriting boldly on the wall, he began to speak the other side's language. He announced that he had suspended all furloughs for lifers for ninety days while his Anti-Crime Council studied the matter; it would make recommendations in March. By then, the New Hampshire primary would be history.

No longer did he repeat the stout defenses that had marked his handling of the issue through the summer. "We recognize this is a serious problem of great concern to people, and it is of great concern to me," he said in announcing the Anti-Crime Council study. And he denied any firm commitment to vetoing Giordano's bill if it should pass that spring.

Another round of hearings began on the bill in the third week of February. Giordano assembled the CAUS crowd—Cuomo, Ruggiero, and Donovan—to testify, and Cliff Barnes came up from Maryland one more time. Angela had decided not to come, saying she had "reached a point of exhaustion" with the political process.

"I'm depressed about being here again," Cliff Barnes said. "I can't believe this is still going on. I don't want to be here." Angela, he explained, could not appear because "she came here and poured her heart out, cried on television, and you people didn't do your job. She felt like she couldn't do it again."

The hearings included opposing views. A Boston University professor named Elizabeth Barker, who had taught prison inmates, argued the case for rehabilitation, insisting that education and furloughs reduce recidivism. "People can change," she said. "It seems to me we're endangering the public. You want people going out the same way they came in? Furloughs give them hope, keep them in touch with the community and their families. Prison families are victims, too."

According to *The Eagle-Tribune*'s account, "Several people in the room groaned and booed, cutting off Mrs. Barker. One man shouted, 'Give me a break.' "

A few days later, the house Human Services Committee approved the bill after having rejected an amendment that would have kept furloughs for lifers but with stricter guide-lines. At that point, leaders of the senate, fearing that waiting too long to act could give Bolling another opportunity to delay the bill to death, took up the measure. They managed to get it before the Ways and Means Committee, chaired by a sympathetic senator, Patricia McGovern. On March 13, her committee gave unanimous approval to the bill, and Bolling declared that he would now oppose it only with reasoned arguments, not with stalling tactics. "Time was on my side before, but it isn't now," he said.

A week later, the governor finally put the issue to rest, going before reporters to announce that he would no longer support furloughs for lifers. He would ask the corrections department to develop other ways for inmates to demonstrate responsibility and maintain community ties. In his announcement, Dukakis recounted the overall success of the furlough program and his continued belief in the idea of community reintegration. But he acknowledged that the Horton escape "raised legitimate public concerns and sparked appropriate public debate."

As the reporters bored in with questions, he made no attempt at elegant explanations for his reversal. "I try to listen, I try to learn," he said. Asked if he remained personally in favor of the furlough program, he responded, "That's irrelevant. The fact of the matter is people in this commonwealth and the legislature aren't."

It would take another five weeks for the ban on furloughs for lifers to win approval of both houses, by lopsided margins, but there were no more fireworks. On April 28, 1988, Dukakis finally signed the bill into law.

Giordano and the leaders of CAUS complained that he did so privately, rather than inviting them and other supporters of the bill to a big public ceremony. "Where were the balloons and the band?" Giordano asked. Maureen Donovan wanted to know if "he signed it in the men's room or the closet." Hermann observed that the governor was "not too enthused about the whole thing."

No, he wasn't, nor was he interested in calling attention to the furlough issue in any way. For by now, the national press had anointed him front-runner for the Democratic presidential nomination, and the harsh spotlights of media scrutiny were swinging toward Massachusetts.

After enactment of the ban on furloughs for lifers, congratulations seemed in order all around. Giordano and Hermann could collect compliments for determined leadership in the interest of public safety. Cuomo, Donovan, and the other members of CAUS could boast an authentic victory for grassroots organizing. And for its coverage of the Horton issue, *The Lawrence Eagle-Tribune* won no less than a Pulitzer Prize for general reporting, journalism's most prestigious award.

It did not seem to matter much to anyone that the furlough ban was mostly a symbolic victory. It affected only first-degree lifers; no more than a few dozen of them ever participated in the program over the course of a year. Most, if not all, were stable people like Omar Abdur-Rahim, whose furlough behavior had been wholly benign. It was hard to make a plausible case that denying people like him furloughs would prevent any crime at all; eliminating the chance for rare replays of the Horton case would make no measurable contribution to overall crime reduction. But this was by now an obscure point.

For tens of thousands of Massachusetts voters, the furlough fight remained a victory to savor, for it had given them a chance to act on their fear. While it also served the political needs of conservative populists out to embarrass a liberal governor, the broader effects could not be overlooked. The public debates that the campaign generated had given sympathetic voice to widespread anxiety and anger. They had subjected vicious criminals to sharp, often vituperative public rebuke, laid bare the supposedly dangerous ineffectiveness of the criminal justice system, and held it up for public censure. Before the roar of outrage, the system and the governor who had dared to defend it fell back in humiliating retreat, ultimately submitting, publicly acknowledging that they were wrong and changing the law to comply with the popular will. On closer examination, however, there were reasons to question the celebrations of triumph, reasons that went well beyond the absence of practical effect.

The CAUS campaign succeeded largely because its promoters hammered two ideas into the public consciousness so relentlessly that they soon were accepted as bedrock assumptions, the points from which the whole discussion of Horton's furloughs had to begin.

The first was that Horton had committed crimes of unspeakable viciousness, that he was capable of behavior so extreme that, like Charles Manson or Jeffrey Dahmer, it separated him from the rest of humanity at a level of elemental morality. The second sprang from the first: If Horton was so monstrous a criminal, no honest or sane prison official could possibly have considered him for furloughs. His release therefore must have been the result of gross malfeasance.

However vividly these ideas played across the stage of Massachusetts politics that year, they remained rooted more in emotion than in provable fact. Many would see no reason to apologize: No one but Horton himself ever seriously argued that he was wrongly convicted of *any* crimes, and there was little basis for such a claim. If he was guilty, who should care if CAUS and its supporters exaggerated a bit? To them, certainly, the end was important enough to justify such means.

Even so, the furlough opponents' casual attitude toward inflammatory allegations—they indignantly rejected accusations of demagoguery—oversimplified the issues in ways that expanded the image of Horton as a villain in a powerful folktale of official betrayal.

What kind of person was William Horton? The story of his life and court records indicate a garden variety criminal, a lowlife who never got much education and never figured out how to function very well in legitimate society. He also bore a burden of unfocused anger, the legacy of a turbulent childhood, that had eroded away basic respect for both the law and norms of ethical behavior. He enjoyed manipulating people for his own purposes. Without compunction, he could lie, cheat, steal, and abuse the feelings or naïveté of those who made the mistake of getting close to him. And he had a proven capacity for violence, especially under the influence of vodka, his favorite drink.

While hardly appealing, this was not an especially unusual profile. The web of social pathologies afflicting American society had been generating tens of thousands of young men like Horton every year. Cops, social workers, judges, and prison wardens all over America recognized the pattern. So did people on the streets.

"William," his friend Dougie Cecil would say, "is an asshole." The vulgarity conveys precise judgment: a person pathetically unable to handle the hard realities of life, a loser through and through.

But a loser is not a vicious monster, a person so depraved as to call his own humanity into question. In 1974, Horton actually managed to combine criminal behavior with a respectable life, holding down straight-world jobs and going home to his family each night. By all accounts, his criminal side was more mundane than monstrous, and in truth, there was no compelling reason to alter that judgment even after the murder of Joey Fournier.

Yet after his 1987 arrest in Maryland, the public clamor about his case permitted no examination of his character or his record in any detail or with any precision. Instead, the story promoted by the furlough opponents required Horton as monster, a criminal larger than life whose horrible deeds should have barred him from furloughs forever. If that Horton didn't really exist, CAUS, the Merrimack Valley politicians, and *The Lawrence Eagle-Tribune* seemed eager to create him. And a fearful public just as eagerly believed in their creation. Lacking a real point of focus, the general fear had brought forth its own, an ugly hologram that hung in the air whenever the subject came up, an image with the power, finally, to liberate bottled-up rage.

The rumors conveniently inflating the luridness of Horton's crimes began almost as soon as news of his arrest in Maryland reached the Merrimack Valley.

One was that Angela Miller was pregnant when Horton had attacked her. References to his having raped a pregnant woman crept into early newspaper accounts and kept being repeated as reporters, without checking further, included the obligatory summaries of Horton's crimes in articles about each new development. Yet Angela was not pregnant on the night of April 3, nor had she ever been pregnant. But that fact did not get reported until August, when Cliff and Angela invited Susan Forrest down to Maryland for the first big interview.

Another rumor arose from recollections of old news stories about the Fournier murder. Police describing the crime scene noted that as his assailants fled, Joey Fournier had fallen onto a wastebasket in the office at Marston Street Mobil. Yet by 1987, furlough opponents would declare with great authority that Fournier's murderer had stuffed the body into an oil drum or heaved it into a Dumpster. Some even thought they recalled that the killer had hacked the arms and legs off the corpse before disposing of it as trash.

Joe Hermann legitimated an even more repellent rumor at a hearing of the Human Services Committee on May 27, 1987. He asserted, according to *The Eagle-Tribune,* that after stabbing Joey Fournier to death, "Horton cut off the boy's genitals, put them in his mouth and then spit them out." In other words, beyond robbing, raping, and assaulting, Horton's crimes included grossly unspeakable acts—sexual mutilation and something that approached either necrophilia or cannibalism.

Two weeks later, in a hearing before the Massachusetts Security and Privacy Council on *The Eagle-Tribune*'s request for Horton's prison records, the newspaper's attorney, Peter

Caruso, repeated the hideous charge with great vehemence. "If you take a look at the court docket," he said, "you will read a graphic illustration of what Horton did to that young man, . . . cutting off his penis and putting it in his mouth."

For many people, this horrible story was enough to settle the furlough question all by itself. What kind of morally idiotic correctional program would grant any favor at all to a person capable of such a thing?

A television talk-show host used the question to ambush a hapless Omar Haamid Abdur-Rahim, the well-spoken, clean-living lifer who appeared opposite the Barneses and Vivianne Ruggiero.

"Are you acquainted with what William Horton did?" the host asked Abdur-Rahim, reading from note cards in her lap.

"Yes, I am," Abdur-Rahim replied.

"All right," the host went on, "for the benefit of people who don't know, he killed a seventeen-year-old boy, and after he killed him, he cut him up in pieces, dismembered his body, and put it in an oil can in the gas station. Do you think a man with this kind of background should have been paroled?"

Ignoring her confusion of furloughs with parole, Abdur-Rahim groped to answer: "Well, I think that was a very horrendous crime, and I think it should have been scrutinized, and personally . . . on the face of it, I would probably have said no."

A short while later, she raised the same question about the murderer of Ruggiero's husband, effectively equating it with the barbaric description of Horton's crime.

"Let me ask you, Omar, a question. Vivianne's husband, shot in the face six times, a police officer, unprovoked, should that man have been furloughed?"

Abdur-Rahim attempted to make a case for change and forgiveness: "When I came in the institution, I was nineteen years old. . . . In most cases you will find extenuating circumstances, such as drug use, alcohol use. . . . We do get caught up into some situations that after you end up in prison you can't believe yourself that you've done." But this succeeded only in drawing a chorus of abuse from Angela Barnes and Vivianne Ruggiero.

"There's no extenuating circumstances," Barnes snapped.

"Once you commit murder, that's it. That's it," Ruggiero insisted. "If you can bring my husband back, then you can get out on furlough."

Concerned with the conversation's drift, Abdur-Rahim sought to explain how he had devoted himself to atoning for his crime by trying "to give something back to the community. . . . I try to give back and show that people who have been convicted of first-degree murder are not necessarily ravaging savages who are going to remain that way for the rest of their lives."

At which point Ruggiero erupted: "You shoot someone in the head six times—how more savage can you get? When you stab someone, you cut them up in pieces—how more savage can you get?

"You can't get much more savage than that," a defeated Abdur-Rahim admitted. And Ruggiero shouted, "That's right!" as the studio audience nodded its approval.

The sexual-mutilation charge was important for reasons that went beyond concentrating the poison in a poisonous debate. The law barred any furloughs for sex offenders. *The Lawrence Eagle-Tribune*'s attorney and its editor, Dan Warner, suggested that the Department of Correction might be resisting release of the records because officials had foolishly approved Horton's furlough only on the basis of his conviction for murder while the records documented an awful sexual aspect to the crime. "Horton's crime in 1974 was clearly sexual," Warner had testified. "We keep finding things that keep us, and the people we serve, confused over what happened."

But at that moment, he had no idea how very confused he was. For, of course, all of the allegations about sexual mutilation and dismemberment were totally false. The autopsy on Joey Fournier found stab wounds to his upper body but no damage below the waist. Not a word about mutilation or dismemberment appears in the voluminous Fournier trial record or in any other official document—or in *The Eagle-Tribune*'s own accounts of the murder and trial in 1974 and 1975.

"I don't know where that came from," Giordano would say later about the mutilation story. "It never happened, but for some reason it came up somewhere along the line. It was just one of those hearsay rumors."

Though its own morgue could easily have set the record straight, *The Eagle-Tribune* continued to repeat the mutilation charge. Susan Forrest says Lawrence police detectives confirmed the story for her; she reported it without reviewing the autopsy results or the Fournier trial transcript. Finally, in its edition of July 29, the paper reported the truth after interviewing Correction Commissioner Fair about the release of Horton's prison file. The article left it to Fair to correct the gross error, briefly and in the nineteenth paragraph, well off page 1. "Fair said earlier statements . . . that Horton sexually mutilated Fournier were not true. . . . Photographs of Fournier in his autopsy report clearly show that he was stabbed 19 times above the waist. There was no damage below his waist."

The distortion of Horton's record involved more than false rumors. Beginning with her earliest stories for *The Eagle-Tribune,* Susan Forrest, relying on the recollections of Lawrence detectives, commonly referred to Horton as a "cold-blooded murderer," an epithet more circumspect newspapers might reserve for editorials. And where other papers might have tempered their reports of the Barneses' understandable bitterness, *The Eagle-Tribune* freely quoted their references to Horton as a "monster" and an "animal."

More substantively, *The Eagle-Tribune* and other Massachusetts newspapers routinely described Horton as "a convicted first degree murderer sentenced to life in prison because he stabbed a Lawrence youth 19 times in 1974." They referred to Joey Fournier as "the Lawrence youth whom Horton stabbed to death" or who "died after being stabbed 19 times by Horton." In recounting the 1987 Maryland crime, Massachusetts newspapers said Horton allegedly "stabbed" or "slashed" Cliff Barnes repeatedly before raping Angela.

Yet there is no conclusive evidence that Horton stabbed either Joey or Cliff. The prosecutors who convicted Horton of felony murder were not required to prove which of the three defendants actually killed Joey Fournier, and they never did. The investigation and trial strongly suggested Alvin Wideman had wielded the knife. Wideman had as much of a reputation for violence as Horton and seemed a more mercurial personality. It was Wideman who confessed the stabbing to J.J. and Thelma Thomas on the night of the crime. And it was

Wideman who tried to borrow one of J.J.'s guns the following day in order to go after Horton and Pickett because, he said, he had done all the work, he had killed the person, and they had stolen his share of the money. Under interrogation by the police, Wideman was the only one of the three who admitted to going into the gas station. Though he insisted that Fournier was alive when he left, that statement was not necessarily inconsistent with his having done the stabbing.

Again, most of this was available to anyone who might have consulted back issues of *The Eagle-Tribune.* Yet in 1987, at the height of the furlough controversy, Susan Forrest reported that "From the beginning of the investigation . . . [prosecutor Michael Stella was] of the opinion that Pickett was the driver of the car, Horton and Wideman went in to rob the gas station, Horton had the knife, and it was Horton who stabbed Fournier 19 times."

Five years later, when asked about who stabbed Joey Fournier, Stella sounded less certain: "Three participated, but there was no way the jurors could determine which one of them did the stabbing," he said. "There was no evidence, no proof coming out of the trial. I suspect Horton did the stabbing. I think Pickett stayed in the car."

Why did he think that?

"Because it was Pickett's car." His investigators, he added, had interviewed people at the party the three had attended that night and determined that Pickett had been driving. But at the trial, Stella's colleague, Robert O'Sullivan, had made much of John Greenwood, who testified that he had seen three black men in a car prowling the streets near Marston Street Mobil. Greenwood said that the driver had the bushiest Afro of the three, a point that suggested Horton, who sported the bushiest Afro, was at the wheel. In any event, it's hardly beyond the realm of reason that Pickett might have left the car even though he was driving.

"I think a lot of the comments that were made were hearsay that wouldn't stand up in a court of law," Giordano says now about the Fournier case. "Nobody really knew for sure who stabbed him."

As for the "stabbing" or "slashing" of Cliff Barnes eleven and a half years later, the trial jury failed to find that it had occurred. Photographs of Cliff's torso taken on the morning after the crime show a series of horizontal scratches that barely break the skin, similar to those that might be inflicted by thorns on a bush.

In fact, when Giordano, in a hearing, asked Angela what Cliff looked like after their ordeal, she replied that "he looked like he had a fight with a rosebush and a bus and didn't fare very well. . . ."

However they might have figured in the infliction of psychological torture, the scratches were hardly serious injuries. No one who had seen the pictures could argue with the jury's decision to acquit Horton of malicious cutting with intent to disable.

Yet neither the furlough critics nor the Massachusetts media seemed to have much patience for careful reporting of such details. As late as December 6, 1987, more than a month after Horton's acquittal on the knife charge, *The Eagle-Tribune* published a statement that Horton had raped Angela and "repeatedly stabb[ed] her fiancé."

The Eagle-Tribune's performance raised some eyebrows in the journalistic community, particularly after the newspaper won the Pulitzer Prize. In May 1988, Alexander Cockburn denounced the award in his sharp-tongued column of media criticism for *The Nation*. He headlined his discussion of the Horton coverage A DISGUSTING AWARD FOR A DISGUSTING PAPER. "*The Eagle-Tribune* used an old and simple formula," Cockburn wrote. "Find a crime, recruit a couple of hyperventilating politicians, and it's simple enough to stir up hysteria, particularly if the objects of the assault are killer convicts and a sensible program."

He declared that Susan Forrest's "prolonged interview with the Maryland couple made Geraldo Rivera look like John Chancellor. . . . [Her] idea of good journalism was to take hatred polls—that is, if you can find enough people before deadline to say killers should be locked up and the key thrown away, such sentiments should determine social policy."

In 1989, the newspaper suffered more criticism in an article that appeared in the *Washington Journalism Review*. The author, Steve Burkholder, read through more than 250 *Eagle-Tribune* clips about the Horton case and concluded that the paper "ran roughshod over complexities and it ran in one direction." In addition to inaccuracies about the stabbing of Joey Fournier, sexual mutilation, and Angela Miller's pregnancy, Burkholder found that the paper had totally abandoned objectivity and often seemed transparently in bed with the politicians pushing the ban on furloughs.

The Eagle-Tribune "piled up facts, figures and sources that focused on the weakness of furlough programs, while skimping on material supportive of furloughs. It allowed itself to be swept up by a crusade in which the voices of news reporters, editorial writers, Op-Ed commentators, politicians and activists became indistinguishable," Burkholder wrote.

Given space to respond, *The Eagle-Tribune's* editor, Warner, complained that the *Washington Journalism Review* article "echoes exactly the point of view of the Dukakis administration." He conceded that the paper had published "incorrect details of the crimes" on the word of the politicians who uttered them, adding lamely that "only *The Eagle-Tribune* pursued the story until we got and reported the correct details," an apparent reference to the downplayed paragraph about the absence of sexual mutilation. On the question of who stabbed Joey Fournier, he asserted that "we have three sources, two of them eyewitnesses," to establish that "Mr. Horton did knife Joey Fournier to death."

If such eyewitnesses existed, however, the paper never printed a word about them, and they apparently never came to the attention of prosecutors. Asked about the discrepancy more recently, Warner declared, "I have a huge lack of interest in this. . . . I don't want to reveal my sources. I don't want to get involved."

Lies have long half-lives. As late as 1992, it was still possible to find well-meaning officials in the Massachusetts criminal justice system who would repeat the sexual-mutilation story as if it were well-established fact. That same year, Rush Limbaugh, the popular right-wing commentator, would write in his best-selling book that "Horton was in prison for murdering a man after castrating him and stuffing his genitals in his mouth."

The elevation of Horton from street criminal to monstrous folk villain implied awful questions about correctional management. No competent prison system could possibly be capable of releasing such a person for any reason, the argument went. Therefore, Fair's administration of Massachusetts corrections had to be hopelessly incompetent or corrupt.

The idea gained weight as the Norfolk penitentiary's Lifers' Group began bad-mouthing Horton. Specifically, its members suggested that Horton was an active drug user and dealer who had also become a "favored" inmate—his furloughs were granted as rewards for informing on others.

On July 13, 1987, Susan Forrest had slipped this idea into a story recalling her weeks of frustration in dealing with a corrections bureaucracy that understandably enough had begun to treat her with active hostility. "Nearly two months ago a group of first-degree murderers in Norfolk contacted me and have since written two dozen or so letters asking that I come visit so they can talk about Horton," she wrote. "They claimed Horton was a drug dealer in prison and a stool pigeon for the guards. They said he was let out on furloughs solely because he snitched on fellow inmates. I still can't get anything verified."

CORI and official stonewalling prevented her from getting to the bottom of the story, she suggested. "Unless Mr. Horton himself wants to talk publicly about why he was furloughed by the Massachusetts Department of Corrections, the final chapter to his story unfortunately may never be told."

A month later, Giordano and members of the Post Audit and Oversight Committee visited with the Norfolk lifers and apparently received an earful. "All of them said Horton was a bad apple," Giordano told *The Eagle-Tribune*. "They are upset with Horton because he has made things bad for them. They all said he was a drug dealer and an informant. They said he was a loner."

The lifers clearly hoped that by discrediting Horton, they could preserve the furlough privilege for themselves, not realizing how such a strategy could backfire. To the legislators and the public, evidence that Horton's furloughs were improperly approved, on top of the portrayal of him as a "ravaging savage," would build a case for getting rid of the program altogether, not preserving it for better inmates.

Notes from the meeting found in committee files record interviews with Billy Doucette, then cochairman of the Lifers' Group, Richard Baptiste, and four others serving first-degree life terms. Doucette, according to the notes, "stated Horton had a bad heroin problem, was selling drugs, was anything but a model prisoner, was a 'snitch' who got to minimum and furlough by doing 'favor for favor.'" Doucette, according to the notes, also said that "Horton was stabbed while in prison over a bogus drug deal."

Baptiste, according to the notes, said that "Horton was far from being a model prisoner," that his "co-defendants also had a serious drug problem," and that "Horton was 'bad news.'"

Two of the other four told the visitors that Horton was a drug addict and dealer and one, Alan Lossier, said that "Horton was dishonest dealer." Lossier himself, the notes said, "was a drug dealer while at Walpole—claims to have had 5 guards, 2 social workers and 1 civilian suppling [sic] him with the drugs—action was from $500 to $1000 per week."

The inmates also told the visiting group that Horton had been transferred from Norfolk shortly after a big drug bust in the prison, suggesting that he might have provided information that led to it.

It was apparently true that Horton had done some drug dealing while at Norfolk. Dougie Cecil had spoken of it, and eventually Horton would admit to it himself. Certainly the atmosphere at the big medium-security pen—"it was more like a city. It was like being set free," Doucette would say—allowed for trafficking in contraband. Whether it continued during Horton's final months at NCC isn't clear, though a drug sale might explain the roll of cash he had with him on the morning of his escape.

While these later acknowledgments of drug dealing would in hindsight raise more questions about Horton's suitability as a furlough candidate, they do not by themselves suggest corrupt reasons for his approval. Prison officials made no effort to cover up the drug offenses for which Horton was disciplined. They may have just assumed, perhaps naïvely, that by the time he applied for his first furlough, he was no longer abusing or dealing drugs. Neither of his sponsors reported any drug activity while he was out on furlough; he passed the drug tests administered when he returned.

And there was nothing at all to confirm the lifers' assertions that Horton was an informer and had been approved for furloughs as a reward. At the time, such scuttlebutt simultaneously served the purposes of lifers trying to save the furlough program and legislators trying to kill it. But it depended entirely on the word of convicted criminals with a good reason to lie.

Nonetheless, the meeting with the lifers pumped up Giordano's confidence. In the first of the October hearings, he would taunt Philip Johnston, the secretary of human services: "I don't know if you are aware, in prison he was a druggie, plus he was a dealer—are you aware of that? Are you aware that he was stabbed in prison?"

Johnston replied, "These are allegations about him that I am not going to—"

Giordano broke in: "OK, we are going to have people come in and testify, and they are going to bring it out publicly."

Later that day, Representative Kollios came before the committee in order to argue passionately in favor of the furlough concept. But he, too, had been meeting with lifers. "In Horton's case," he said, "you have got to come to either two conclusions. One, it was either extremely slipshod, bad management of his particular furlough application or a huge mistake; either that or he was a favored inmate. . . .

"Now I tell you, that is a very plausible thing. . . . It certainly makes sense that within the system there are people who are going to play ball with the administration. . . . This isn't my idea totally. Inmates have told me this about Horton. You can't believe how bullshit the lifers are about Horton. Their program may go down the drain because of that rat, and they know it."

Still, neither Giordano nor Kollios ever produced more objective evidence to support the lifers' stories, and corrections officials denied them vigorously.

"Was [sic] you ever aware that he was stabbed in prison?" Giordano asked Dennis Humphrey, associate commissioner of correction.

"No, I wasn't aware that he was stabbed in prison."

Giordano: "Now if an individual was stabbed in prison, how would it get back to the superintendent?"

Humphrey: "Well, it would get back very quickly. If an individual was stabbed in prison, the officer obviously would know that was in the area and would take the person to the infirmary. The superintendent would then start an investigation, an internal investigation in terms of what the circumstances were. He would also have to, because that is a felony, refer it to the district attorney for prosecution."

But no records could be found to document a stabbing, medical treatment for stab wounds, or referral of such a case to the district attorney for prosecution. That meant that in order to believe the lifers, one had to believe in a broad cover-up that extended beyond the prison system. It would also have to include prosecutors who had no love for the furlough program and the independent doctors and other medical staff who routinely signed off on reports of matters as minor as hemorrhoids and skin rashes for inmates' medical files.

When Representative Joseph Herron questioned him, Humphrey grew even more adamant. "I was here for Representative Kollios's testimony, and I disagree personally with his evaluation that the review was slipshod and that there was any lack of professionalism on our part in terms of how we evaluated that case. . . . And I vehemently deny . . . that we had any deal with Willie Horton to get him on the furlough program. What Representative Kollios is basing that information on I have no idea."

Herron: "It is not within the realm of possibility that inmates may be given favored treatment during their stay at a particular institution? Does that happen? Are you telling me that it doesn't happen?"

Humphrey: "No . . . first-degree lifer is going to be put on furlough as part of that favored treatment. . . . Favored treatment I would define as a preferred housing setting, . . . you know, or someone that works outside the gate may get a preferred housing assignment because of that trusting status that they have."

When Representative Cerasoli, chairman of the committee, put the question of favored status to Judy Davis, who had been Horton's counselor, she said, "I never heard of that about William Horton before."

Cerasoli: "Or anyone?"

Davis: "Not to the extent of furloughs and pre-release. Housing assignment, you know, a room on the sunny side of the building."

Commissioner Fair, asked about the lifers' allegations, cautioned the committee not to believe them: "I think perhaps some of the inmates who think they can salvage the program by coming in and saying that Horton was a no-good inmate and everybody knew it—I think that is unfortunate, especially if it is not true. It is their attempt after the fact to salvage the program by discrediting a person who obviously violated the trust. No one needs to discredit William Horton. He has done a fine job of discrediting himself for the rest of his life."

In the end, however, the lifers themselves would back away from their earlier statements about Horton, preventing Giordano from delivering on his initial threat to Johnston. In the public hearing, before reporters, TV cameras, and the sobering awareness that they were suddenly at the center of a potent political debate, Baptiste and Doucette sounded nothing like the people in the interviews recorded in the committee's files.

Asked about the stabbing story, Baptiste responded, "No, I can't say that that is a fact." Doucette added that "it was all hearsay and conjecture."

Asked about Horton's having been given favored status in exchange for information, Baptiste stated that "when this Horton incident came out, there was a lot of angry people that made a lot of statements. . . . I couldn't perceive in my mind that Horton was let out because he snitched, because this snitch line is as long as this room in the penitentiary, and you have to have damn good information that you're going to be let out on such a program as that because you snitched. . . . We have had men gone before the Commutation Board that have saved officers' lives and still are not out. To get a favor like that . . . and I don't think Mr. Horton had the intelligence to even think of a game like that . . . there's nothing in Norfolk that he could have told that got him where he was. I think Mr. Horton—when I looked through everything later—that Mr. Horton was eligible."

This rankled, Baptiste suggested, because he had not yet succeeded in getting approved for furloughs himself. "Deep down inside, very jealous of Mr. Horton then, I think I was a better candidate, and I think a lot of us feel that way."

On the favored-status issue, Doucette would say only that "like I said before, it's all hearsay; it's nothing I could tell this committee factually, and I wouldn't want to mislead you."

As members of the committee went back over all the allegations about Horton based on the interviews at Norfolk a month before, the lifers refused to repeat any of them. Did Horton use drugs? "From what I read and what I was told,"

Baptiste said. "Only by what I was read and what I was told, you know—I never actually saw Horton take drugs."

What about Horton's alleged transfer after a big drug bust? "You know, we all have a habit," Baptiste said. ". . . Like every time someone moves, we say, 'Oh yeah, he must have . . .' You know, but it's like I said—it takes more than that, believe me. I don't think that's why. I don't think that's why he moved."

Giordano sought to cover his growing embarrassment with anger: "OK. You say that you are angry [with Horton]. You don't think I was angry when I asked questions why Mr. Horton was let out, right. You don't think the forty thousand people I represent didn't call me, and they were angry, and they want some answers. But yet the people at the correction department didn't want to speak to me about it. This is how this whole thing came about. You don't think I was angry. How would you feel if you were a state representative and you didn't receive any answers?"

Baptiste's response arose directly from the profound alienation of the incarcerated convict. "You know, Mr. Giordano, you know how we look at it in the penitentiary when we deal with a senator or a legislator? . . . When you [say] . . . you have to have answers, what it looks like to convicts in prison is that anytime an incident happens, that's the only time that you people speak up. So to us, it looks very political, and we take it very political. . . . No matter we're convicted, we have very deep feelings also."

The credibility of that emotion could not be challenged, certainly, but the facts remained murky at best. As they contradicted themselves, the lifers made their stories impossible to believe without independent corroboration, which no one ever produced.

"You've got to remember they're not altar boys," Giordano would say later. "They could have said what they wanted me to hear and just changed their minds."

The inquiries and emotional debate had continued for the better part of a year. Yet to any fair-minded observer, the furlough opponents never managed to shake the corrections officials' assertion that despite its terrible consequences, Horton's release had occurred as the result of familiar policies and procedures that were for the most part followed properly. No one turned up any evidence of corruption or gross incompetence on which to pin the blame. Horton's escape had occurred because Horton had managed to manipulate the system for a change of sponsors. But that was an unusual event that exposed only a weakness in procedure, not a scandalous neglect of duty or an abuse of public trust.

Aspects of the debate in Massachusetts plainly demonstrated the triumph of expressiveness over older beliefs in rational crime control and rehabilitation.

The furlough program's opponents were openly contemptuous of people who cited statistical findings documenting that prison furloughs posed no real threat to public safety. For a time, in fact, "statistics" became a code word for softness on crime and callousness toward its victims. Gravely abused crime victims and all who feared a similar fate painted the furlough program for first-degree lifers as an intolerable menace. First-degree lifers were only a tiny percentage of all the prisoners furloughed or paroled each year, some of whom would commit crimes after getting out. But no one seemed particularly passionate about any but the first-degree lifers.

And who were the first-degree lifers? Some, like Horton, were charged and convicted of first-degree murder because they were part of a group responsible for a violent crime even though they may not have committed any violent acts themselves. Some, like Abdur-Rahim's codefendant, may have done the killing and then agreed to testify against their confederates in exchange for a reduction of the first-degree charge to second-degree murder or manslaughter. Thus could the banning of furloughs for first-degree lifers needlessly deprive the nonviolent of the privilege while leaving it in place for those with undeniably violent records.

Should furloughs then be banned for all prisoners in order to protect the public? The much maligned statistics clearly document that furloughs reduce recidivism for those eventually released. In 1984, for example, 31 percent of offenders released without having gone out on furloughs committed new crimes, compared with only 12 percent of those with furlough experience. The research conducted by LeClair and Guarino-Ghezzi, published in 1991, confirmed that the furloughs of the 1970s and '80s sharply reduced recidivism, producing a net prevention of crime.

But the climate in the Merrimack Valley that year would not tolerate these facts. On one talk show, an intrepid young woman who introduced herself as a furlough sponsor for a prison inmate sought to justify the program before an angry Cliff and Angela Barnes and a hostile studio audience.

If the purpose of the correctional system is to promote public safety, she argued, then it makes no sense to get "rid of the entire program because of one bad person."

Cliff Barnes immediately rose to the challenge: "So you use statistics."

"Excuse me," the sponsor continued evenly. "The recidivism rate for men who have been out on furlough is much lower—"

"So you use rates and ratios?" Cliff interjected. And Angela chimed in: "Thank you. I'm a dispensable person. Thank you very much."

"Absolutely not," the sponsor responded.

"That's what you're saying," Cliff shot back.

"Statistics only work in finances," Angela added.

The sponsor tried again: "It's very unfortunate that I find myself arguing against your pain, which I really feel for. . . . And I don't think anyone is arguing that what happened with William Horton shouldn't have been prevented, and we all wish that it had been prevented."

But Cliff was adamant. "How do you use statistics and ratios when you're dealing with human lives? You're not talking about how much your CDs yield. If he had killed us, would that have been proof enough?"

"If we're just talking about public safety, the men who have been on the furlough program are safer when they are released," the sponsor explained.

But Cliff wasn't impressed. "Every one of these men gave up their rights. If even one person dies because of them, is that right?"

"I'm saying," the sponsor persisted, "that if we didn't have the furlough program, unfortunately, more people would die . . . because the recidivism rate in places that do not have furlough programs is much higher."

As the audience gasped in disbelief, the host announced a break for commercials.

A second current of public feeling caused violent eruptions of skepticism with every mention of rehabilitation and forgiveness. As Omar Abdur-Rahim had explained to an unsympathetic audience, he believed it important to demonstrate "that the people who have been convicted of first-degree murder are not necessarily ravaging savages who are going to remain that way for the rest of their lives." He and others tried to point out that horrible murders could be committed by young people in the heat of adolescent anger or other passions liberated by drugs or alcohol. Such people were in fact capable of growth and change, even in prison, so that by the time they reached mid-life, many might no longer be capable of such behavior.

What should society do with them then? Should it continue to lock them away, based on the theory that retribution for the suffering of their victims ought to supersede all else? Or should it grant some forgiveness, some recognition of positive change?

In the Merrimack Valley, the answers were clear. On another talk show that year, the furlough sponsor Chris Dotson appeared with Vivianne Ruggiero. Speaking of the man who murdered her husband, the police officer, Ruggiero said, "This man just walked up to my husband's cruiser at three-thirty one morning and shot him five times in the face. I mean, you know, and to serve seventeen years—that's not right."

"How do you respond to that?" the host asked Dotson. "You certainly can't blame Vivianne for feeling that way. . . ."

"No, no, . . . I do understand that," Dotson said. "I also do believe, though, that people can change. I do. I simply do, and I think that when it's all said and done, it does come down to that."

"It's too bad they have to murder someone first to change, though," Ruggiero responded, eyes flashing. "Isn't it? Isn't it?"

To which Dotson responded, "One of the things that I've thought about in all of this is that there is that five minutes in somebody's life that forever changes their life and the lives of everyone around them—the victim, the victim's family, and all of their family as well and to be frozen forever in time in that five minutes, to never be able to be recognized for any strides, any gains, anything that you've done productive in your life after that because of that—"

"Well," Ruggiero interrupted, "I'm frozen forever in that five minutes' time, too."

By April of 1988, few in Massachusetts were left to argue the case for either reason or compassion when it came to crime and criminals. The state's legislature, its news media, and its public seemed willing to consider the Horton case closed, even as it began its rise to nationwide notoriety.

Washington

1 9 8 8

*In the first days of December, honchos of both campaigns
gathered in Cambridge for what turned out to be an extraor-
dinary confrontation. Here were Susan Estrich and Lee
Atwater, Paul Brountas and Ed Rogers, Roger Ailes and John
Corrigan. Though all still tasted victory or defeat, they could
speak more freely now, having some distance from the drama
that had consumed them for more than a year.*

*It was Estrich who chose to turn up the heat under what
had been a relatively cordial discussion. "I do want to talk
about this furlough issue and Willie Horton in particular," she
began and then added a statement that startled some of those
present: "I happen to have been a rape victim and taught
about rape and wrote about rape. I saw [the Horton issue]
coming right between the eyes. We tried to deal with it as an
issue about crime. We tried to deal with it as an issue about
furloughs. . . .*

"But my sense . . . is that it was very much an issue about race and racial fear. . . . You can't find a stronger metaphor, intended or not, for racial hatred in this country than a black man raping a white woman. And that's what the Willie Horton story was. I talked to people afterward, men and women. Women said they couldn't help it, but it scared the living daylights out of them. . . . I talked to men who said they couldn't help it either, but when they saw the leaflets later and the ads and the like, they couldn't help but thinking about their wives and feeling scared and crazy."

Atwater, the street fighter, was ready with his answer: "When I first heard about this issue, I didn't know who Willie Horton was. I didn't know what race he was. I was told a story about a guy—I didn't know the name—who had gone to a gas station. There was a seventeen-year-old kid there who was trying to work his way through college. The guy stabbed this kid twenty-four times, cut his sexual organ off, stuck it in his mouth, cut his arms and legs off, and stuck the guy in a trash can. This guy was then thrown into jail and received a furlough under the Massachusetts furlough program, went out on furlough, and raped and brutalized a woman.

"You know, it was sickening to me, but what was sickening was that it defied common sense."

No one in the room made a move to correct the gross factual errors.

Within three years, Lee Atwater would be gone, the victim of a massive brain tumor. But in the spring of 1988, at the age of thirty-seven, his future seemed limitless. Intelligence, arrogance, and a sure sense of who certain American voters were and what they wanted had borne him into the stratosphere of American politics. Managing Vice President George Bush's campaign to succeed the phenomenally popular Ronald Reagan, he saw himself as field commander of a deadly earnest struggle to protect America from liberal Democrats.

"I . . . approach politics as only a slightly politer form of ground battle," he would write later. "We are hired guns. That's why I rely on three books of military and political wisdom: Plato's *Republic,* Machiavelli's *The Prince* and Sun Tzu's *The Art of War.*"

It was Sun-tzu, the fourth century B.C. Chinese military philosopher, who taught Atwater to focus "on finding my opponent's weak point, striking there and striking hard." On April 12, 1988, hardly realizing what was happening to him, Michael Dukakis exposed a weak point and handed Atwater a fateful opportunity.

It was a week before primary day in New York, and a large Democratic field had been reduced to three: Dukakis, Jesse Jackson, and Senator Al Gore. On the morning of the twelfth, the candidates met for a debate before a raucous audience of three thousand at the Felt Forum in Madison Square Garden.

Hoping to salvage his sinking candidacy, Gore was on the attack. He needled Dukakis about welfare and the Middle East. And he told the crowd that as governor of Massachusetts, Dukakis had allowed weekend passes for prison inmates, "including those convicted of first-degree murder and serving life sentences without parole." Some of these prisoners committed new crimes while out on furlough, Gore said. "If you were elected president, would you advocate a similar program for the federal penitentiaries?"

Dukakis thought he knew how to handle Gore: by emphasizing his own experience as a hands-on executive; Gore had served only as a legislator. "Al," Dukakis said, "the difference between you and me is I have to run a criminal justice system—you never have. I'm very proud of my record fighting crime." And he pointed to declining crime rates in Massachusetts.

Then he tried out the policy-wonk response: "Any correctional system in America has got to recognize that the vast majority of people who go into that system are going to come out sooner or later. So we're tough on violent criminals, but we also work very hard to make it possible for those people who come out not to commit crimes over and over again, and I'm very proud of that."

But the audience sensed a dodge. Some hooted and scoffed, and a woman shouted for Dukakis to answer Gore's question.

"We have tough gun control," Dukakis offered, losing his balance. "We're tough on violent criminals."

More jeers, and a gleeful Gore closed in for the kill. "Can we get an answer to the first question?" he insisted. "Would you advocate it or not?"

"We have changed our program," Dukakis finally admitted. "We will not furlough lifers any more."

It was an awkward stumble, but it gave no cause for worry. By that time, Dukakis wasn't really in trouble in New York, and the debate didn't count for much. On April 19, he won a decisive victory. Gore's White House aspirations would have to wait another four years.

Still, the furlough question had provoked one of the discussion's sharper exchanges; news reporters would feature it in their accounts of the ninety-minute event. More important, the incident occurred at a time when Atwater was making basic strategy decisions.

After the Illinois primary, on March 15, the Bush campaign assumed that the vice president had secured the nomination. Atwater and his lieutenants could stop worrying about Senator Robert Dole, the chief Republican threat, and start worrying about Democrats. After the March 26 Michigan caucuses, won by Jesse Jackson in a surprising landslide, and the April 5 Wisconsin primary, when Dukakis trounced Jackson 48 percent to 28 percent, the Bush people assumed the Massachusetts governor would be their opponent.

The polls that spring gave the Republicans no reason to feel comfortable about that prospect. Published surveys had Dukakis leading Bush by sixteen percentage points, while the Bush campaign's private polling suggested the gap might be as much as ten points wider. And although as many voters said they liked Bush as disliked him, those who liked Dukakis outnumbered those who didn't by a margin of five to one. Some in the Bush camp downplayed the numbers as reflecting no more than fickle turns of voter sentiment at the early stages of a campaign.

But Atwater saw plenty of reason for worry. The Republicans had been in power for two terms. He believed that voters who saw no big difference between two candidates were likely to vote for a change just for the sake of change. Furthermore, the swing votes in the states that mattered were the Reagan Democrats, people who identified with the Democratic party but could be lured from it by a populist conservative Republican. If they saw no big difference between

Bush and Dukakis, they would vote for the Democrat because they were Democrats.

"It was obvious that the Dukakis campaign was going to try not to allow issues to drive the campaign, to try to make competence or some other obscure issue drive the campaign," Atwater would say afterward. "If they were able to do that, they would have won." The Dukakis people understood this well enough. Their job, they figured, was to sustain the governor's reassuring image of managerial talent, the technocratic prowess that had brought off the "Massachusetts miracle" of economic growth.

The vice president's most important task, his main hope for victory, would be to puncture that image, to redefine the "real" Dukakis as an incompetent, softheaded liberal. In such a process, the Bush campaign enjoyed a powerful advantage: The vice president was a familiar figure nationwide, but the Massachusetts governor was little known outside the Northeast. The campaign would turn on a battle for the definition of Dukakis, not Bush.

"The good news" Atwater would tell his people, "is that we do not think the other side will plug into this." They considered the liberals from Massachusetts hopelessly elitist and out of touch with the feelings of ordinary Americans, including those crucial Reagan Democrats. "It would take them a long time to figure out what was going on," Atwater predicted.

If he could find a few issues on which to set up Dukakis as a liberal weirdo, out of the mainstream, Atwater sensed that he could keep the governor off balance. "Our personality profile of Dukakis," recalls Ed Rogers, who served as Atwater's deputy through 1987 and 1988, made clear that "he will defend himself. So if you go on the attack on anything having to do with his record in Massachusetts, you will get him on the defensive."

"We had the feeling that the candidate—Dukakis—would dig in and defend from a legal standpoint issues that the American people just had an instinctive feeling about, i.e., the pledge," Roger Ailes, who contracted to handle the Bush media effort, would say. He was referring to Dukakis's veto of a law that required teachers to lead students in the Pledge of Allegiance. The governor, he said, was "a guy who said, 'I'm right, you're wrong, and here are the reasons,' with no regard to how or why people responded emotionally to an issue. In other words, he may be right technically, but the American people react instinctively to issues like the flag, not technically."

To pursue his strategy, Atwater set up an "opposition research" team that may have been a first for presidential campaigns. He had one of his brightest operatives, James Pinkerton, assemble an office of "about thirty-five excellent nerds" to comb through Dukakis's record for foolish statements, stumbles, screwups—anything that might be used to define his negative image.

"We need five or six issues, and we need them by the middle of May," he told Pinkerton. He emphasized that the issues had to be simple to state, simple to understand. Enforcing that point, "I gave him a three-by-five card, and I said, 'You come back with this three-by-five card, but you can use both sides, and bring me the issues that we need in this campaign.'" So those were the marching orders for the nerds: Find defining facts or anecdotes that could be reduced to a few words or a single idea, a line on a three-by-five-inch card.

On April 12, Pinkerton tuned in the New York debate, and as he watched the exchange with Gore over Horton and furloughs, he got excited. He immediately called up Andrew Card, a New England organizer for Bush who had served in the Massachusetts legislature and had hoped to run against Dukakis for governor in 1982. Card was the campaign's main source of expertise on Dukakis's background and personality.

With competitive juices flowing, Pinkerton was known to speak in machine-gun bursts. "Do you know anything about this Willie Horton case?" he shouted in a staccato voice. "What's this Willie Horton thing all about?" Card gave Pinkerton a quick summary of the case as he recalled it—a guy who murdered a kid and threw him into a Dumpster and then got furloughed from a Massachusetts prison and raped a woman. The Horton case, he opined, could well be used to demonstrate Dukakis's philosophical approach to the crime issue. For more information, he said, Pinkerton should read *The Lawrence Eagle-Tribune*.

After he had done so, "I thought to myself, 'This is incredible,'" Pinkerton would say later. "It totally fell into our lap." What most impressed him as he read through *The Eagle-Tribune* coverage was that Dukakis had so stubbornly refused to change the furlough program in the face of a mounting political firestorm. He hurried to Atwater with the news. "The more people who know who Willie Horton is," he told his boss, "the better off we'll be."

However persuasive the case for a negative campaign, Atwater and his lieutenants weren't sure they could talk the vice president, who preferred serving in office to campaigning for it, into going along. They planned to pitch the idea at a meeting set for Memorial Day weekend at Kennebunkport. The Thursday before, they set up focus groups at a shopping mall in Paramus, New Jersey. The purpose was to test out possible campaign themes on a group of suburban Reagan Democrats. As the sessions began, all said they favored Dukakis.

Atwater, Ailes, and others huddled behind a one-way mirror as researchers explained how Dukakis had vetoed a law requiring teachers to lead students in the Pledge of Allegiance, how Boston Harbor had become polluted—and how Massachusetts prisons furloughed convicted murderers serving life without parole. By the end of the evening, half the voters no longer supported Dukakis. "I realized then and there that we had the wherewithal to win," Atwater recalled later. "The sky was the limit on Dukakis's negatives."

The Paramus group also impressed him with another point that may well have been a decisive factor in the 1988 election. The voters did not seem much concerned with big basic concerns like the economy or national defense. Instead, Atwater recalled, "the issues that were popping up were issues like drugs, moral-fabric-type issues." All the more reason, then, not to let Dukakis define the campaign as a test of relative administrative competence.

Atwater brought tapes of the focus group to Kennebunkport. But as it turned out, the vice president didn't require a hard sell. In a Sunday morning meeting on the porch of Bush's summer home, he agreed that Dukakis's attitudes on prison furloughs and the Pledge of Allegiance seemed "out of the mainstream," and in any case, given the dismal poll results, he would do what he had to do to win. "Bush stared into the abyss," Rogers recalls, and decided "yes, I will engage, and I will do it sooner rather than later."

In speeches that June, Bush gave the furlough issue full throat. Dukakis, he told the Illinois Republican State Convention, had let "murderers out on vacation to terrorize innocent people. . . . Democrats can't find it in their hearts to get tough on criminals. . . . What did the Democratic governor of Massachusetts think he was doing when he let convicted first-degree murderers out on weekend passes, even after one of them criminally, brutally raped a woman and stabbed her fiancé? Why didn't he admit his mistake? Eight months later, he was still defending his program, and only when the Massachusetts legislature voted by an overwhelming majority to abolish this program did he finally give in. I think Governor Dukakis owes the American people an explanation of why he supports this outrageous program."

In a Kentucky speech to the National Sheriffs' Association, Bush said that Horton "was sentenced by a judge sentenced to life in prison. Before eligibility for parole, Horton applied for a furlough. He was given the furlough. He was released. And he fled—only to terrorize a family and repeatedly rape a woman. So I'm opposed to these unsupervised weekend furloughs for first-degree murderers who are not eligible for parole. Put me down as against that. When a judge says life without parole, it should mean just that."

The prison-furlough question fit nicely with Dukakis's rejection of the death penalty that Bush so heartily endorsed. "Michael Dukakis on crime is standard old-style sixties liberalism," Bush would shout, adding that Dukakis "has steadfastly opposed the death penalty" and (exaggerating the truth)

that "he supported the only state program in the whole country—the only one!—that gives unsupervised weekend furloughs to first-degree murderers!"

These early displays of the Horton issue demonstrated its
powerful bite, for the anxieties of the Merrimack Valley
turned out to be shared by millions of Americans across the
land. The need for ways to release that tension, the developing shift to expressive justice, was not something much on
politicians' minds at the time. But the Republicans welcomed
the results: Far more than Boston Harbor or the Pledge of
Allegiance, the Horton issue could define Dukakis in a way
likely to repel millions of voters. The heart of the case as it
had played out in Massachusetts involved an issue—furloughs
for vicious murderers!—that appeared to pit voters' common
sense against the convoluted explanations of ideologues or
bureaucrats. "You can never escape the common sense of
this," Atwater would say. "This is salient." But what he kept
referring to as common sense also reflected darker, wilder
feelings: fear for physical safety and a sense of betrayal by
government.

Thus did William Horton become an effective tool for
defining the governor the way the Republicans wanted him
defined. "It said, all in one breath, he's against capital punishment, he's more for criminal rights than victims' rights, he's
cold and insensitive to people," Card observes. It also said
"something that all politicians strive never to have said about
them: He doesn't care."

Discussing the issue later on, the Bush managers would
vehemently deny that race played any part in their thinking as
they developed the Horton issue that spring and summer.

Atwater insisted that when he first heard of the case and decided to make use of it in the campaign, he was unaware of Horton's race; it was the idea of furloughing murderers that caught his attention.

"Finally, obviously, when it came to our attention that Willie Horton was black," Atwater would say at Harvard, "we made a conscious decision—Roger [Ailes] was there at the meeting when I took the lead—not to use him in any of our paid advertising, on television or in brochures. We figured at the time that we would have to try to police other people." This was a reference to the supposedly independent political action groups and committees that were springing up to purchase pro-Bush advertising on their own.

In any event, given the previous year's controversy in Massachusetts, how could one discuss the furlough program *without* focusing on William Horton? No public records document any discussion of how the use of his case could win racist votes. But of course the Republicans didn't have to acknowledge the case's racial aspect in order for it to have an effect in the context of anxiety about crime. By 1988, the assumption that black men were dangerous had soaked deeply into America's urban consciousness, powerfully reinforced by the steady flow of news coverage depicting black men under arrest, in court, in prison. The image of Horton's face caused heads to nod in grim affirmation all over America. Those who sought to learn more discovered the ravaging savage who had dominated the news in the Merrimack Valley—many, no doubt, reading no further than the early accounts that reported as fact the false rumors about the sexual mutilation of Joey Fournier.

Word that the Bush campaign had discovered the Horton case stirred more than the obvious concern in Michael Dukakis's campaign manager, Susan Estrich. It was not just that she could understand how the issue would play from a female point of view. As it happened, she was also an innocent, middle-class victim of random violence, a white woman who had been raped by a black man. The crime had occurred some fourteen years before; since then, she had given the subject of crime and race a great deal of thought as she wrote about it and discussed it in her law school classes.

She recalled how as she sat in a police car after the assault, "the first question was, 'Was he a crow?' As in Jim Crow. As in, was he black? When I answered yes, it became a lot easier to deal with the police. Now they believed me. 'Nigger' was a term I heard a lot of that night."

The event affected her own feelings as well. "For months, I wanted to cross the street or run inside or lock my door every time a strange black man looked at me 'funny'—or at all," she would write. "I hated myself for it, and I managed to conquer my fear, but that's not the point. The point is how easy it is to confuse race and crime."

She also grasped what the Republicans were trying to do. Like Atwater, she also knew that "by June or July of 1988, a majority of the people thought that the country was on the right track" in terms of the big issues like the economy and foreign affairs. "When that happens, questions of values become even more important." And plenty of Americans had doubts about Michael Dukakis's values. Republicans could point to Horton as evidence that Dukakis "doesn't understand people like you."

She recognized that the issue was far more emotional than rational. An effective response required an appeal to the heart before the head. To neutralize the Horton issue in a mood favoring expressive justice, Dukakis would have to persuade the country on an emotional level that he understood the fear of crime, the pain of victims, the general outrage.

He was not without his own stories to tell. His father, a doctor, had once been assaulted and tied up in his office by an intruder seeking drugs. And his brother had died in an automobile crash caused by a drunk driver. Of course he understood the pain and tragedy crime could inflict on innocent people, he could say. It had touched his own family just as it had so many others.

In June, even before the convention, Estrich and her lieutenants proposed that Dukakis feature a forthright anticrime message on a campaign trip to North Carolina and Florida. They had "the first inklings" of a Republican ad using Horton to portray the Massachusetts governor as soft on crime. "We decided we should serve notice that we were going to take on the crime issue and do it in the South." But the candidate vetoed the idea.

In planning for the convention that summer, Estrich recalls trying again. "We wanted to do a whole shtick about crime. . . . It was clear to everybody that Willie Horton was a symbol of the crime issue and if we didn't do something, we would get killed on the crime issue. . . . It was important to establish Dukakis as somebody who was on the side of people who were raped and killed by criminals."

She suggested that the candidate include the emotional anticrime material in his speech accepting the nomination, the most widely watched hour of the whole affair. But to her considerable frustration, Dukakis again nixed the idea. Estrich had her writers insert the anticrime message in the speech Olympia Dukakis delivered to introduce her cousin. But a lot fewer people would watch that.

What was Dukakis's problem? How could a man with the political skills to win his party's nomination for president suffer from such a blind spot? To an extent, he had been neutralized by the fight over furloughs in Massachusetts. Acknowledging the need for some emotion on the victim side of the crime issue would be an admission that it had been a terrible mistake not to meet with the Barneses and extend an apology. It would vindicate *The Lawrence Eagle-Tribune* and all those people up in the Merrimack Valley who had given him such a hard time for so many months. These were things Michael Dukakis would never do.

Beyond that, some said, he associated sympathy for victims with the cynical law-and-order politics that substitutes tough-sounding rhetoric for serious crime control. The emotion behind the crime issue was simply no basis for sound, practical policy on an issue that remained complicated even as it stirred elemental feelings. But America in 1988 did not have much patience for such an idea, principled as it might be. The acknowledgment of crime victims' suffering had to come first. "If you don't say those things, almost nothing else you say matters," Estrich laments.

In the middle of June, the July issue of *Reader's Digest* became available, granting the Horton case more legitimacy as a campaign issue. The magazine contained a long article by Robert James Bidinotto on Horton's escape, his attack on Barnes and Miller, and the ensuing uproar in Massachusetts.

This turned out to be so happy a coincidence for Republicans—polls showed that Dukakis had lost half his lead by the end of June—that Democrats and news reporters suspected high-level coordination. Bidinotto told a writer for the *National Journal* that he had become aware of the CAUS effort in the fall of 1987 and proposed the article to the *Digest* in December, well before it was clear that Dukakis would be the Democratic nominee. He received approval for the assignment in January.

Reader's Digest's executive editor, Kenneth Tomlinson, a former director of the Voice of America, told the *National Journal* that he had rushed the Bidinotto piece into print in the July issue to avoid publishing it after the campaign heated up later that year.

But the *National Journal* also reported that Andrew Card was acquainted with Bidinotto's wife, who had run for the Massachusetts legislature, and quoted Card as saying he had spoken with Bidinotto "between the time that he wrote [the furlough article] and the time that it was published." Though Card denied that Bidinotto had written the piece at the request of Bush organizers, he described the author as "a fellow who has a political instinct."

Whatever the level of its involvement, the Bush campaign could not have been happier with the article. In retrospect, it also read like a basic text for the politics of expressive criminal justice. Titled "Getting Away With Murder," it described the killing of Joey Fournier, stating flatly that "prosecutors were convinced . . . that the actual killer was Horton." And it detailed Horton's crimes against Barnes and Miller, exaggerated somewhat for lurid effect. "For the next seven hours, a laughing Horton punched, pistol-whipped and kicked [Cliff Barnes]. Horton also cut him 22 times across his midsection.

"Later that night, Angela returned. Bound and gagged, Cliff listened in helpless horror to Angie's screams as Horton savagely attacked her."

Bidinotto depicted *The Eagle-Tribune*'s campaign, the legislative inquiries, and the CAUS ballot-initiative drive as heroic struggles against an inexplicably unfeeling Dukakis administration. "After the hearings, CAUS members worked feverishly to collect and deliver signed petitions to city halls across the state. Late at night on December 1, 1987, nine bone-weary volunteers crowded into Joan Bamford's living room to tally the results. They needed 50,525 signatures. They had 52,407. There were screams, tears and hugs all around."

A theme that ran through the article echoed the point that frustrated Estrich even as it intrigued Pinkerton and Atwater: Dukakis's inability to show much more than perfunctory respect for the feelings of crime victims and their families. As middle-class fear and anger over crime burst into the political arena, Dukakis remained the cool technician, the iceman.

Looking back on the *Reader's Digest* article, Pinkerton marveled at how it "created a firestorm at the grass roots." Atwater, vacationing on the Fourth of July at Luray, Virginia, found himself in the middle of a motorcyclists' gathering. Always on the alert for insight into the electorate, he overheard two biker couples discussing the *Reader's Digest* piece in a Chinese-American restaurant.

He had, he recalled later, been "trying to figure out whether the pledge would work better or the furloughs." In the booth behind him, "this one woman starts talking to the other woman. . . . And one of them said, 'I just read this thing in the *Reader's Digest* that you would not believe.' And the other woman said, 'What?' And she said, 'This criminal furlough thing that Michael Dukakis did is the most amazing thing I've ever seen.'"

Atwater noted that one of the couples was white, the other black. It also impressed him that the women were the ones who seemed most animated about the issue. "It interested me because, obviously, we had a gender problem at the time." So without identifying himself, Atwater joined the conversation—as did other customers, the cook, and two waitresses.

"Before it was all over, everybody in the restaurant was over there talking about the thing," Atwater remembered. "The waitresses closed the restaurant, and we sat around talking about his whole furlough thing all night. I said to myself this issue has a real life, this issue counts to Americans."

Atwater called Robert Teeter, the Republican pollster, who told him that mention of the *Reader's Digest* article in an Alabama focus group had demolished support for Dukakis. "A woman in the focus group started talking about the *Reader's Digest*," Teeter told him. "She almost had it memorized verbatim. And the whole focus group shifted." For whatever reason, it was clear that they were onto something big. From then on, Atwater would think of Horton and prison furloughs as the Bush campaign's "silver bullet." At a meeting of state party leaders, he boasted that the campaign would lead voters to think Horton had become Dukakis's running mate.

The *Reader's Digest* article spread the Horton story further by bringing it to the attention of other news media. Cliff

Barnes and Donna Cuomo began getting calls from the talk shows, and Cliff responded with enthusiasm.

He and Angela had different reactions to the attention that came their way as Horton's victims. Though she saw an obligation to speak out, she never felt good about it. She hated having to relive the whole business again for a public that however sympathetic, still seemed prurient. She longed for privacy and peace, an end to pain, an end to embarrassment, a way to make the whole thing go away.

"Angie didn't heal when we talked about it," Cliff explained. He thought it was a gender thing. "When a woman is hurt, she withdraws," he said. "When a man feels attacked, his first instinct is to counterattack."

Cliff still was haunted by the helpless impotence he had felt while tied up in the basement as Horton assaulted Angela. That April, Susan Forrest had returned for another interview to run on the anniversary of the crime and learned that Cliff had developed a new temper, a new pugnacity. Before Horton's attack, she reported, he had never fought with another adult. But in the past year, he had gotten into four fistfights. Most recently, Forrest wrote, "Barnes punched and threw a drunken stranger to the ground after the man made a verbal pass at Mrs. Barnes."

"I'm ashamed about the fights," Cliff said, "but I'm still afraid I'm going to really hurt someone someday."

"No matter what I tell him," Angela said, "Cliff will always feel responsible for what happened. . . . It has nothing to do with his ego or his love for me. He just hated not being able to help me."

Now the political storm Horton's escape and their case had set off gave Cliff another way to fight back, a way to vent more of the anger and pain—good therapy. He had reached out to Susan Forrest, guaranteeing that their story would play a big part in the Massachusetts controversy. And when CAUS invited him and Angela to testify against furloughs, he was glad to go.

The following spring, as the presidential primaries dominated the news, he had taken it upon himself to call all the candidates, who at that point still included not only George Bush but six of Michael Dukakis's Democratic-primary opponents. He told his story over and over, explaining that he thought the Massachusetts governor should be called to account for the Horton case. At that point, the Bush people showed little interest. Of the Democrats, only Al Gore picked up on the idea, introducing it at the April 12 primary debate in New York.

But now the journalists, the talk shows, and the Republicans finally were calling, and Cliff was glad to oblige. People would tell him that the Republicans were using him, but given the outlet the campaign provided for his feelings, he didn't feel exploited at all. The Republicans weren't using me, he would say; I was using them. And so he was.

On June 28, for example, he, Donna Cuomo, and Bidinotto appeared with Geraldo Rivera. It would be the first of several television appearances and press-conference tours they would make for the Republicans that summer and fall.

On Geraldo's show, Cliff and Donna gave dramatic accounts of Horton's crimes. "A point I wanted to make was that he was never satisfied that night," Cliff said about the beatings, robbery, and rapes. "I think there was a crescendo that evening that was never met because we managed to escape. I think he would have killed us."

"It was very upsetting that this man was let out to hurt somebody else," Donna said. "The evidence was there in the beginning to keep him in jail. Basically what we found out is Massachusetts had routinely commuted the sentences of many first-degree murderers, and the furlough program was one tool that they used as a reason to say, 'Well, now this person is able to go back and live a normal life into society.' "

Alan Dershowitz, the liberal law professor, also appeared on the show. He attacked Bidinotto's *Reader's Digest* article as "political" and "total nonsense." He asserted that Massachusetts is "one of the safest states in the United States" and observed that "more murders are committed by people who are released at the end of their sentence than who are placed on furlough."

But the television format remained far more hospitable to expressive justice than to explanations of the issue's complexities. Toward the end of the program, an audience member asserted that "prison isn't a picnic. Prison is punishment. As far as I'm concerned, they can herd them all up, they can stick them in like cattle, and they can stay there for the rest of their lives."

Roger Ailes went to work on the furlough issue and produced a commercial for the Bush campaign that won praise from admen and political consultants on all sides for its concept and effectiveness. It showed a line of prison inmates marching through a revolving gate while the voice-over talked about the temporary release of "first-degree murderers not eligible for parole. While out, many committed other crimes, like kidnapping and rape." The evocation of incompetent revolving-door justice made a powerful point.

"Now Michael Dukakis says he wants to do for America what he has done for Massachusetts," the ad said at the end. "America can't afford that risk."

But his would not be the only furlough ad that year. For the *Reader's Digest* article had gained the attention of the independent consultants and political action groups that were running parallel campaigns. These groups sought to remain legally and financially independent of the official Bush operation even as they advanced projects clearly intended to help it. Their activities were supposed to be paid for with "soft" money—contributions to the Republican party rather than to the campaign.

The nature and extent of their independence would become a matter of some contention (and eventually a cause for litigation) since a demonstrable link between the supposed independents and the official campaign would require that the independents' expenditures count as direct spending on the Bush campaign. That could push the campaign's total spending over the legal limit for presidential candidates. Formal separation of the independent groups also made it possible for the campaign to disavow commercials that risked creating a backlash.

One of the independents was the Los Angeles–based Dolphin Group, a Republican political-consulting firm led by Fred Karger. Dolphin had a track record on politics and crime. In 1986, it had set up a group called Crime Victims for Court Reform to campaign for the ouster of Rose Bird, liberal chief justice of the California Supreme Court.

Sensing the potential of the Horton issue, Karger called up Donna Cuomo and Cliff Barnes and persuaded them to make campaign commercials for a group he created called the

Committee for the Presidency. Simply conceived, the two thirty-second ads focused closely on the victims' faces as they talked earnestly about Horton's crimes and Dukakis's complicity.

Donna said: "Governor Dukakis's liberal furlough experiments failed. We are all victims. First Dukakis let killers out of prison. He also vetoed the death penalty. Willie Horton stabbed my teenaged brother nineteen times. Joey died. Horton was sentenced to life without parole, but Dukakis gave him a furlough. He never returned. Horton went on to rape and torture others. I worry that people here don't know enough about Dukakis's record."

Cliff said: "Mike Dukakis and Willie Horton changed our lives forever. He was serving a life term without the possibility of a parole when Governor Dukakis gave him a few days off. Horton broke into our home. For twelve hours, I was beaten, slashed, and terrorized. My wife, Angie, was brutally raped. When his liberal experiment failed, Dukakis simply looked away. He also vetoed the death-penalty bill. Regardless of the election, we worry that people don't know enough about Mike Dukakis."

The "regardless of the election" was apparently inserted at Cliff's request. Dolphin had wanted him to endorse Bush, he says, but he objected. Though they favored Bush, both he and Angela considered themselves independents. To this day, Cliff insists his main objective in 1988 was to publicize his concerns about criminal justice in general and furloughs in particular, not to advance the fortunes of George Bush or the Republicans.

"The criminal justice issue is pretty much an issue of common sense," he says, echoing Atwater. "If they'd used common sense, [Horton would] never have done anything to us. I don't care if you're a Democrat or Republican. It's common sense."

The ad that aroused the most controversy—and made Horton the symbol of negative campaigning for years to come—was created by another independent group, called the National Security Political Action Committee. It was founded in 1986 by a woman named Elizabeth Fediay, who had been working for the right-wing Institute of American Relations, headed by her father.

With retired Admiral Thomas Moorer, a former chairman of the Joint Chiefs of Staff, as a cofounder, NSPAC would become one of the nation's largest spenders of political soft money. In two years, the group, sometimes calling itself Americans for Bush, raised about $9 million, mostly in small contributions solicited by direct mail and telephone banks. Federal campaign-spending records show that NSPAC spent more than $7 million to promote the Bush candidacy.

During the 1988 campaign, Bush officials publicly denounced NSPAC and filed a complaint with the Federal Election Commission, accusing the group of misrepresenting itself as part of the Bush campaign in order to line its own pockets. News reports at the time suggested a cozy relationship between NSPAC and a group of companies owned in part by Ronald Kanfer, an old friend of Fediay's. NSPAC paid Kanfer's direct-mail companies $3.4 million of the $7 million spent in behalf of Bush. Jan Baran, the Bush campaign's general counsel, called NSPAC "bloodsuckers."

After the election, however, Democrats would complain to the FEC that NSPAC had in fact colluded with the Bush campaign in violation of the public-financing law. When the agency refused to pursue the charge despite an initial investigation that suggested substantial contact between NSPAC and the campaign, the Democrats filed a lawsuit against the FEC, seeking to force further inquiry.

The Democrats' annoyance with NSPAC arose primarily as a result of the thirty-second commercial the group commissioned in August of 1988 and aired on cable-TV channels for four weeks in September and early October. It was considered the most inflammatory of all the Horton ads because it dared to display the now famous mug shot.

To produce the ad, NSPAC turned to Larry McCarthy, a former senior vice president of Roger Ailes's advertising firm, Ailes Communications. Elizabeth Fediay asked McCarthy to work up some ideas for ads attacking Dukakis. On August 24, he spoke with her as well as three others she had hired: Floyd Brown, a political organizer; Craig Shirley, a public relations man; and Tony Fabrizio, who purchased television time for political commercials. The group discussed ads that would contrast Bush and Dukakis on different issues: defense, the American flag, and crime—specifically, the Horton case, which McCarthy, like so many others, had read about in *Reader's Digest*.

McCarthy went off to draft possible scripts. "It became clear to me as I was writing that furloughs was [*sic*] going to stick," he recalled later. "It was based on nothing other than my own gut instinct. I thought the Pledge of Allegiance was going to fade away. . . . But I thought people—and this is based on my . . . experience in political campaigns— . . . take crime real seriously. . . . So I said I think we should do an ad on the furlough issue. And they agreed with me."

Fediay recalled that "there was [sic] like three scripts, and by far the one that was the most compelling was the crime issue. . . . In my mind, it was the one with the most substance."

Their decision came as polls showed that the Horton strategy was working. Gallup surveys found that Dukakis's negative rating had risen to 42 percent by September, nearly triple the July figure of 15 percent. A poll for the Times Mirror Company found that 61 percent of respondents said the furlough issue had soured them on Dukakis. Only 47 percent opposed him because he vetoed the bill requiring schoolteachers to lead the Pledge of Allegiance; only 42 percent disliked him because they found him "too liberal."

After the August discussions, McCarthy went to work on a Horton ad with the help of a TV producer and director named Jesse Raiford, who had also worked for Ailes. In their lawsuit, the Democrats would make much of so cozy a history, though all three men vigorously denied any collusion on the Horton ad or on any other commercials.

McCarthy and Raiford put the Horton ad together over the space of a week, relying on information from *Reader's Digest* and *The Lawrence Eagle-Tribune*. By the Tuesday after Labor Day, the commercial was finished. NSPAC paid McCarthy about $6,000 for his few days of work.

The commercial began as the voice-over announced, "Bush and Dukakis on crime." Pictures of the two candidates appeared on-screen and then alternated as the announcer stated that "Bush supports the death penalty for first-degree murderers. Dukakis not only opposes the death penalty, he allowed first-degree murderers to have weekend passes from prison." Then the Horton mug shot appeared, and the announcer said, "One was Willie Horton, who murdered a boy in a robbery, stabbing him nineteen times. Despite a life sentence, Horton received ten weekend passes from prison." The picture on the screen shifted to a fuzzy news photo of Horton being escorted by police. "Horton fled, kidnapping a young couple, stabbing the man, and repeatedly raping his girlfriend." The picture of Dukakis reappeared as the announcer concluded, "Weekend prison passes. Dukakis on crime."

The ad would lead to the broad reprinting and rebroadcasting of the mug shot; now Horton's image was no longer just an idea, an ethereal hologram, but a real photo, in ink on paper, on tape on the tube. As such, it gained even greater power to focus public emotion.

McCarthy and Raiford had obtained the photo from an archive, where it had wound up after newspapers acquired it from the police in Maryland. The photo that would become etched in the national consciousness was the visual equivalent of rumors about the sexual mutilation of Joey Fournier. The unshaven, unkempt face with slack jaw and half-closed eyes looked subhuman, dirty, and dangerous. And it barely resembled William Horton, who normally paid serious attention to his appearance.

Jeffrey Elliot, the political science professor who had befriended Horton and visited him in prison from time to time, took a picture of him looking well-groomed, as he usually did, and showed it to his classes at North Carolina Central University, asking the students whether they knew who it was. Invariably, they didn't. Female students sometimes were even moved to inquire, Such a nice-looking man—is he married?

Does he have a steady girlfriend? When Elliot told them it was the infamous Willie Horton, they were shocked.

Horton told Elliot that police in Prince George's County snapped the disheveled image sometime after his arrest, as he recovered from wounds inflicted during the Indian Head Highway chase and shooting. When he tried to get up from his hospital bed one day, he said, he frightened a nurse, who thought he was trying to escape. As a result, he was put into a more secure unit, where for several weeks he had no chance to shave. "It was then they took the picture," he said. "That's why I looked like a zombie. . . . They chose the perfect picture for the ads. I looked incredibly wicked."

McCarthy told the *New Republic* how he agonized over his decision to use the photo:

> This guy looked like an animal. . . . And frankly, because he was black, I thought longer and harder about putting him in there. . . . If he looked like Ted Bundy, [the serial murderer executed in Florida], I probably wouldn't have used his picture, because he looks perfectly normal—like a YR [Young Republican]. But then I said, as an advertising guy, I should have been shot if I didn't use Horton's picture because the picture says it all. It says this is a bad guy and Dukakis let him out. If it was a picture of a guy who looked like a crazy—an animal—but was white or Hispanic or Oriental, you'd use it. So I decided to put a criminal's picture on the screen.

With the ad in hand, he then gave some thought to the timing of its release. He insists that he did not consult Ailes to coordinate the event. "I know Roger very well," he said. "I just tried to run it as if I were Roger. I tried to spare him from doing some of these things. I figured they'll go negative by mid-September. So I said, I'm going to lead them by about a week or two."

Succeeding with the ad containing the awful picture of Horton might not have been so easy, however, because the cable networks from which he would buy time retained the power to refuse an independent group's ad that looked like too crude a racial appeal. No slouch at manipulating television, McCarthy devised a plan based on two versions of the commercial. Both followed the same script, but only the second included the photos of Horton. The first made greater use of the two candidates' photos instead.

McCarthy knew that network officials who reviewed ads carefully scrutinized them when they first came in. But they paid only perfunctory attention if an advertiser sent in a revised version of a tape to be substituted for the first one. So McCarthy submitted the first Horton ad, waited a few days, and then sent the second, asking that it be aired in place of the first. The cable networks accepted the first ad and never questioned the substitution.

NSPAC used a second ploy to achieve a vast increase in exposure of the ad. Though the group lacked funds to purchase time for it on major networks, it sent a copy to *The McLaughlin Group* talk show, where it became the basis for a panel discussion. Thus it became the focus of controversy and fair material for network news reports on the campaign. As the networks reported on the debate, they aired snippets of the commercial, including Horton's face, over and over again to their immense national audiences.

As controversy over the ad built, NSPAC would insist that it had the tacit blessing of the Bush campaign. Just before the election, Fediay told *The New York Times* that "officially, the campaign has to disavow themselves from me. Unofficially, I hear that they're thrilled about what we're doing." She also produced an October 22 letter signed by Bush's running mate, Senator Dan Quayle, praising NSPAC as "a source of real encouragement as well as a great boon to our efforts."

"The campaign was schizophrenic over it," Ed Rogers says of the ad. Some felt that "anybody that's running an ad that's bad for him and good for us is OK." But Atwater, he says, believed that "we don't need this. This takes the issue to a level that it doesn't need to be taken to. . . . This could be trouble."

Hoping to fend off trouble, the Bush campaign produced a copy of a letter from James Baker, the campaign chairman, restating the campaign's complaint that NSPAC continued to raise money under Bush's name without permission. But NSPAC pointed out that Baker had waited until September 27 to send the letter, only a few days before the Horton ad would finish its scheduled run. "If they were really interested in stopping this, do you think they would have waited that long to send us a letter?" Floyd Brown asked a *Times* reporter.

In its November 14 issue, *Time* magazine reported that "Bush press secretary Mark Goodin pasted a mug shot of Horton on the wall above his desk" and that some state Republican organizations had distributed fliers bearing the photo. It also quoted Ailes during the campaign: "The only question is whether we depict Willie Horton with a knife in his hand or without it."

In depositions to the Federal Election Commission two years later, Fediay said she could not recall making the quote to *The New York Times*, and Roger Ailes vehemently denounced the now notorious ad.

"My first reaction to it was this is awful, we have to get it off the air," Ailes testified. He worried about backlash: "It was very clear to me as a media strategist that we needed to be on offense in September and October, and it was my feeling that the Willie Horton ad would generate a position where we were on defense. And you don't win on defense."

As for the "knife in his hand" quote, "It was meant as a joke. . . . It got a big laugh at the time, but when you read it in the press it isn't quite as funny."

In October, the Republicans sniffed blood. The NSPAC ad finished its limited run, but Horton's image continued to be broadcast and published as the furlough issue enlivened the campaign. Ailes's revolving-gate ad continued to appear, as did the Dolphin Group's Donna Cuomo and Cliff Barnes testimonials.

In campaign appearances around the country, Bush emphasized the issue with rising scorn. He evoked cheers and laughs in Texas when he said that if Clint Eastwood greeted criminals with "Go ahead, make my day," Dukakis said, "Go ahead, have a nice weekend."

Republican groups at the state level delivered lower blows. A flier distributed in Illinois read, "All the murderers and rapists and drug pushers and child molesters in Massachusetts vote for Michael Dukakis. We in Illinois can vote against him." A fund-raising letter to Maryland Republicans carried pictures of Horton and Dukakis and read, "Is this your pro-family team for 1988?" As with the NSPAC ad, Bush campaign officials deplored such tactics and denied any responsibility for them. Journalists and other campaign watchers found the denials hard to believe, given James Baker's authoritarian, controlling approach as campaign chairman.

The Committee for the Presidency flew Cliff Barnes and Donna Cuomo to California, Texas, and other states for press-conference tours. In addition to repeating their stories of Horton's crimes, they attacked Dukakis for indifference. "He fought us tooth and nail," Cuomo would say of the CAUS campaign. "He has never agreed to meet with us." Cliff would add that "my wife and I have never heard from the Dukakis administration. There has never been even an apology."

On October 4, Cliff appeared on Oprah Winfrey's show in Chicago, along with some criminal justice experts and a local woman allegedly raped by a man recently released from the county jail because of overcrowding. In a disconcerting coincidence for Cliff, the rape victim, reluctant to reveal her identity, called herself Angela.

Cliff repeated his story about the night of terror on Proxmire Drive and the CAUS campaign against furloughs for first-degree lifers in Massachusetts. "There are no words to describe what it feels like to be, you know, victimized this way, . . ." Oprah responded. "There are no words to describe what it feels like. But I'm—I imagine that the feeling is compounded when you recognize that one of the reasons why it did happen to you is because the system failed you."

For once, however, Cliff found himself upstaged as the Chicago Angela told her story. Not only had she been forcibly raped by a stranger who hit her in the face with a wine bottle after picking her up on an elevated train; the crime occurred in public, as strangers watched. Now she gave a much broader public another look.

"When I got my left leg out of the nylons," she said, "he stood up in front of me and unzipped his pants and took himself out and told me to put it in my mouth. And then there was another threat, you know, that if I didn't, I would get the bottle in the face again."

Oprah: "And so, he forced you to have—forced oral sex upon you as people walked by—"

Angela: "Right."

Oprah: "And saw it?"

Angela: "Right. . . ."

Oprah: "So what were people saying? I mean, people didn't say anything? People didn't say something? . . ."

Angela: "I could hear chattering, but it's not registering what people are saying right then because I'm scared if this man's going to hit again in the—you know, with the bottle again. This time, you know, who knows what would happen? He kneeled down and he actually had sex with me at that point—"

Oprah: "As people were walking by."

Angela: "Well, at this point, they were gathering."

Audience [groaning]: "Oh, no."

Angela: "And they—I could hear people saying, 'God . . . you know . . . never in the city of Chicago had they ever seen anything like this.' The laughing I could hear, and I just felt like, God, you know, why are they just standing there talking? And I just felt alone, you know. There was no hope. . . ."

Once again, an innocent person had suffered a random attack by a total stranger, this time in a way that suggested a wholesale meltdown of morality, values, and social control.

"Listen," Oprah told her audience at the end of the show, "sometimes shows like this always leave me so frustrated because I still don't know what we can do. I know it's an election year, and people should keep that in mind when they're voting, I think." Whether or not she intended the implicit endorsement of Bush wasn't clear.

A week later, on October 12, Cliff appeared on national television again, this time with his own Angela in a segment of *The MacNeil/Lehrer News Hour.* A correspondent reporting the case had reduced them to sound bites:

Cliff: "I don't think any of you could understand what it's like to be tied up in a basement and listen to your wife being violated and beaten."

Angela: "Even after the second assault on me—I mean, having a first assault on me was bad enough, OK. You figure the guy would leave. He got that. I mean, if that is what he was waiting for, if he was watching the house because it was me and that's what he wanted, he had that, and then he did it again."

Candidate Bush had a sound bite, too: "What did the Democratic governor of Massachusetts think he was doing when he let convicted, first-degree murderers out on weekend passes?"

Dennis Humphrey, the Massachusetts corrections official, offered the Dukakis administration's limp-sounding defense: "[Horton's] work reports continued to be positive; his housing reports while he was at the institution continued to be positive. In general, there was nothing that gave us any indication that he could become dangerous to the community on that furlough."

Though experts and politicians on both sides of the issue followed up with a fairly moderated discussion, it did little to dull the point.

With his campaign in trouble, Dukakis finally agreed to fight back. He aired some commercials that ridiculed the Bush ads for their negativism and distortions of truth. And he began pointing out that the federal prison system, administered by Republicans for eight years, routinely furloughed prisoners. So did the state of California, where furloughed prisoners had committed murders when President Ronald Reagan was governor.

He even found a couple of Horton equivalents to pin on Bush. One was a resident of a correctional halfway house in Texas who escaped to rape and murder a minister's wife. The halfway house was funded with federal money, and even after the disastrous escape, Vice President Bush visited the place to give it a presidential award.

Another was a Hispanic man who murdered a woman while on furlough from the federal prison system. The Dukakis campaign put together an ad that showed her being carried from the crime scene in a body bag, followed by a picture of the murderer's recognizably Hispanic face. "I had to call the victim's parents," Susan Estrich recalls. "I had to call the Hispanic caucus." Both gave her the go-ahead. But the ad remained a defensive gesture, too late to do much good. By the time it was aired, Estrich observes, the crime issue was "not about the Bush-Reagan furlough program. . . . It's about your values and your toughness."

"The only purpose of that ad," she would say, ". . . was to show 'You want to play this game? You want to debate furloughs? Fine. You can come up with an ugly story on our side; we can come up with an ugly story on your side. What does it prove?' George Bush, we were making the point, is a hypocrite."

What no one appeared to understand was that by now, the substance made no difference. Succeeding with the politics of fear depended much more on tone and attitude, pushing the right buttons that released the anger. Bush had seized that ground early; Dukakis's discomfort with it showed through whatever he did or said.

He displayed that discomfort most spectacularly on October 13, when the candidates met at UCLA for the second, and final, nationally publicized debate.

Most observers had scored Dukakis the winner of the first debate, on September 25 at Wake Forest University in Winston-Salem, North Carolina. For most of the evening, he had stayed on the attack, besting a flustered Bush in sharp exchanges on health insurance, the federal budget deficit, and abortion. When Bush brought up the Pledge of Allegiance, Dukakis handily responded by accusing Bush of "questioning my patriotism. . . . My parents came to this country as immigrants. They taught me that this was the greatest country in the world. I'm in public service because I love this country. I believe in it. And nobody's going to question my patriotism. . . ."

Prophetically, however, Bush managed to land a solid punch on one issue. The discussion had turned to his support of the death penalty for drug dealers. Dukakis reflexively reached for one of his lines designed to respond to Horton questions even though Bush had not raised that issue. The Bush administration, Dukakis asserted, "has a federal furlough program which is one of the most permissive in the country, which gave last year seven thousand furloughs to drug traffickers and drug pushers, the same people that he says he now wants to execute."

Bush did not fumble the opportunity. "When a narcotics wrapped-up guy goes in and murders a police officer, I think they ought to pay with their life," he shot back. ". . . So I am not going to furlough men like Willie Horton, and I would meet with their, the victims of his last escapade, the rape and the brutalization of the family down there in Maryland."

When the second confrontation convened two and a half weeks later, both sides worried that the other would try a bold stroke, a ploy that might force his opponent to commit a major blunder.

The Republicans believed that they now enjoyed a lead substantial enough that a debate that ended in a draw would give them victory. They therefore worried that Dukakis might try something dramatic or bizarre—walking away from the lectern, perhaps, to dispense with the moderator and challenge Bush directly. Dukakis's handlers feared that Atwater might arrange to seat the Barneses in the audience so that Bush could point them out and demand that Dukakis apologize to them on the spot.

As it turned out, however, Atwater did no such thing. Instead, it was the moderator, Bernard Shaw of the Cable News Network, who extended to Dukakis a length of rope with which to hang himself.

Shaw began with the ritual welcome to the audience, introduced the candidates and the other journalists on the panel,
and went over a few rules. Then, without missing a beat, he
asked Dukakis a heart-stopping question. "Governor, if Kitty
Dukakis were raped and murdered, would you favor an irre-
vocable death penalty for the killer?"

The question should have been easy to answer, so easy, in
fact, that some would say later Shaw had asked it in hopes of
helping Dukakis out, a suggestion Shaw would deny. Here
again was a chance for Dukakis to repeat the stories of his
father, assaulted and robbed by a thief seeking drugs, and his
brother, killed by a drunk driver. Of course he understood
crime, he could say. Of course he understood pain. And sure,
he might have said, he would personally feel as angry and
vengeful as any man would about someone who raped his
wife; make no mistake about that. How could the impertinent
reporter have put the issue in such tasteless terms? But as
president, he would have to put aside such personal passions
and do what he knew was right. And he knew that vengeance
is a poor basis for sound policy on crime or anything else. He
also knew that the death penalty doesn't work to reduce
crime, even though crime demeans society, diminishes us all.

That is what he might have said. But Dukakis had been ill
that day, as the stresses of campaigning had begun to catch
up. He had slept all afternoon. Now his mind worked too
slowly even to come up with the answer that had been in his
repertoire for so many weeks. So did he favor the death
penalty for a man who raped and murdered Kitty?

"No, I don't, Bernard," Dukakis responded calmly. "And I
think you know that I've opposed the death penalty during all

of my life. I don't see any evidence that it's a deterrent, and I think there are better and more effective ways to deal with violent crime. We've done so in my own state, and it's one of the reasons why we have had the biggest drop in crime of any industrial state in America."

He then moved into a familiar lecture about the need to do more about drugs—drug law enforcement and drug education to "make it possible for our kids and our families to grow up in safe and secure and decent neighborhoods"—as if he had quickly forgotten the matter of Kitty's rape and murder.

Confronted with his wife's brutal violation, in other words, he simply regurgitated dull campaign rhetoric. Here, clearly, was a man who had no comprehension whatsoever of the humiliation and outrage a crime victim might feel, no sense of the fear crime had introduced into the daily lives of millions, perhaps no capacity for emotional response at all.

In a room nearby, Baker, Atwater, Rogers, Ailes, and other Bush campaign celebrities had gathered to watch a closed-circuit feed of the event. High spirits and nervous wisecracking filled the room as Shaw made his introductions and spelled out rules. But when he asked his first question, the group quieted down.

"Every pol in the room instinctively knew what he could have done with that question," Rogers says. "The room went dead silent, waiting for the ball to sail out of the park." But as Dukakis droned on, they began looking at one another in disbelief. When it was over, "Ailes said, 'Hope for a power failure. . . . If we could just freeze it now and walk off, it's over.' "

As it turned out, no freeze was necessary. After the second debate, whatever life had remained went out of Dukakis's campaign. "It was clear that [the first question] was an opportunity that we missed," Estrich acknowledged after it was all over. "Whether it was fair or unfair, I thought we could have won the debate in the first five minutes. We didn't."

William Horton had claimed his latest victim. The Barneses and their millions of sympathizers had a new satisfaction to savor.

The presidential campaign of 1988 spread the Willie Horton story, luridly inflated in the Merrimack Valley the previous year, to all America. In doing so, it made clear to politicians everywhere that they could find themselves in trouble if they did not find a way to acknowledge an expressive response to crime.

Although it was a development that transcended party and ideology, conservative Republicans felt much more comfortable with the new expressiveness than did liberal Democrats. The emphasis on the death penalty and long mandatory prison terms, the disparagement of rehabilitation and social programs to prevent crime—all of it fit with traditional Republican positions. And the expressive contempt for government's supposedly callous betrayal of public trust resonated with the deeply felt beliefs of the radical right.

In the wake of the Dukakis debacle, perhaps still not fully aware what had happened to them, Democrats bitterly accused the Bush campaign of foul play. The deliberate negative strategy was unseemly, they suggested, and the use of Horton, they said, was a blatant appeal to racism that violated an important taboo.

In a remarkable conference convened at Harvard University's Kennedy School of Government, for example, Susan Estrich was able to confront Lee Atwater and Roger Ailes. Of course the use of Horton was an effort to exploit racism, Estrich insisted. "We weren't going to deal with Willie Horton by emphasizing our crime record in Massachusetts, for goodness' sakes, let alone the federal furlough policy or Ronald Reagan's furlough policy [as governor of California]. All of that was fine, and all of that we put out there. . . . Whether it was intended or not, the symbolism [of a black man raping a white woman] was very powerful."

Atwater came on just as strong in response. "There was nothing racial about Willie Horton," he declared. "We resent the fact that it was used racially in the campaign [by the independents] because we certainly didn't [use it that way], and we were very conscious about it. I think the furlough issue was a very important issue in this campaign. I think it was symbolic. I think it was a value issue, and we didn't back off at all from using that issue in the campaign. We are very sorry if anyone took it racially, because we had a concerted effort in our campaign to make sure that race was not used in any way, shape, or form in the development of this issue."

And he disclosed—"this has never been told before"—that concern about race had caused a revision of the revolving-door ad. For the first version, Roger Ailes had used prison inmates selected randomly, but so many were black that he and Atwater decided to reduce the number of blacks for a retake.

Democrats and journalists present went on to grill Atwater and Ailes about why they had not tried harder to control the independents who took a more gleeful approach to the racial aspects of the Horton issue.

Ron Brown, who had managed Jesse Jackson's campaign, asserted that "the Republican National Committee or somebody didn't meet their responsibility in dealing with this issue. You knew what it was causing. You knew what was happening. Maybe you couldn't control everything, but nobody stepped up to the plate and said, 'It's divisive, it's dangerous, it's wrong.' "

"So you're saying that because he's black, we cannot use the issue," Ailes shot back. "Despite the fact he was a murderer and a rapist, you're saying he should have been given special treatment because he was black."

With that, the debate ended in a draw, frustrating Estrich, who published a long meditation on race, crime, and the campaign in *The Washington Post Magazine* ("Willie Horton and Me") the following year. After recounting her own experience, she went on to argue forcefully that "when Democrats are attacked as soft on crime—by a campaign using a black rapist as a symbol—our substantive response on the 'crime issue' is largely beside the point. The point is race, not crime."

The deeper point, however, the one the Republicans had turned to their advantage so effectively, was middle-class fear; race was responsible for some of it but certainly not for all of it, and it was a fact of life that nothing seemed likely to change.

Further fallout from the election occurred as prison administrators all over America reviewed furlough and other programs that permitted temporary release of inmates, even those that had been functioning well. In February of 1989, a *Boston Globe* reporter found that at least five other states— Texas, Virginia, Maryland, Louisiana, and Michigan—had revised their furlough policies or had them under review. By

1990, a census found 28,849 of the 739,980 inmates in the nation's state and federal prisons participating in furloughs, for a rate of 3.9 percent. That represented a sharp decline from 1987, pre-Horton, when another survey had found a furlough rate of more than 9 percent for that year's 560,812 prison inmates.

Alvin Bronstein, director of the American Civil Liberties Union's National Prison Project lamented that "the campaign and the Horton issue have had a very dramatic and serious impact on all kinds of programs like furlough programs, work release, and house arrest. . . . There's been a real backlash against these programs. Politicians see that it's a way to win."

Anthony Travisono, executive director of the American Correctional Association, observed that "every state has taken a look at the issue and where they can tighten up the restrictions they have. We're tightening the entire system, and the entire system, being tightened, will at some point be a difficult thing to operate."

The chairman of the board of the Texas Department of Corrections acknowledged the political influence on prison policy. "We really hadn't had problems," Charles Terrell said of the furlough program. "What caused all this was the Willie Horton thing during the presidential campaign. Our local paper did a story on our program compared to Massachusetts's program, and the board looked at that and tried to make changes." The changes, barring more serious offenders and allowing furloughs only for those within six months of parole eligibility, reduced the number of Texas inmates going out on furloughs by more than half.

Corrections officials worried that curtailing furloughs would lead to more violence inside prisons and result in poorer decisions about whom to release on parole. Idaho's corrections commissioner resigned amid a controversy over furloughs. Edward Morris, deputy director of the Virginia Department of Corrections, voiced the professional's frustration with a popular trend toward the more primitive penology of a different era. "The fact that politicians can demagogically come forward at any time and scream law and order and put up the Willie Horton face—the black male murderer, rapist, every stereotypic horror nightmare of white America—and say, 'This is what the liberal agenda is,' and lock them up and throw away the key, vengeance becomes the total basis of our criminal justice system. Forget rehabilitation, forget all that. America seems ripe for accepting anything that could be wrapped up in those racial terms."

Whatever the implications for prison management, the practical consequences for public safety were slight. The tougher attitude toward furloughs and other temporary-release programs reduced the number of prison convicts on the streets of America. But there was no way this would make those streets discernibly safer. Crimes committed by inmates on temporary release from prison—a figure that by the widest stretch of the imagination could not have totaled more than a few hundred each year—made a barely noticeable addition to the thirty-four million crimes being committed annually in the mid-1980s. And those furlough-generated crimes surely were more than offset by the new offenses committed by ex-cons released without the benefit of furloughs to ease the shock of reentry. The nationwide result, nowhere measured, was most likely a small increase in crime.

But again, in an era of expressive justice, crime control was no longer the point. The Willie Horton story aroused politicians' self-protective instincts. The bottom line was that few officeholders who wished to remain where they were could afford to oppose the wave of popular feeling revealed, and further aroused, by the Bush campaign's use of the Horton case. Those who preferred not to ride it to their advantage would have to hunker down as it rolled by.

And that, it soon became apparent, would take some time. In 1991, Kathleen Hall Jamieson, dean of the Annenberg School of Communications at the University of Pennsylvania, convened a focus group of Louisiana voters and asked them, "Can you tell me what you remember as being important in the 1988 presidential campaign?"

She transcribed the group members' responses:

"Hmmm."

"I'm trying to think. . . ."

"Dukakis."

"That was Dukakis. . . ."

"I just knew I couldn't vote for him. . . ."

"I think the big thing against him was that—wasn't his criminal . . . I mean, not his criminal record but his . . . the handling of, um . . ."

"The handling of his state programs."

"His state programs. I think that influenced a lot of people—how they voted . . ."

Focus group leader: ". . . Can you think of any specific issues?"

"Well, I think right off, the . . . the one I'm thinking about was his . . . his handling of a criminal, um, and I can't right now . . ."

"What do you mean, a pardon of someone who has . . ."

"Willie Horton."

"Yeah. A pardon."

"Pardon."

"Yeah. He pardoned that guy that went out and killed someone."

"Afterwards. You know, he released this known . . . I guess he was a murderer, wasn't he? Originally. And they released him anyway, and he went out and killed . . ."

"Immediately and killed people again."

"Right after getting out."

"And this was brought out, that he was releasing people really without seemingly too much thought. I think that had a lot to do with it."

Jamieson comments: "William Horton and Michael Dukakis are now twinned in our memory. The fact that the memories are factually inaccurate does not diminish their power."

The Horton case also remained on the minds of Republicans as they prepared to defend George Bush's presidency in the election of 1992. Worried that New York's governor Mario Cuomo might pose the strongest challenge to the president, the opposition researchers, now an essential part of the campaign team, quickly unearthed what appeared to be a Horton equivalent: a man named Arthur Shawcross.

Imprisoned in New York on a manslaughter conviction for killing a child in 1972, he was paroled in 1987, having served fifteen years of a twenty-five-year term. He used his new freedom to become a serial murderer. Between 1987 and 1989, he killed 10 women in the environs of Rochester, New York. The case didn't quite fit the pattern: Many of the victims were prostitutes, not nice middle-class folks.

But it would do. "If Mario Cuomo had been tougher on crime," the narrator of the attack ad might say, "this vicious killer would not have been set free to kill again," as pictures of the unsavory-looking Shawcross filled the screen. Some in the Bush campaign, it was said, looked forward to using the case in a Horton-like campaign because Shawcross is white. They could demonstrate once and for all that the issue with Horton had been crime, not race.

But Cuomo knew how to fight back and even relished the chance. As soon as he learned that Republicans were researching Shawcross, his office counterattacked with a document that expanded on it in a way that fought expressiveness with expressiveness. Shawcross, it pointed out, had been paroled only two years before he would have completed his full sentence, given time off for good behavior. The real issue in his case wasn't his release on parole but the original conviction for manslaughter. A murder conviction would have carried a sentence of twenty-five years to life. The manslaughter conviction was the result of a plea bargain, and there was wide agreement, the governor suggested, that the prosecutor who negotiated it had erred on the side of leniency. *There* was the real official incompetence, the real betrayal of public trust—*and that prosecutor was a Republican.*

But Arthur Shawcross would not get the chance to star in his own Willie Horton story, for Cuomo would soon announce that the state's budget problems required so much of his attention that he could not afford to enter the presidential race.

With Bill Clinton, governor of Arkansas, moving toward the Democratic nomination, Republican strategists looked over his record and found suitable cases there, too. In fact, any governor, ultimately responsible for a prison system and a parole board, could be expected to have on his watch a few cases of inmates who committed new crimes after release on furlough or parole. The new politics of expressive justice threatened to bar any governor from running for president.

Arkansas, for example, had a furloughed inmate who embarrassed Clinton that April. Charles Lloyd Patterson had been serving a forty-year term for a number of convictions, including one for hiring a man to murder his ex-wife's divorce lawyer. Patterson escaped while on furlough and commandeered two airplanes, one in Arkansas and another in Colorado, before his recapture in Texas.

For a while, it looked as if Patterson might become the Willie Horton of 1992—in fact, when he came to trial that September, he claimed that Arkansas Republicans had encouraged him to escape with promises that he would be "taken care of by the Republican party" if he absconded in a way that embarrassed Clinton. (The Republican officials he accused denied the charge, and a jury refused to believe it.)

As it turned out, however, the Republicans could do little to turn that or any other prisoner-release case against Clinton in the 1992 campaign. They had not reckoned with a crucial bit of history: The Arkansas governor had already suffered the bite of expressive justice, and it had scarred him so deeply that there was simply no way he would ever let it get the better of him again.

In 1978, Arkansans elected Clinton to his first term; all of thirty-two years old, he was the youngest governor in the United States. During his term, he regularly commuted sen-

tences of prison inmates, including those of thirty-eight murderers serving life sentences. One of these was a seventy-
three-year-old man supposedly now so ill that his medical
treatment could cost the state two hundred thousand dollars
if he remained in prison. But shortly after his release, he committed another homicide, shooting a sixty-one-year-old man
in the course of a robbery.

The following year, Arkansas voters turned Clinton out of
office in favor of a Republican who had made much of
Clinton's liberalism and softness on crime. "The astonish-
ment of that repudiation was a trauma that, by all accounts,
hugely sobered and altered Clinton," Marshall Frady wrote
in *The New Yorker*. ". . . One almost metaphysical lesson it
provided him was never to range, whatever his own
impulses, too far beyond the standing disposition of the general populace."

A greatly changed and chastened Bill Clinton campaigned
to reclaim the statehouse in 1982. He apologized for the many
commutations he had granted as governor and begged for a
chance to show he had learned to respect people's feelings
about crime. The people complied. In office once more,
where he would remain for a decade, he took a more parsi-
monious approach to commutations, granting only seven in
ten years, and a more generous approach toward executions.
During that time, he set seventy-one execution dates for
twenty-seven convicts condemned to death and presided over
four executions of those who had exhausted their appeals.

This stark feature of Clinton's political persona, familiar
enough in Arkansas, was exposed for national scrutiny at a
particularly rocky moment in the 1992 campaign. That

January, as the governor appeared headed for a salutary victory in the early New Hampshire primary, his quest for the presidency tripped over Gennifer Flowers, an Arkansas state employee who came forward to claim that she had been carrying on a prolonged affair with the governor and released tapes of telephone conversations with him to prove it.

As Clinton battled reporters fomenting a classic feeding frenzy and huddled with campaign aides to plan a response, Arkansas corrections officials prepared to execute a man named Rickey Ray Rector. Few outside Arkansas had ever heard of him, but locally his case had stirred strong emotion. In March 1981, Rector shot three men, one fatally, in a dispute over admission to a dance hall in the town of Conway. A few days later, he shot to death a well-respected local police officer, Bob Martin, who had come to arrest him. Then Rector lifted the gun to his head and shot himself through the temple. Instead of succeeding with suicide, however, he inflicted massive brain damage that left him grossly impaired. Even so, prosecutors trading on outrage over the death of Officer Martin prevailed in their determination to try Rector as a normal person and have him sentenced to death.

His IQ in the sixties, Rector sat in prison for more than ten years, displaying erratic thinking and behavior, a childlike personality, and a gravely limited comprehension of his circumstances. Attorneys pursued appeals on his behalf, arguing that the man sentenced to die was not the same man who had committed the crime and in any case was in no shape to help lawyers with his appeals.

To many, it seemed incomprehensible that the law could allow Rector's execution, given his condition. Yet in June of

1991, a Supreme Court impatient with the rising volume of death-penalty appeals refused to hear his case for the second time. Now only Bill Clinton could spare his life.

But with friends and relatives of Rector's victims repeating their demands for retribution and Gennifer Flowers dominating the news, Clinton wasn't about to intervene. He returned to Little Rock on the day of the execution, a Friday, and spent most of his time planning the dramatic rescue of his candidacy: He and his wife, Hillary, would appear on national television after the Super Bowl that Sunday, submitting to an interview that would put the Flowers issue to rest.

That afternoon, Rector ate his last meal of steak and chicken—and set aside his pecan pie apparently because he believed he would be returning to eat it just before bedtime, as was his custom. He died by lethal injection that night.

Clinton's efforts to deal with the Flowers issue dominated national political news that weekend; outside Arkansas, the Rector execution remained a secondary story. But as time passed, it became clear that Clinton had deprived Bush of a powerful issue. For Bush could no longer claim to be sole proprietor of expressive justice.

The political consultant David Garth marveled to Frady that Clinton "had someone put to death who had only part of a brain. You can't find them any tougher than that." And Jay Jacobson, head of the Arkansas chapter of the American Civil Liberties Union, declared that "you can't law and order Clinton. If you can kill Rector, you can kill anybody."

America

1 9 9 5

On paper, it looked like just another driving-under-the-influence case, a woman spotted by cops shortly after midnight, weaving slowly along the interstate. Pulled over, she failed all the tests of sobriety.

But when Judge Femia looked down at her from the bench, he connected the name with the face: Angela Barnes. What on earth? he thought to himself, hating for a moment the job he basically loved. Showing no recognition, he listened while her lawyer explained that she had been the victim of a rape; it continued to devastate her emotions, disrupt her life.

He recalled then how she had sat so stoically through the trial of William Horton two and a half years before. She had never betrayed a feeling, and when it came her turn to testify, she had spoken quietly, almost in a monotone, about the night of abuse on Proxmire Drive. Along with a lot of meanness, he had read a lot of pain on the faces of people who passed before

his bench in the nineteen years he had been a judge. The suf-
fering on hers was as plain as any he had ever seen. His
impulse was to take her aside, ask how she was doing, express
his concern. But the law is the law. He fined her $250 and
costs.

Back in the Merrimack Valley, Maureen Donovan and her friends vowed to keep CAUS going and campaign for other criminal justice legislation. But as time passed, the group faded. Donovan herself, however, found she had discovered a taste, as well as considerable talent, for public life, and in 1991, she won a seat on the Methuen Town Council.

Donna Cuomo, who had worked as a housewife, a school-teacher, and a real estate agent, also found a new vocation. On October 26, 1989, the fifteenth anniversary of her brother's murder, she went down to the site of Marston Street Mobil, where she held a little ceremony to announce the establishment of a new organization called Joey Fournier Services. The not-for-profit group would seek grant money to develop programs for crime victims. The furlough campaign had put her in touch with a great many victims' families, she says, "and I could see there was a need to do more."

The office opened the following March 1, offering support groups, counseling, and other social services for families devastated by crime. Cuomo also promoted a violence-prevention curriculum for elementary schools and from time to time lent support to criminal justice measures coming before the state legislature.

Then in 1993, Joe Hermann, the North Andover representative who had cosponsored the furlough ban with Larry

Giordano, died of cancer. Cuomo stepped in to campaign for his seat on the basis of what was now a substantial record of public service. That November she won the election and the chance to push victims' rights in the legislature herself.

Down in Baltimore, William Horton remained in prison, working in the kitchen to prepare lunch and dinner on a shift that began at one o'clock each morning. During the 1988 campaign, he had made a point of not granting interviews to the many reporters who called. Well aware that he had become an evil star of the Bush campaign, he figured that anything at all he might say could only be used against him, not to mention Michael Dukakis.

At one point, he claims, a woman who identified herself as a Republican-party official managed to get him on the phone— she apparently had previously worked at the prison and placed her request through the warden, who summoned Horton to his office. She asked Horton whom he supported in the election, trying to get him to say he favored Dukakis. That would have laid the basis for the ultimate attack ad—"Michael Dukakis picked up another endorsement the other day . . ."— but Horton saw what was going on and refused to bite.

After the election, he gave more attention to the interview requests, hoping he could somehow turn his dubious celebrity to his advantage. The right kind of publicity might attract a liberal lawyer willing to press new appeals of both his cases pro bono. Or perhaps there were people who would pay enough for his story that he could hire big-time attorneys. A sharp lawyer might still find some unsettled issues in the Fournier conviction to pursue, he thought, and he loved telling visitors about the big hole he perceived in the Barnes case—no eyewitnesses had placed him at the scene except for Angela Barnes, and she had admitted she was near-sighted and had seen his face only without wearing her glasses.

Even so, not much cash materialized. Some people seemed grossed out by the very idea of paying him for an interview. When others made offers, he worried about how much control he would have over the slant they might take. The wrong kind of exposure could do more harm than good.

In the end, he spoke for public benefit with only two people, Sam Donaldson of ABC News and his friend Jeffrey Elliot, the political science professor. Elliot had built a second career for himself, getting to know prison inmates convicted in celebrated crimes, then selling interviews with them to magazines.

In December 1989, *Playboy* published an Elliot interview with William Horton. For the first time, Horton gave his reaction to the use of his story and image in the Bush campaign. The Republicans, he said, "succeeded in portraying me as the Devil incarnate. . . . Was the ad racist? Hell, you know it was. And I'm not the only victim of racism. All poor people and minorities are portrayed in a similar manner by people who exploit their woes in order to whip up public anger and fear."

Brazenly, he went on to deny murdering Joey Fournier and raping Angela Miller, admitting only that he had stolen the car from the Barnes-Miller house.

Horton granted Donaldson an interview a few months later. It aired on *Prime Time Live* on March 29, 1990. Asked what he thought of the Republican ads that featured him, he responded, "I guess I think, as any other normal person would, how could people create such a negative picture of an individual that they don't even know. . . ." He again denied his guilt and asserted that the ads "reminded me of some of the racism that went on back in our history."

At one point, Donaldson marveled at his civilized appearance and demeanor. "You know, some people watching this interview are going to say, 'Well, William Horton is nice looking, he's soft-spoken, he seems reasonable. But he's a monster. He must be an actor.'"

"There's no way I could be acting," Horton responded. "I'm very sincere."

Three years later, Horton was in regular communication with Elliot and granted him twelve hours of interviews, which prison officials, no doubt frustrated with their famous inmate, insisted take place over the course of a few days between the hours of 2:00 and 6:30 A.M. Horton again denied his guilt of major violent crimes and told a story he repeated to other visitors, in which he alleged two Massachusetts lawyers offered him a bribe. One of the lawyers, Anthony DiFruscia, was representing the Barneses in the lawsuit they hoped to file against the state of Massachusetts in order to recover damages and, as Cliff had said, "teach Massachusetts correction officials a good, hard lesson in accountability."

The suit was never filed. It turned out that Massachusetts state agencies and their employees enjoy sovereign immunity against liability for the consequences of legitimate conduct in the course of their official duties. And try as he might, DiFruscia could find no more hard evidence that Horton's furloughs were improperly approved than could the state's investigators, the Merrimack Valley politicians, or *The*

Lawrence Eagle-Tribune. In the end, DiFruscia had a falling out with the Barneses over how to proceed, and they never found another lawyer to represent them.

But in February of 1989, DiFruscia was still at work on the case, and he apparently decided that it would be worth talking to Horton to see whether he would admit to his prison drug dealing and thus give DiFruscia something with which to embarrass the correction department in court. He arranged to visit Horton at the Maryland Penitentiary, bringing along Charles Capace, who was helping him with the suit, and Dougie Cecil, Horton's childhood friend. Dougie, the lawyers hoped, could help establish their bona fides with Horton.

This proved to be a good strategy. Dougie, Horton told Elliot, "was part of the reason I agreed to see them. They discussed the details of their investigation. Basically, they wanted me to say that Massachusetts—and Governor Dukakis—had made a terrible mistake in approving my furlough, for which they would put $20,000 in a trust fund for my daughter." According to Horton, they then left him alone with Dougie, who supposedly added that the lawyers might also be able to get him transferred back to Massachusetts or perhaps to more comfortable digs in a federal prison.

If all this were true, it would be a sensational footnote to the whole saga—agents of the Barneses now offering favors to Willie Horton!—and evidence of how perverse the politics of expressive justice might become. But DiFruscia and Capace stoutly denied making any such offers. The bribe story is "absolutely an outrageous lie," DiFruscia declared. "I can't imagine that I would ever offer anybody any money for getting involved with any litigation. It's unethical, and I wouldn't dare do it. . . . I can say without question that no money was ever offered to Mr. Horton or for anyone on his behalf. I was just interested in finding out the truth and finding out if I had a witness." Capace dismissed Horton's story as "pure, unadulterated bullshit."

As for transfer to Massachusetts or a better prison, it seemed beyond the capacity of DiFruscia and Capace to accomplish even if they had been inclined to do so. Later on, Dougie Cecil would confirm the lawyers' version. After William asked why he should help DiFruscia with the case, "Tony told him straight up that he couldn't promise him anything," Dougie said.

Elliot sold some of the interview to *The Nation* and other parts of it to *Emerge*. Both magazines published the Horton material in 1993. That same year, in May, after *The Lawrence Eagle-Tribune* had published an article to celebrate the fifth anniversary of the furlough ban victory, the paper received a letter from Horton's daughter, Tara Mays, who was five months old, asleep in her crib, the night the police came to take her father away.

Now a young woman of eighteen who had seen her father only on prison visits, she wrote to ask that the newspaper leave him alone. "I know for a fact that he is not the kind of person that you and a whole lot of other people describe him to be. He might have made a lot of mistakes, but he shouldn't be called a pathological killer."

In Maryland, the Barneses continued their struggle to heal. Immediately after the crime, they had moved into a house that a friend owned and happened to have available for rent.

A few months later, they purchased a new home down closer to Port Tobacco and their boat.

Their different reactions to the crime and its aftermath put a huge strain on their marriage. Much as she understood Cliff's need to do it, Angela hated his campaigning, which paraded their pain and humiliation before national audiences. They compromised on the issue, agreeing that he would suspend his activism after the 1988 election. He accepted the deal but continued to wonder, Could he have done more for crime victims when all the attention was focused on the Horton case? Could he be an effective spokesperson even now?

For more than two years, Angela remained overwhelmed by the aftermath of the attack. Her self-confidence shattered, she now lived in a constant state of distraction, her face often falling into a dull mask of anger. She lived with high anxiety that produced a wholly understandable, if excessive, paranoia.

She was terrified of being in the house alone. The police returned the Bernardelli .22; the Barneses taped up the handle that had broken when Horton dropped it on the highway, and they kept it close at hand. When Cliff's stepfather retired and moved to Mexico, he left them the Colt .45 he had carried while in the army. Its big bullets afforded Angela an additional measure of comfort.

If she entered the house when Cliff was away, she would take a knife or a gun and walk from room to room, checking each one to make sure no one was there. She insisted that the house and garage be heavily locked down before they went to bed each night. She also sank into a depression from which there seemed to be no relief. Struggling constantly with the anger and pain, she took to drinking heavily and gained weight.

For a time, she found herself obsessed with true-crime books, especially the works of Ann Rule, who had written about Ted Bundy, the serial killer, and Diane Downs, convicted of shooting her own children. Angela found it gratifying to read how criminals convicted of horrible crimes were brought to justice.

She tried counseling, but she turned out to be a frustrating case, uncomfortable sharing her most intimate feelings with a relative stranger. One therapist, declaring that she had to act if she wanted to get better, encouraged her to try going through the empty house without a weapon, even if she shook with fear, just to see if she could do it, and then try it again the next night. But nothing seemed to work.

In the end, it took a crisis to shock her into recovery. Shortly after midnight on September 9, 1989, troopers pulled her off the Beltway, where she had been weaving along after having had too much to drink. In court the following March, she found herself face to face with Vincent J. Femia, the judge who had presided so sternly over the trial of William Horton. His most merciful act that day, surely, was to betray no recognition as he imposed a $250 fine.

Cliff was furious—she could have hurt herself, driving that way, or hurt somebody else. And Angela was deeply chagrined. She hated the idea of drunk driving. She wasn't irresponsible. What was happening to her? She realized then how tired she was of it all, of being fat, of feeling stuck. Why, after all, should she let William Horton ruin the rest of her life?

And at that point, she began to get better. She stopped drinking and decided to quit her job with the land-development company. She went back to school for a real estate broker's license so that she could work for herself.

After two more years, she and Cliff were making commitments to the future. He quit his job with the auto dealership and opened his own shop with a partner; they would offer dealership-quality service at independent prices. In addition to selling real estate, Angela kept the books for the family business. And she and Cliff decided to have a baby. Their little boy, born in March 1993, filled a big place in a life that had shifted around to take a new shape, as healthy lives should now and again.

Even so, friends might still sense traces of the attack in Angela's quietness, the reserve that had taken hold as a permanent part of her, the angry mask that still appeared once in a while. Cliff for the most part seemed affable as ever, but if a visitor should suggest that with the new job, the new business, and the new baby, he and Angela were doing well, he could turn pensive.

"I kind of wish that all that meant everything is OK," he would say quietly. "But it doesn't. . . . I would give up everything Angie and I have right now and start from scratch . . . no money, not a roof over my head, not a car to drive . . . if I could take back what happened. . . . [Willie Horton] took something from me that I can't replace."

A memorable early scene from Mark Twain's greatest novel describes the effort of a town judge to reform Huckleberry Finn's degenerate father. After the judge denies the application of decent folk to become Huck's guardians ("He said courts mustn't interfere and separate families if they could help it"), Huck's father forces his son to find money so he can celebrate. When Huck borrows three dollars, "Pap took it and got drunk and went a-blowing around and cussing and whooping and carrying on, and he kept it up all over town, with a tin pan, till most midnight; then they jailed him and next day they had him before court and jailed him again for a week."

Undaunted, the judge takes Pap to his house and gives him clean clothes and family meals. After supper one night, he delivers a temperance lecture that seems to strike home: "The old man cried and said he'd been a fool and fooled away his life but now he was a-going to turn over a new leaf and be a man nobody wouldn't be ashamed of, and he hoped the judge would help him and not look down on him. The judge said he could hug him for them words; so he cried and his wife she cried too. . . . Then the old man he signed a pledge—made his mark. The judge said it was the holiest time on record."

But the reform lasts only a few hours. "They tucked the old man into a beautiful room, which was the spare room, and in the night some time he got powerful thirsty and clumb out on to the porch-roof and slid down a stanchion and traded his new coat for a jug of forty-rod, and clumb back again and had a good old time; and towards daylight he crawled out again, drunk as a fiddler, and rolled off the porch and broke his left arm in two places and was most froze to death when some-body found him after sun-up."

That brings the chapter to an abrupt conclusion: "The judge . . . said he reckoned a body could reform the old man with a shotgun, maybe, but he didn't know no other way."

• • •

America's shift to expressive criminal justice takes place amid great confusion, without much public acknowledgment. Is it really such a reason for concern?

The question is perfectly valid. If crime continues to drag down a society's morale and the prospects for crime control remain uncertain, why *shouldn't* people use the political and legal systems as therapy? Why not exorcise collective fear and anger, and perhaps buck up morale, with laws and policies that gratify emotion, whether or not they achieve a more practical result?

One answer is that the question is premature. The prospects for crime control may remain uncertain, but that doesn't mean it is time to give up on them altogether. Promoters of expressiveness pay lip service to crime control—isn't it common sense that executing more convicts and putting more in prison for longer terms ought to reduce the number of criminals on the streets and therefore reduce the amount of crime? Yet in fact expressiveness and crime control aren't compatible.

The arithmetic, the much disparaged statistics, convey a point that can't be ignored. During the 1980s, state legislators responding to expressive demands of constituents tripled America's prison capacity, from 316,000 to nearly 1 million. This turned corrections into a $25-billion-per-year growth industry with a political constituency of its own. As a result of that expansion, by far the largest, most determined effort to punish criminals in the nation's history, the United States now locks up a larger percentage of its population than any other free country.

Even so, crime continues to plague America. The reason is simply that prison isn't very effective as a crime-control device right now, if ever it was, because compared with the number of criminals committing crimes, so few are locked up. Even after the immense prison buildup, the total put behind bars each year remains less than 3 percent of all criminals. Locking enough criminals up to make a noticeable difference would cost hundreds of billions of dollars and would force an impossible choice between higher taxes for prisons and sharply reduced money for schools, health care, housing, and other government services.

Yet prisons are also by far the most expensive element of criminal justice. The $25 billion spent to keep less than 3 percent of criminals locked up amounts to fully 30 percent of the nation's total spending on law enforcement. So long as that disparity continues, criminal justice officials are hard-pressed for resources to deal with the other 97 percent of criminals who don't go to prison. Thus does the new expressiveness perpetuate financial gridlock.

What could be done about the 97 percent? Plenty, given the kind of money routinely spent on prisons—and likely to increase by the tens of billions if expressiveness continues. Funds on that scale could vastly augment the nation's police departments; with more officers, police managers could develop more creative, proactive strategies that involve working with communities on crime control.

New money could finally make possible drug treatment for all who request it as well as for tens of thousands more ordered by the courts to receive it. So obviously necessary a step might quickly make a big dent in crime rates. More billions could make possible more effective sanctions and programs in the lower courts for first offenders. As a result, large numbers of teenagers before judges for their first crimes might receive meaningful punishment or treatment rather than getting off with minimal supervision by overworked probation officers.

The trend toward expressiveness forecloses all these possibilities. Yet if given a real chance to work, they could begin to reduce both crime and fear and give a beleaguered public reason to recover lost faith in government. The stakes are simply too high to abandon that wholly plausible hope.

The most important reasons to resist the trend, however, are moral. The Horton case demonstrated amply and alarmingly the power of expressiveness to torture the truth. The politics of fear make a casualty of it, just as wartime passions nurture propaganda.

The Constitution might bar the courts from imposing cruel and unusual punishments, but in the Horton case, tried in the arena of politics and public opinion as well as in court, politicians and the news media imposed their own grotesque punishments fashioned from legitimized falsehoods. They inflated Horton from a sadly inadequate person who may not even have participated directly in the murder for which he was first convicted into a monster guilty of sexual mutilation, dismemberment, and necrophilia.

Of course it's a mistake to squander too much concern on Horton. Though falling short of unspeakable, his crimes were serious, and he deserves to remain right where he is, serving out his eighty-five-year minimum term in Maryland. But the inflation of his evil for popular consumption constitutes a gross insult to truth and to the idea, fundamental to any democratic tradition, that people are to be judged on the basis of what they have done, not on how angry others may feel. More important still, the escalation of Horton from lowlife to ghoul served to bolster the case for malfeasance, in reality nonexistent, on the part of the government and its criminal justice system. The powerful emotion stirred up by inflammatory falsehoods, repeated as true with great authority, made public officials appear as callous, monstrous, and dangerous as the expressiveness-enhanced image of Horton himself.

In the election of 1988, Republican tacticians moved quickly to exploit this view of public officials in the heat of political combat—caring little about the powerful side effect: a corrosion of faith that can't ever be restored in full by a change of party or people in office. Since the presidential campaign of 1988, millions of Americans still carry the false impression that in allowing a furlough for Horton, the government of Massachusetts demonstrated incomprehensible softheadedness or outright stupidity. The idea that any government entity was capable of such a thing creates a doubt that lingers and gets reinforced with every new crime that follows the Willie Horton pattern.

Beyond official credibility, however, lies an even deeper issue. Expressiveness assumes that evildoers are evil for life, that bad people may not be converted to good, that lost souls may never be reclaimed. There are practical reasons to hope this is not always the case. It costs a lot of money to imprison people for life, even more to conduct the legal appeals required for the death penalty. Why incur those expenses for people who might one day become law-abiding, productive, taxpaying citizens?

But there are larger reasons for questioning a massive shift to a darker view of human nature. The idea of rehabilitation became discredited in the 1970s, when researchers of the era failed to show that programs designed to rehabilitate criminals could do so reliably or for large numbers. But much has changed since then in both theory and practice. Today, thousands of criminals are rehabilitated annually, one way or another. Some succeed with the established programs; others pursue private journeys. Progressive prison administrators have no trouble at all making sense of their work: In addition to housing and guarding, it is to help those inmates with the will and the ability to rehabilitate themselves.

And in nearly every state, prison officials can point to successful cases. In Louisiana there is Wilbert Rideau. While serving a life term for a vicious murder, he has become the nationally recognized editor of an award-winning prison magazine and exhibits remarkable maturity and peacefulness of spirit. In New York, there is Clayton Williams, a former drug abuser and gangster who now leads a productive life as a senior manager for one such program, finding job placements for criminals sentenced to do community service work. And in Arizona, there is James Hamm. Convicted of a drug-related murder after a youth spent drifting in and out of a marijuana fog, he used his time in prison to study Jungian philosophy, Taoism, computers, and law. Now released and married to a former court magistrate, he is studying for a law degree at the University of Arizona.

There is tantalizing evidence, furthermore, that those who proclaim the death of rehabilitation grossly overstate their case. Jerome Miller, a psychiatric social worker who has headed correctional agencies and programs in a number of states, tirelessly defends the assertion that rehabilitation remains alive and well. He points out that researchers are finding significant rates of success with new programs offering "chronic care"—ongoing counseling, support, and other resources for former offenders to call on whenever they feel they may be headed for trouble. Miller also observes that a public outraged by crime may wrongly dismiss a program as worthless when it deserves credit for partial success.

He points to a study of family therapy for juvenile career criminals that found a recidivism rate of 60 percent after fifteen months. So much recidivism prompts many to judge the program a waste of time and money. Yet a matched control group continued to commit crimes at a rate of 93 percent. "A medical procedure that suppressed symptoms in 40 percent of a group of chronically ill patients, 93 percent of whom deteriorate without treatment, would be seen as a virtual triumph," Miller writes. "In corrections, however, such results are usually regarded as failure."

Religious groups also claim some progress in recent years. During the 1970s, the Black Muslims enjoyed growing influence among prison inmates. Many submitted to the faith's strict prohibitions against drugs and alcohol and embraced its teachings about family and community solidarity—thereby effectively turning their lives around. Fundamentalist Christians have also widened their prison outreach in recent years. One prison fellowship was led by Charles Colson, the Watergate conspirator.

The sponsors of such programs point out, with reason, that they have received less attention from students of penology than they deserve. Nonetheless, researchers examining the effectiveness of one program in the Washington, D.C., area found that when compared with a control group eight to fourteen years after release, prisoners who had participated in the Christian seminars had lower rates of recidivism, had a longer crime-free period following release, and committed less serious offenses when they did return to crime.

Meanwhile, recent studies of drug treatment, a field whose potential now remains limited only by the reluctance of the federal and state governments to provide funds, have come up with surprisingly encouraging results. Researchers find significant declines in both drug use and criminal behavior among participants in a variety of programs. The most dramatic are for those who remain in residential programs for at least three months. The most important single finding may be that such results are the same for addicts who are forced into treatment by the courts as for those who sign up voluntarily.

Even so, public tolerance of talk about rehabilitation wanes as crime victims continue to display their anger and grief. Why so much attention to helping the criminals turn their lives around and so little to the devastated lives of their victims? That wholly valid question deserves much better answers than criminal justice now provides.

To be sure, as the crime issue developed in the 1980s, so did a movement to help victims. Joey Fournier Services, started by Donna Cuomo, was one of many voluntary groups to offer counseling for individual victims, promote the teaching of conflict resolution in the schools, and provide other services. Similar groups sprang up all over America in response to a growing awareness that the criminal justice process too often considers the victims of a crime worthy of attention only to the extent that they might provide evidence to help the prosecution. In some places, governments also created new agencies to provide victims with social services and financial compensation.

These were positive steps, long overdue, but they continue to fall far short of the need. Real help for victims ought to be universally available, automatically, immediately, and extensively on proof of serious victimization. The government that still claims responsibility for public safety should stand squarely behind it everywhere, managing it as dependably and efficiently as it manages Social Security.

Do the Barneses, for example, need medical care that isn't covered by their insurance? A victims program would make sure they got it free of charge. Have they lost property and days of work? They could be fully compensated. Do they need psychological help? The program would pay for all the counseling they need in the form that suits them best for as long as they need it. Has an intruder damaged their house? The program would take care of repairs. Or are they afraid to move back into the house? Then the program would help them sell it, perhaps to the government, and find a new one of equivalent value. In addition, the program would assign a caseworker to help them apply for everything they need, to make sure the government follows through, to deal with special problems that come up as the victims try to put their lives back together, and generally to serve as a reassuring, sympathetic presence.

Doing this well, of course, would be a formidable undertaking. Mechanisms would have to be devised to guard against fraud. But government has plenty of experience addressing such problems in other big programs. Likewise, by now, the individual agencies for victims around the country have developed a considerable body of knowledge regarding what victims are likely to need and how those needs can best be met.

Such a benefit would also cost a great deal of money every year. But then, so does the prison expansion driven by the politics of fear. Once in place, moreover, a victim-benefit program could alter the emotional and political atmosphere of a crime-ridden America. It would ease the countless human tragedies that have now become so routine that they hardly receive much notice. The loneliest crime victim would never have to go without symbolic and substantive comfort.

In effect, the creation of a crime-victim benefit would constitute a renegotiation of the social contract. The state would admit the truth it now avoids: It cannot control crime completely. And it would guarantee to make victims whole when crime occurs. The taxpaying, law-abiding citizen would have less reason to feel betrayed. Whether Americans are now prepared to muster the energy and resources to make such a thing happen remains to be seen, of course. But the idea establishes the proper context for debate.

One kind of society gives up on reducing crime, resigns itself to more victims, more anguish, and more fear, and then ventilates the resulting anger with vengeful laws. Another kind of society preserves the old ideals of rehabilitation and enlightened crime control, investing serious resources in them as well as in real help for the victims of those crimes that cannot be prevented.

The Willie Horton story and the new expressiveness starkly outline this historic choice. They raise no less an issue than how Americans are to think of themselves, what kind of people they are to be.

Note on Sources

This book is based on the small mountain of documents generated by William Horton's crimes—thousands of pages of court and prison records, newspaper and magazine articles, tapes and transcripts of televised commentary and political advertising—supplemented by interviews with many of the most important figures in the story.

A partial list includes:

Transcript of *Commonwealth of Massachusetts* v. *William R. Horton, Roosevelt Pickett and Alvin L. Wideman* heard in District Court of Lawrence, Massachusetts, beginning December 6, 1974.

Files pertaining to William Horton's years in the custody of the Massachusetts Department of Correction.

Transcript of *State of Maryland* v. *William Robert Horton aka Tony Franklin* tried in Circuit Court for Prince George's County, Maryland, beginning October 13, 1987.

Transcript of hearings conducted by the Massachusetts House of Representatives' Post Audit and Oversight Committee from October 14, 1987, to November 5, 1987.

Notes of investigators for the House Committee on Post Audit and Oversight.

Department of Correction: Furlough Program, final report of the House Post Audit and Oversight Committee.

Final Report on the Investigation of the Furloughs Granted to William Horton, prepared by the Office of General Counsel and Investigation of the Commonwealth of Massachusetts Executive Office of Human Services.

Final ruling on *Devlin & others* v. *Commissioner of Correction and others* filed in Supreme Judicial Court for the County of Suffolk, Massachusetts, on October 10, 1973.

Press releases, correspondence, and other documents issued by the office of Governor Michael Dukakis, the Massachusetts Executive Office of Human Services, the Massachusetts Department of Correction, and the Lifers' Group at the Massachusetts Correctional Institution at Norfolk, Massachusetts.

Filings, deposition transcripts, and other documents relating to *Eugene Branstool, James M. Ruvolo, Ohio Democratic Party, William L. Mallory, Ray Miller and Black Elected Democrats* v. *Federal Election Commission* filed in United States District Court for the District of Columbia.

Daily newspaper articles published in *The Lawrence Eagle-Tribune, The Boston Globe, The Boston Herald, The New York Times, The Washington Post,* and other newspapers from 1974 through 1992.

Magazine articles published in *Corrections Magazine, Emerge, Life, The Nation, National Journal, The New Yorker,*

New Republic, Playboy, Reader's Digest, Time, and *Washington Journalism Review.*

Transcripts of *Geraldo* aired June 28, 1988; *The Oprah Winfrey Show* aired October 4, 1988; *MacNeil/Lehrer News Hour* aired October 12, 1988; *Prime Time Live* aired March 29, 1990.

General statistics on crime and law enforcement are from *The Sourcebook of Criminal Justice Statistics,* published annually by the Justice Department's Bureau of Justice Statistics, and from reports supplied by CEGA Services of Lincoln, Nebraska.

Statistical discussions of the Massachusetts prison furlough program relied in part on documents released by the Massachusetts Department of Correction: *Position Paper: The Massachusetts Furlough Program* by Michael W. Forcier and Linda K. Holt, released in May 1987. *1986 Annual Statistical Report on the Furlough Program* by Lisa Lorant, released in August 1987. *The Massachusetts Department of Correction's Community Reintegration Program* by Michael V. Fair, released in March 1988. *The Effect of Community Reintegration on Rates of Recidivism: A Statistical Overview of Data for the Years 1971 Through 1985* by Daniel P. LeClair and Michael V. Fair released in July 1988.

Other sources on furlough statistics and research: "Getting Away With Murder: Supplementary Information" by Robert James Bidinotto, unpublished and undated. "Does Incapacitation Guarantee Public Safety? Lessons from the Massachusetts Furlough and Prerelease Programs" by Danield P. LeClair and Susan Guarino-Ghezzi, published in *Justice Quarterly,* March 1991.

Books consulted and/or quoted in the text include:

Picture Perfect: The Art and Artifice of Public Image Making by Kiku Adatto (Basic Books); *What It Takes: The Way to the White House* by Richard Ben Cramer (Random House); *Whose Broad Stripes and Bright Stars: The Trivial Pursuit of the Presidency 1988* by Jack W. Germond and Jules Witcover (Warner Books); *Dirty Politics: Deception, Distraction, and Democracy* by Kathleen Hall Jamieson (Oxford University Press); *The Way Things Ought to Be* by Rush Limbaugh (Pocket Books); *Campaign for President: The Managers Look at '88* edited by David R. Runkel (Auburn House).

Index

and Horton's participation in furlough program, 157; and Joey Fournier Services, 258, 274–76; and media, 165, 223–24, 225–26, 227, 228; and Post Audit and Oversight Committee, 171–72; and presidential campaign, 223–24, 225–26, 227, 228, 236, 237
Cuomo, Mario, 251–52

death penalty: and Clinton, 254–56; as collective revenge, 17; as deterrent, 17; and drug dealers, 241–42; and expressive justice vs. crime control, 15–16; for federal crimes, 16; and presidential campaign issue, 215–16, 228, 231, 241–42, 243–44, 245
DiFruscia, Anthony, 131, 132, 261–63
Dolphin Group, 227–29, 236
Donaldson, Sam, 260–61
Donovan, Maureen, 139, 161, 167, 180; and ballot initiative, 140, 160, 162, 163, 164; and CAUS, 162, 163, 164, 258; as elected official, 258; and Giordano-Hermann bill, 155–59, 178, 180
Doucette, Billy, 94, 96, 194, 195, 198–99
drugs/drug-related crimes, 10, 18, 49–52, 241–42, 244, 274. See also specific person
Dukakis, Michael: acceptance of nomination by, 219–20; apologies to Barneses by, 160, 161, 166, 220, 237, 242; and death penalty, 215–16, 228, 231, 241–42, 243–44; delegations' meetings with, 139–40, 160, 161; Eagle-Tribune campaign against, 148–49; and emotional issues, 166, 218–20, 222, 244; furlough program support by, 4, 160, 161, 179, 209, 213, 239, 242; and Giordano-Hermann bill, 177, 179–80; misjudgment of, 159–61, 166; values of,

218–20, 240–41; as victim, 245; and victims, 244. See also presidential campaign (1988)

Eagle-Tribune. See The Lawrence Eagle-Tribune
economic issues, 52–53, 92, 268–70, 274, 276
Eighth Amendment, 15–16
Elliot, Jeffrey, 29–30, 132, 133–35, 232–33, 260, 261, 262, 263
Emerge magazine, 134–35, 263
Estrich, Susan, 206–7, 218–20, 222, 240–41, 245, 246, 247
expressive justice: Bolling's attack on, 176–77; as cause for concern, 24–25, 268–72; crime control vs., 15–16, 268–77; and death penalty, 15, 16; and economic issues, 268–70; and grassroot campaigns/petitions, 19; history of, 14–15; Horton case as example of, 24–25, 55–56, 201–5, 216; and human nature, 15, and mandatory sentencing, 17–19; meaning of term, 14–15, political aspects of, 245–51; and presidential campaign, 245–47; and punishment, 15, 20; and social contract, 21; and statistics, 201; and television, 226; as therapy, 268

Fair, Michael, 92, 93, 173; defense of furlough program by, 158–59, 168–69, 174–75; and exaggerations about Horton, 187–88; and Fournier case, 187–88; Giordano-Hermann meet with, 143–44; lack of defense of furlough program by, 143, 144, 145, 146–47; and malfeasance issue, 193, 198; and Post Audit and Oversight Committee, 168–69, 171; and privacy issues, 144, 146–47, 150
Farrell, Hubert, 45–46, 47, 126

ABOUT THE AUTHOR

David C. Anderson has worked as a reporter, editor, and editorial writer for *The Wall Street Journal* and *The New York Times,* where he wrote extensively about criminal justice. He also served as editor of *Police* and *Corrections* magazines; his previous books include *Crimes of Justice.* He lives in New York City.